2nd Edition

Fundamentals of Music

EARL HENRY

Webster University

Prentice Hall, Englewood Cliffs, New Jersey 07632

Library of Congress Cataloging-in-Publication Data

Henry, Earl.
   Fundamentals of music/Earl Henry.—2nd ed.
     p. cm.
   Includes index.
   ISBN 0-13-337288-X
   1. Music—Theory, Elementary. 2. Musical notation. I. Title.
MT7.H49 1993
781—dc20

                      92–16644
                      CIP
                      MN

Acquisitions editor: *Norwell Therien*
Editorial/production supervision
   and interior design: *Carole R. Crouse*
Copy editor: *Carole R. Crouse*
Cover designer: *Ray Lundgren Graphics, Inc.*
Page makeup: *Debbie Toymil*
Prepress buyer: *Herb Klein*
Manufacturing buyer: *Bob Anderson*
Editorial assistant: *Lee Mamunes*

© 1993, 1988 by Prentice-Hall, Inc.
A Simon & Schuster Company
Englewood Cliffs, New Jersey 07632

Printed in the United States of America

10 9 8 7 6 5 4 3 2 1

ISBN 0-13-061904-3 (with compact disc)
ISBN 0-13-337288-X (text only)

PRENTICE-HALL INTERNATIONAL (UK) LIMITED, *London*
PRENTICE-HALL OF AUSTRALIA PTY. LIMITED, *Sydney*
PRENTICE-HALL CANADA INC., *Toronto*
PRENTICE-HALL HISPANOAMERICANA, S.A., *Mexico*
PRENTICE-HALL OF INDIA PRIVATE LIMITED, *New Delhi*
PRENTICE-HALL OF JAPAN, INC., *Tokyo*
SIMON & SCHUSTER ASIA PTE. LTD., *Singapore*
EDITORA PRENTICE-HALL DO BRASIL, LTDA., *Rio de Janeiro*

In Memory of

EUGENE ORNER

Professor of Music
East Tennessee State University

Contents

APPENDIXES

Preface

This text is designed to provide an introduction to the notation and performance of traditional music as well as to present and explain basic materials and theoretical concepts such as meter, scales, triads, and chords. *Fundamentals of Music,* second edition, is intended to meet the needs of two different groups of students. First, the book will serve as a text in college, secondary, or preparatory school courses where the aim is to provide a solid, pre-professional background that will precede one or more courses in music theory. For these students, concepts and terms employed in the text are those that constitute the basic vocabulary of traditional music. Experiences are also provided in basic areas of musicianship such as sight singing, ear training, and keyboard performance. Finally, Chapters 11 and 12, as well as several appendixes, include topics that are often excluded from courses in fundamentals but that may be needed as a background for music theory or applied music study.

The text is also intended to serve those students engaged in other disciplines (perhaps with no prior musical training) who must acquire a working knowledge of traditional music notation or the fundamentals of musicianship. For these students, terms and concepts are presented in straightforward language with many examples and are reinforced through numerous fundamental and musicianship skill exercises throughout the text. Students for whom an introduction to music is sufficient, however, may make less use of the musicianship exercises and some of the advanced theoretical concepts such as seventh chords and part-writing procedures.

USING THE TEXT

Each of the twelve chapters in *Fundamentals of Music,* second edition, is based on four areas of study: text, fundamental and musicianship skill exercises, a self-test, and supplementary exercises. Each of these four areas provides a different approach to the topic, and each should be studied in succession.

Text.   Chapters center on a relatively brief discussion in prose of the major topic or topics. Note carefully the list of essential terms that precedes the discussion, and be sure that you understand each of these terms when you have completed the chapter. Read the chapter material at least once, and try to formulate an understanding of that material in a broad sense. Next, review the chapter looking only at the headings of each section; try to put into your own words the central facts about each. If that proves difficult, read the section again.

Skill Exercises.   The skill exercises—both fundamental and musicianship— are distributed throughout the chapter material so that topics can be mastered in "bite-sized" chunks. Some instructors will assign the exercises to be done at home and turned in, and then either graded and returned or discussed in class. Other instructors will use class time for the exercises, with students working either independently or as a group. If success on the exercises is unsatisfactory, review of the chapter material may be necessary.

Self-Tests.   In a subject like music, in which each small topic serves as a foundation for the next, keeping up is essential. The text discussion and the exercises are included for this purpose; these areas can be studied in whole or in part and over several periods of time if desired. The self-test included in each chapter, however, should be completed in one timed situation. In music fundamentals, it is often not sufficient merely to get a correct answer; one must arrive at the correct answer quickly. So whereas the fundamental and musicianship exercises may be studied leisurely, the self-test should be taken under "real" conditions. Your instructor will probably suggest an appropriate length of time; most tests, however, are intended to be completed in fifteen or twenty minutes. Because the questions are generally objective, right and wrong answers should be determined easily. Occasionally, two or even several answers are correct.

Supplementary Exercises.   Included with each chapter are a number of supplementary exercises, which are designed to present familiar material in new contexts. Some of these problems require creative activities, such as composition; others center on analysis and drill. Still other projects provide additional drill on crucial topics. After you have studied the chapter, worked through the fundamental and musicianship exercises, and taken the self-test, complete the supplementary exercises as directed by your instructor.

USING THE OPTIONAL COMPACT DISC

This text is available both with and without a compact disc. Forty of the most important and instructive text examples have been recorded. The numbered examples in the text correspond to tracks on the disc. Consult the notes accompanying the compact disc for the correlation between examples and disc track numbers.

If you have purchased the version of the text without a disc, your instructor will probably play the examples for you in class. Some instructors may want to make a master disc available to students so that they can make audiocassette copies.

FEATURES OF THE SECOND EDITION

The second edition of *Fundamentals of Music* is a complete revision of the first edition, undertaken in response to user requests and changing trends in pedagogy. First, chapters have been reordered so that experiences in rhythmic and pitch notation are parallel rather than consecutive. In addition, although a substantial amount of new material has been added, the original topics have been condensed to make a total of twelve rather than fourteen chapters.

The format of each chapter has also been changed. The programmed review questions, for example, have been replaced with numerous drill exercises throughout the chapters themselves. Likewise, the performance and listening exercises of the first edition have been replaced with many more sight-singing, ear-training, and keyboard experiences. New material on seventh chords and basic part-writing procedures has been added.

All dictation material was included in the first edition; however, the aural exercises have been so greatly expanded in this edition that the notated music can no longer be included in the text. This material is heard on the compact disc, of course, and is notated fully in the Instructor's Manual that accompanies *Fundamentals of Music.*

ACKNOWLEDGMENTS

I appreciate the comments of many instructors and students across the country who used the first edition of *Fundamentals of Music* and took the time to point out to me their perceptions of the book's various strengths and weaknesses. I have tried to retain the best and most popular features of the first edition while adding the musicianship exercises, basic music theory, and other topics that many users requested. I also want to thank my students and colleagues at Webster University who class-tested both editions and recommended many changes, additions, and improvements. I am grateful to the following reviewers for their advice and helpful comments: Joel Kramne, University of Missouri—Rolla; Tom Risher, University of Alabama; and Edwin F. Avril, Glassboro (N.J.) State College. Finally, I am especially indebted to Carole Crouse, the Prentice-Hall production editor for the second edition, whose experience and insight were invaluable.

Earl Henry

The Notation of Rhythm

MUSIC is sound in time. Throughout the history of music, composers and performers have devised various means of representing sounds with symbols—a process we call NOTATION. Conventional music notation originated in the Middle Ages. As music changed over the centuries, notation was slowly revised and refined until, by about 1600, the system we use today was in place. Traditional Western musical notation is based on two sets of symbols. One group of symbols indicates the *duration*, or length, of a sound; another designates *pitch*—the sensation of relative highness or lowness.

THE NOTATION OF RHYTHM

RHYTHM is the element of time in music. In traditional Western music, rhythm is measured in *beats* or their fractional parts. One of the duties of a modern conductor is to outline those beats so that the ensemble members can perform their parts at exactly the right time. A BEAT is a regular pulse like the heartbeat or the ticking of a clock.

Note Values

The NOTE (o) is the basic symbol for sound and can be altered in a variety of ways to indicate differences in duration. The largest single traditional value is the WHOLE NOTE (o); other notes have fractional relationships to the whole note and receive one-half its value, one-quarter its value, and so on.

Note Name	Note Symbol	Value
WHOLE NOTE	o	[-]
HALF NOTE	♩	$\frac{1}{2}$ value of whole note
QUARTER NOTE	♩	$\frac{1}{4}$ value of whole note

The half note includes a STEM; the quarter note has both a stem and a solid notehead.

stem ⟶ ♩ ⟵ notehead

The value of rhythmic symbols is set in beats. Any rhythmic symbol can have the value of one beat, but once that designation is made, other symbols relate to it as multiples or fractions of the beat unit. The quarter note is often assigned the value of one beat. In that case, the whole note has the value of four beats; the half note, two beats.

♩ = 1 beat

Whole Note	Half Note	Quarter Note
o	♩	♩
4 beats	2 beats	1 beat

If the whole note receives four beats, two half notes or four quarter notes are required to fill the time occupied by a single whole note (four beats).

♩ = 1 beat

o	♩ ♩	♩ ♩ ♩ ♩
4 beats	4 beats	4 beats

If the half note has the value of one beat, the fractional relationships among the notes are the same: The whole note receives twice the value of the half note; the quarter note, one-half the value of the half note. Notice that in this instance, the quarter note receives *less* than one beat; two quarter notes are required to make up the time of one beat.

Whole Note	Half Note	Quarter Note
2 beats	1 beat	½ beat

Regardless of the value of the whole note, the half and quarter notes stand in the same relationships to it. Two half notes have the same value as a single whole; four quarter notes represent a combined duration equivalent to the whole note.

2 beats	2 beats	2 beats

exercise 1–1 Fundamental Skills
Notating Whole Notes, Half Notes, and Quarter Notes

Follow the model and complete each line with notes of the same value. Make the noteheads oval in shape and extend the stems down from the left side or up from the right as shown.

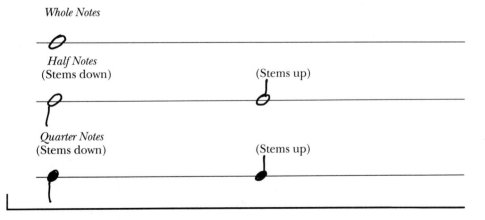

Whole Notes

Half Notes
(Stems down)   (Stems up)

Quarter Notes
(Stems down)   (Stems up)

exercise 1–2 Fundamental Skills
Larger Note Values

A. Given the quarter note as the beat unit, compute the value of each note shown.

♩ = 1 beat

1. ♩ _____
2. o _____
3. ♩ _____

If the half note is the beat unit, compute the total value of each note shown.

♩ = 1 beat

1. o _____
2. ♩ _____
3. ♩ _____

B. With the quarter receiving one beat, compute the cumulative value of the series of notes shown in each line.

♩ = 1 beat

1. ♩ ♩ ♩ o _____
2. ♩ ♩ ♩ _____
3. ♩ ♩ ♩ ♩ o _____
4. ♩ ♩ ♩ ♩ ♩ _____
5. ♩ o ♩ ♩ _____
6. ♩ ♩ o ♩ _____
7. o o ♩ _____
8. ♩ ♩ ♩ ♩ ♩ ♩ _____

Given the half note as one beat, compute the cumulative value of the notes in each line.

♩ = 1 beat

1. ♩ ♩ o _____
2. ♩ ♩ ♩ _____

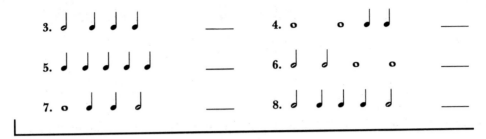

Lesser Rhythmic Values

When composers want durational values smaller than the quarter note, other symbols are available that follow the familiar pattern of relationships.

Note Name	Note Symbol	Value
EIGHTH NOTE	♪	$\frac{1}{8}$ value of whole note
SIXTEENTH NOTE	♬	$\frac{1}{16}$ value of whole note
THIRTY-SECOND NOTE		$\frac{1}{32}$ value of whole note
SIXTY-FOURTH NOTE		$\frac{1}{64}$ value of whole note

Notes smaller than the quarter note include one or more *flags*, which are affixed to the right side of the stem. A FLAG is a curved line attached to a note stem to indicate lesser value. When two or more flagged notes occur in succession, the flags may be replaced by BEAMS for easier reading.

	Eighth Note	*Sixteenth Note*	*Thirty-second Note*	*Sixty-fourth Note*
Flags	♪ ♪	♬ ♬		
Beams				

If the quarter note receives one beat, lesser note values have fractional relationships to the quarter:

- The eighth note receives one-half beat.
- The sixteenth note has the value of one-quarter beat.
- The thirty-second note gets one-eighth beat.
- The sixty-fourth note has the value of one-sixteenth beat.

Quarter	Eighth	Sixteenth	Thirty- second	Sixty- fourth
$\mathmark$				
1 beat	$\frac{1}{2}$ beat	$\frac{1}{4}$ beat	$\frac{1}{8}$ beat	$\frac{1}{16}$ beat

Observe the values of the most common note symbols in relation to the whole note.

Note Name	Note Symbol	Value
WHOLE NOTE	o	[-]
HALF NOTE		$\frac{1}{2}$ value of whole note
QUARTER NOTE		$\frac{1}{4}$ value of whole note
EIGHTH NOTE		$\frac{1}{8}$ value of whole note
SIXTEENTH NOTE		$\frac{1}{16}$ value of whole note
THIRTY- SECOND NOTE		$\frac{1}{32}$ value of whole note
SIXTY- FOURTH NOTE		$\frac{1}{64}$ value of whole note

exercise 1–3 Fundamental Skills
Notating Lesser Durational Values

Follow the model and complete each line with notes of the same value. Make the noteheads oval in shape, and extend the stems down from the left side or up from the right side. The flags should fall from the right side of the stem. See Appendix C for more information about notating music.

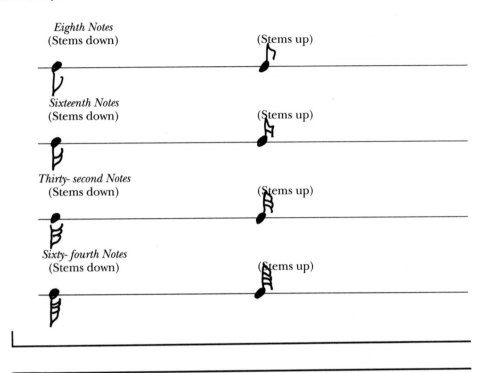

exercise 1–4 Fundamental Skills
Reading Lesser Note Values

A. Given the quarter note as the beat unit, compute the value of each note shown.

♩ = 1 beat

1. ♪ _____   2. ♩ _____

3. 𝅝 _____   4. ♩ _____

5. 𝅘𝅥𝅲 _____   6. 𝅘𝅥𝅯 _____

With the quarter still valued at one beat, compute the cumulative value of the series of notes shown in each line.

♩ = 1 beat

1. ♩ ♩ ♫ _____   2. ♬ ♫ ♩ _____

3. ♩ ♫ ♪ _____   4. ♫♫♫ ♪ _____

5. ♩ ♩ ♪ ♪ ♪ _____ 6. ♩ ♩ ♪ ♪ _____

7. ♫ ♫ ♫ ♬ _____ 8. ♩ ♪♪ ♪♩ ♪ ♪ _____

B. If the half note is the beat unit, compute the value of each note shown.

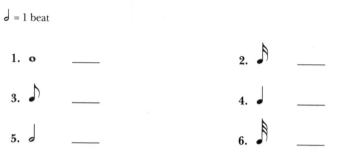

♩ = 1 beat

1. o _____ 2. ♪ _____

3. ♪ _____ 4. ♩ _____

5. ♩ _____ 6. ♪ _____

Compute the combined value of the series of notes shown in each line. The half note is the beat unit.

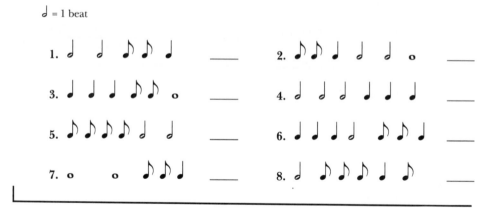

♩ = 1 beat

1. ♩ ♩ ♪ ♪ ♩ _____ 2. ♪ ♪ ♩ ♩ ♩ o _____

3. ♩ ♩ ♩ ♪ ♪ o _____ 4. ♩ ♩ ♩ ♩ ♩ ♩ _____

5. ♪ ♪ ♪ ♪ ♩ ♩ _____ 6. ♩ ♩ ♩ ♩ ♪ ♪ ♩ _____

7. o o ♪ ♪ ♩ _____ 8. ♩ ♪ ♪ ♪ ♩ ♪ _____

Rests

Silence in music can be as important as the sounds themselves. The symbols for silence are called RESTS and correspond to the values of note symbols. The WHOLE REST lies below the line; the HALF REST above the line. Observe, too, that the number of rest "flags" duplicates that for the notes.

Note Symbol	Name	Rest Symbol
o	WHOLE	▬
♩	HALF	▄

Note Symbol	Name	Rest Symbol
♩	QUARTER	𝄽
♪	EIGHTH	𝄾
𝅘𝅥𝅯	SIXTEENTH	𝄿
𝅘𝅥𝅰	THIRTY- SECOND	𝅀
𝅘𝅥𝅱	SIXTY- FOURTH	𝅁

exercise 1–5 Fundamental Skills
Notating Rests

Follow the model and complete the lines with rests of the same value. Quarter rests are made like an angular number *3*. Flags for eighth, sixteenth, and thirty-second rests should extend from the right side as shown.

Whole Rests   *Half Rests*

Quarter Rests   *Eighth Rests*

Sixteenth Rests   *Thirty- second Rests*

exercise 1–6 Fundamental Skills
Note and Rest Values

A. Given the value of the quarter note (and rest) as one beat, compute the value of each rest shown.

♩ = 1 beat

1. 𝄽 ____   2. ▬ ____

3. ▬ ____   4. 𝄾 ____

5. 𝄾 ____   6. 𝄾 ____

With the quarter note still the beat unit, compute the total value of the series of notes and rests shown in each line.

♩ = 1 beat

1. ♩ ♩ 𝄽 ♩ 𝄽 ____   2. 𝄽 𝄾 ♪ ♩ ▬ ____

3. ♪ ♩ 𝄽 ♫ 𝄽 ____   4. ♩ ♫ 𝄾 𝄽 ▬ ____

5. ▬ 𝄽 𝄾 ♪ ▬ ____   6. ♬ 𝄾 ♫ 𝄾 ____

7. ♩ 𝄽 𝄾 ♫ 𝄽 𝄽 ____   8. ♩ ♩ ♩ ♩ 𝄾 ♪ ♩ ____

B. If the value of the *eighth note* is one beat, compute the value of each rest shown.

♪ = 1 beat

1. 𝄾 ____   2. ▬ ____

3. 𝄽 ____   4. 𝄾 ____

5. 𝄾 ____   6. ▬ ____

Calculate the total value of the series of notes and rests shown in each line. The eighth note is the beat.

♪ = 1 beat

1. ♩ 𝄾 𝄾 ♪ ____   2. ♬ ♩ 𝄽 𝄾 ♪ ____

3. ♬ ♩ ♪ ____   4. ♩ 𝄾 ♪ 𝄾 ♪ ____

5. ♩ 𝄾 ♪ 𝅘𝅥𝅰𝅘𝅥𝅰𝅘𝅥𝅰𝅘𝅥𝅰 ＿＿＿ 6. 𝅗𝅥 𝅗𝅥 ▬ 𝄾 ＿＿＿

7. 𝅘𝅥𝅯𝅘𝅥𝅯𝅘𝅥𝅯 𝄾♩ 𝄾♪ ＿＿＿ 8. 𝄾 𝅘𝅥𝅯𝅘𝅥𝅯♩ 𝄾 𝅘𝅥𝅯𝅘𝅥𝅯 ＿＿＿

The Breve

An older note value found occasionally in modern scores is the BREVE (▭), which has double the value of a whole note. The corresponding rest has the same value.

▭ = o‿o

𝄎 = ▬ ▬

The Dot

The DOT (·) is employed to extend the value of a note or a rest by one-half its original value. If the half note, for example, receives two beats, the *dotted* half note has the value of three beats.

𝅗𝅥 = 1 beat

𝅗𝅥   .   𝅗𝅥.

2 beats + 1 beat = 3 beats

If the half note receives one beat, the *dotted half note* receives one and one-half beats—an increase of one-half the original value.

𝅗𝅥 = 1 beat

𝅗𝅥   .   𝅗𝅥.

1 beat + $\frac{1}{2}$ beat = $1\frac{1}{2}$ beats

Whereas the quarter note divides into two eighth notes, the dotted quarter note comprises *three* eighth notes. A DOTTED NOTE is one that includes a dot; notes without dots are classified as SIMPLE. As we will discuss more fully in a later chapter, the use of a dotted note as the unit of beat permits the composer to divide the beat into three rather than two smaller parts.

Simple Note   Dotted Note

The principle of the dot applies to rests as well. If the quarter note and the quarter rest each receive one beat, the dotted quarter rest has the value of one and one-half beats.

♩ = 1 beat

1 beat + ½ beat   =   1½ beats

If the whole rest has the value of four beats, the dotted whole rest receives six beats.

♩ = 1 beat

4 beats + 2 beats   =   6 beats

The Tie

Whereas the dot increases the value of a single note or rest, the TIE (⌢ or ⌣) combines the values of two or more notes of the same pitch (see Chapter 2). If the half note receives two beats, a half note tied to a quarter note has a combined value of three beats.

♩ = 1 beat

2 beats + 1 beat   =   3 beats

If the quarter note receives one beat, an eighth note tied to a quarter receives a beat and a half.

♩ = 1 beat

½ beat + 1 beat   =   1½ beats

exercise 1–7 *Fundamental Skills*
Reading Dotted and Tied Notes

A. Rewrite the tied notes as one simple or dotted note of the same duration as the original. Given a quarter-note beat, compute the value.

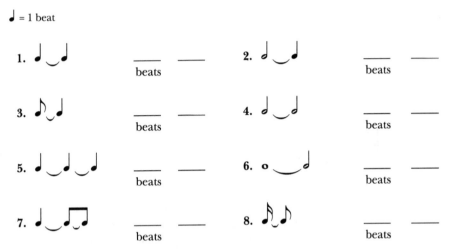

B. Compute the total value of the notes and rests shown in each line. The quarter note is the beat.

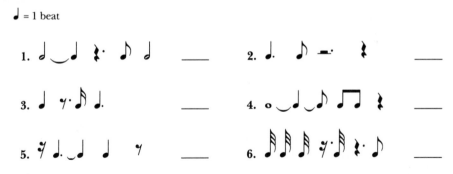

If the eighth note is the beat, compute the combined values of the notes and rests shown in each line.

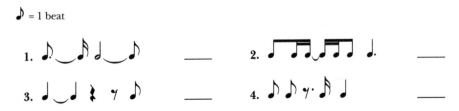

Using Beams and Flags

Composers and arrangers of instrumental music often use beams rather than flags to make the music easier to read. For example, the following series of notes is confusing when written with flags but is much clearer with beams.

Flags   *Beams*

The second example above is clear because beats are separated and beamed together. Even reading the music at sight, performers can see groups of notes that add up to a full beat's value. As shown below, however, incorrectly beamed notes can be more confusing than flags.

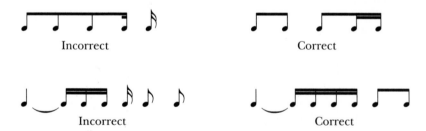

In your own notation, be careful to observe the principle of beaming beat groups. Although in vocal music, flags are used for notes that constitute a syllable of text, flags appear generally in instrumental music only for single notes.

exercise 1–8 Fundamental Skills
Beaming

Replace flags in the following passage with beams where appropriate. Single flagged notes may occur in some cases.

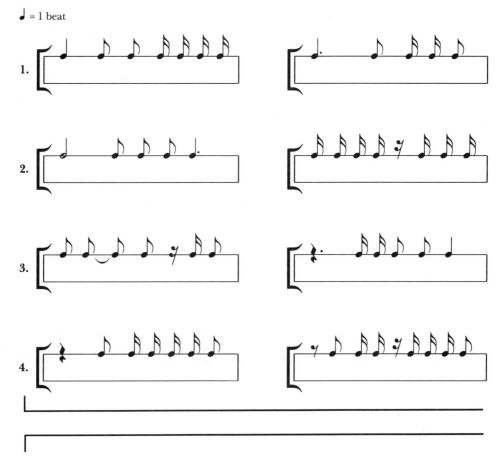

♩ = 1 beat

exercise 1–9 Musicianship Skills
Developing Rhythmic Memory

CLASS ACTIVITY

A. Your instructor will play, sing, or clap several short rhythmic patterns. As directed, repeat the patterns exactly as you heard them. Concentrate on feeling the beat and the length in beats of each pattern.

INDIVIDUAL PERFORMANCES

B. For each pattern your instructor performs, *improvise* a different pattern of the same length. If the instructor's pattern is four beats, for example, make up a four-beat pattern of your own. If the pattern performed by the instructor is three beats, your pattern should be different, but of the same length.

SELF-TEST

1. Match the note or the rest on the right with the appropriate name on the left.

_____ Sixteenth note   **a.** ▬   **d.**

_____ Whole rest

_____ Quarter note   **b.**   **e.**

_____ Dotted eighth note

_____ Half note   **c.**   **f.**

_____ Dotted half note

2. If the eighth note has the value of one beat, compute the values of the following notes and rests.

♪ = 1 beat

3. With the *half note* having the value of one beat, supply one *rest* (it may be simple or dotted) that has the value indicated.

♩ = 1 beat

_____ 2 beats   _____ 1½ beats   _____ 3 beats

_____ ½ beat   _____ ¼ beat   _____ 1 beat

4. Rewrite the dotted notes as tied notes.

♩. _____   ♩. _____   ♪. _____   o. _____

5. Identify the following terms:

    a. Beat

    b. Rest

    c. Dot

    d. Tie

    e. Flag

1. For each given note, supply the corresponding rest as well as the value of both note and rest. The beat is given in each case.

	Beat	Note	Rest	Value
a.	𝅗𝅥	𝅘𝅥	_____	_____
b.	𝅗𝅥	𝅝	_____	_____
c.	𝅘𝅥	𝅘𝅥𝅮	_____	_____
d.	𝅘𝅥	𝅗𝅥.	_____	_____
e.	𝅘𝅥𝅮	𝅘𝅥	_____	_____
f.	𝅘𝅥𝅮	𝅘𝅥𝅮.	_____	_____
g.	𝅘𝅥	𝅘𝅥𝅯	_____	_____
h.	𝅘𝅥	𝅘𝅥𝅮.	_____	_____

2. Add one note to that given so that the total number of beats will be 2, 3, or 4 as indicated.

	Beat	2 beats	3 beats	4 beats
a.	𝅘𝅥	𝅘𝅥 𝅘𝅥 _____	𝅘𝅥 𝅗𝅥 _____	𝅗𝅥 𝅗𝅥 _____
b.	𝅘𝅥	𝅘𝅥𝅮 _____	𝅗𝅥 _____	𝅘𝅥 _____
c.	𝅘𝅥𝅮	𝅘𝅥𝅯 _____	𝅘𝅥𝅮 _____	𝅘𝅥. _____
d.	𝅘𝅥𝅮	𝅘𝅥𝅮 _____	𝅘𝅥 _____	𝅘𝅥𝅮 _____
e.	𝅗𝅥	𝅘𝅥 _____	𝅗𝅥 _____	𝅝. _____
f.	𝅗𝅥	𝅗𝅥 _____	𝅝 _____	𝅝 _____

3. Add two equal notes (dotted if necessary) to the one given so that the total number of beats will be 2, 3, or 4 as indicated.

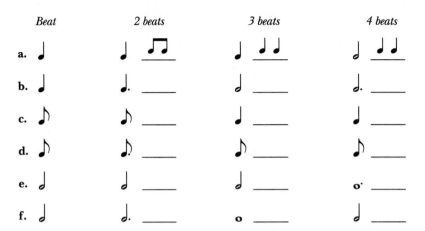

4. The notes below are rhythmic reductions from compositions by well-known composers. In the space provided, rewrite each passage with values twice those of the original or half those of the original, as specified.

The Notation of Pitch

ESSENTIAL TERMS

- *alto clef*
- *bass clef*
- bassa
- *grand staff*
- *interval*
- *ledger lines*
- loco
- *movable C-clef*
- *octave sign*
- *staff*
- *tenor clef*
- *treble clef*

Like the practices associated with rhythm, the notation of pitch evolved over many centuries. Although some early systems of pitch notation employed letters of the alphabet as note symbols, for about a thousand years, traditional Western music has been based on the symbols we now call NOTES. As we discussed earlier, the shape of a note designates its relative duration; relatively higher or lower pitch is represented simply by placing the note higher or lower on the page. The first three notes below, for example, represent increasingly higher pitch; the second three represent increasingly lower pitch.

The Staff

Although the notes above are obviously higher or lower in a relative sense, the performer must know *exactly* how much higher or lower. Another part of the notational system, the *staff*, permits exactness in notating pitch. The STAFF is a grid of five lines (with four spaces between them) upon which the notes are written. Placing the notes on the staff allows them to be identified more precisely.

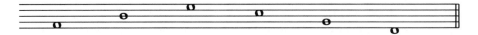

Stem Direction. When stemmed notes appear on the staff, correct stem direction (up or down) is important. If the note is on the third line or above, stems go down from the left side of the notehead. For notes below the third line, stems go up from the right side. Flags are always placed on the right side of the stem.

When several notes are beamed together, stems go up or down according to where most of the notes in the group lie.

Whole Rests and Half Rests on the Staff. On the staff, the half rest lies on the third line. The whole rest appears below the fourth line. Other rests should be written close to the notes immediately before and after them.

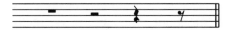

Note Names. There are seven basic notes, named according to the first seven letters of the alphabet: A B C D E F and G. On the staff, these BASIC PITCHES always appear *in order* over consecutive lines and spaces. If the name of any one line or space is identified, all are specified, because the pattern is invariable. In ascending patterns after the note G, A is used again; in descending patterns after A, G is the next note. In the following example, the pitch C is identified with an asterisk.

* = the pitch C.

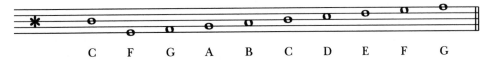

C   F   G   A   B   C   D   E   F   G

The Clef

Where the asterisk was used above to identify the pitch C, a CLEF is the traditional symbol employed to assign notes to specific lines and spaces.

The Treble Clef.   The TREBLE CLEF (𝄞), used for relatively higher sounds, identifies the note G as being on the second line. If G is on the second line, the pitch A occupies the space above it; the pitch F occupies the space below it.

G   E F G A B C D E F   F A C E E G B D F

The Bass Clef.   The BASS CLEF (𝄢) is used for relatively lower sounds and identifies the position of the pitch F as the fourth line. If F is on the fourth line, the space above is G; the space below is E.

F   G A B C D E F G A   A C E G G B D F A

Note the identification of pitches on the two STAVES (plural of *staff*) below.

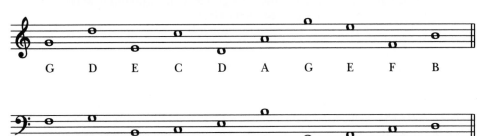

G   D   E   C   D   A   G   E   F   B

F   G   B   C   E   B   G   A   C   D

exercise 2–1 *Fundamental Skills*
Notating Treble and Bass Clefs

Follow the model and complete the lines of treble and bass clefs. Make your notation as clear and precise as possible.

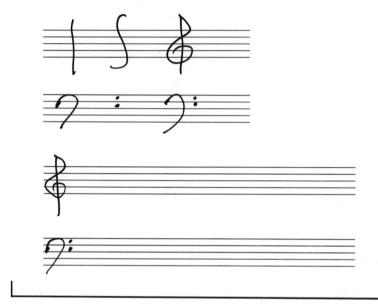

exercise 2–2 *Fundamental Skills*
Notating Pitch

A. In the treble clef, write the notes indicated in their proper positions. When note names are repeated, use different staff locations if possible. Make all the notes *half notes*, with oval heads and correctly placed stems.

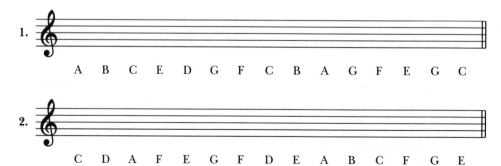

1.   A   B   C   E   D   G   F   C   B   A   G   F   E   G   C

2.   C   D   A   F   E   G   F   D   E   A   B   C   F   G   E

Using the bass clef, write the notes indicated. Make them *eighth notes*, with properly placed stems and a single flag attached to the right of each stem. As before, when note names are repeated, vary the staff locations if possible.

1.

B G D E F C A B F E G A C B D

2.

C G E B F D G B C F D A E B C

Notate rests on the staff as indicated.

Whole Half Quarter Whole Eighth Sixteenth Half Whole Eighth

B. Some of the stems and flags on the notes below are incorrectly placed. Use the second staff to rewrite each passage with correct placement. (In some cases where notes are beamed together, stem direction is chosen for ease of reading rather than through clear-cut rules.) Symbols such as ♯, ♭, and ♮ are called *accidentals* and will be explained in the next chapter. These accidentals are necessary to reproduce the composers' music accurately, but you may omit them in your revision.

1. Corelli

2. Brahms

3.   Handel

4.   Mozart

exercise 2–3   Fundamental Skills
Identifying Pitch

Write the name of the note in the blank.

Identify the pitches of the next three compositions.

The Octave

In the last line of Skill Exercise 2-3, notice that the pitch A is written in two different places; these pitches are an *octave* apart. An OCTAVE is a natural element in music upon which virtually all systems of notation are based. Given any note on the staff, the note with the same name immediately above or below is by definition an octave higher or lower. When pitches are an octave apart, the sounds are so similar that they are often incorrectly perceived as being the *same* pitch. The difference (distance) between two pitches is called an INTERVAL; the interval between the bracketed notes below, therefore, is one octave.

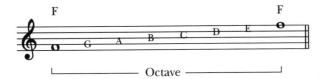

To hear an octave now, however, listen to or sing the opening phrase of the popular tune "Over the Rainbow" (Recorded Example 1); the notes between the words "some" and "where" and between "bow" and "skies" lie an octave apart.

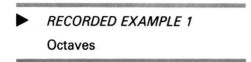

RECORDED EXAMPLE 1

Octaves

Some - where   o - ver the rain - bow,   skies   are   blue.

"Over the Rainbow" by Harold Arlen & E. Y. Harburg. Copyright © 1938, 1939 (Renewed 1966, 1967) METRO-GOLDWYN-MAYER INC. Copyright © Assigned to LEO FEIST, INC. All Rights of LEO FEIST, INC. Assigned to EMI CATALOGUE PARTNERSHIP. All Rights Controlled and Administered by EMI FEIST CATALOG, INC. International Copyright Secured. Made in USA. All Rights Reserved.

Ledger Lines

Theoretically, any pitch can be represented on either the treble or the bass staff, since the staff can be extended up or down as necessary to accommodate pitches outside the standard five lines and four spaces. These additional lines (which are added only temporarily) are called LEDGER LINES. Note the use of ledger lines in the following passage.

Beethoven

The Octave Sign. Because the octave is so basic in traditional notation, a special symbol is used to indicate a pitch *sounding* an octave higher or lower than written. The OCTAVE SIGN (*8va*..............) is used primarily to avoid ledger lines when parts are especially high or low. The Italian word *bassa* is added when the octave sign indicates an octave lower. In addition, observe that when several notes are included in an *ottava* passage, they are delineated by a dashed line. Finally, note that the word *loco* is used at the end of an *ottava* section.

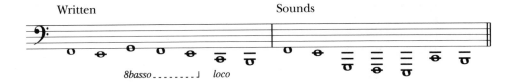

Another type of octave sign is associated with the treble clef. The symbol indicates that pitches are to sound an octave lower than written.

The Grand Staff

In keyboard music, a SYSTEM (set of staves) consisting of both treble and bass staves is used; this traditional arrangement is known as the GRAND (or GREAT) STAFF. In the next example, the pitch C occurs in several different locations. Except for those circled, each pitch C is an octave from its closest neighbor.[1]

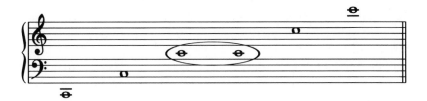

---

[1] Additional information concerning octave names will be found in Chapter 3.

exercise 2–4 *Fundamental Skills*
Octaves and Ledger Lines

A. Write sixteenth notes an octave higher or lower than those given. Use the treble clef and name both pitches.

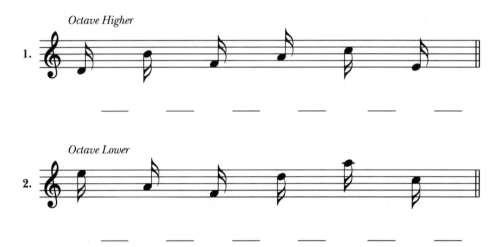

In the bass clef, write half notes an octave higher or lower than those given. As before, name both pitches.

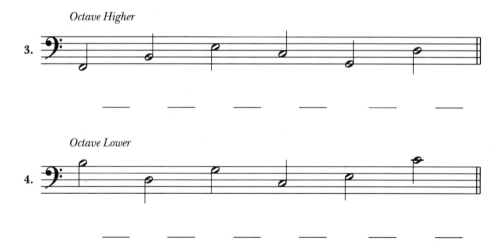

B. The following notation includes *ottava* passages. Rewrite the entire line using ledger lines as necessary to eliminate the use of the octave sign.

1.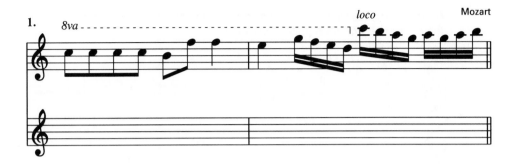

Mozart

2.

Ravel

3.

Beethoven

C. Use the octave sign to eliminate ledger lines in the following compositions. Rewrite the entire passage on the staff provided.

1.

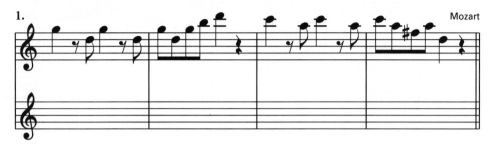

Mozart

2.

Schumann

Boccherini

3.

exercise 2–5   Musicianship Skills
SIGHT SINGING: Matching Pitches

The first step in learning to sing music at sight is matching pitches—that is, hearing a pitch sounded on the piano or another instrument and then singing that same pitch in its correct octave (if possible). Your instructor will play a series of pitches; listen carefully to each new pitch; then, sing it in the same octave if you can. The first two lines lie generally within the ranges of most men's voices. Some women will need to sing these pitches one or more octaves higher. Likewise, the second two lines are higher pitches, and men may need to sing them in a lower octave. As a further exercise, write the pitch name of each note in the blank.

1.

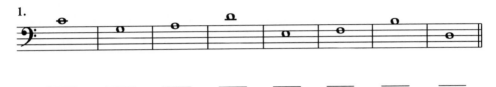

2.

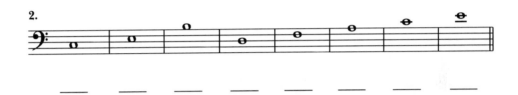

3.

4.

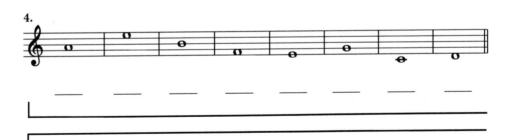

exercise 2–6 *Musicianship Skills*
SIGHT SINGING: Octaves

Sight singing (often called solfège) is an important element of musicianship. The following exercises will introduce you to sight singing.

In the following lines, play the first pitch on the piano or another instrument; then, match the pitch (an octave higher or lower if necessary). Next, repeat the first pitch and sing an octave higher or lower as appropriate. Check the second pitch on an instrument if you doubt your accuracy.

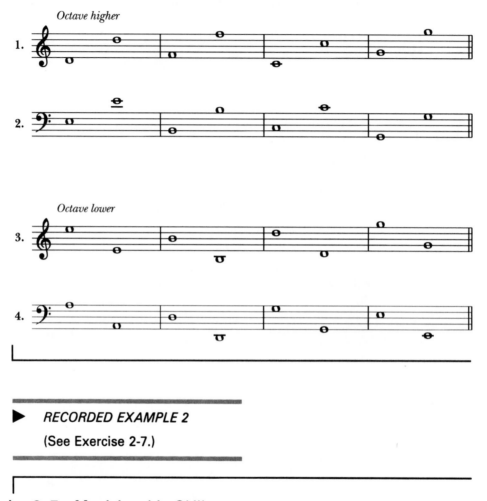

▶ *RECORDED EXAMPLE 2*

(See Exercise 2-7.)

---

exercise 2–7   Musicianship Skills
EAR TRAINING: Pitch Discrimination

You will hear several series of pitches and will be asked to indicate whether the last pitch in the series is the same as (S), higher than (H), or lower than (L) the first. The first series of pitches includes three notes; gradually, more pitches are added until you are listening to five pitches in each series. Each line includes four different series of pitches.

    Circle S if the last pitch is the *same* as the first.
    Circle H if the last pitch is *higher* than the first.
    Circle L if the last pitch is *lower* than the first.

Three Pitches

1. S H L   S H L   S H L   S H L
2. S H L   S H L   S H L   S H L

Four Pitches

3. S H L   S H L   S H L   S H L
4. S H L   S H L   S H L   S H L

Five Pitches

5. S H L   S H L   S H L   S H L
6. S H L   S H L   S H L   S H L

The C-Clefs

In addition to the treble and bass clefs, another clef is often encountered in traditional music. The MOVABLE C-CLEF (𝄡) locates the pitch C on the line that runs through the center of the symbol. Especially in older music, a variety of C-clefs is found. The SOPRANO CLEF identifies the first line as C.

C D E F G A B C D E

Soprano Clef

The MEZZO-SOPRANO CLEF places the pitch C on the second line.

A B C D E F G A B C

Mezzo-Soprano Clef

The alto and tenor clefs are used in a similar manner.

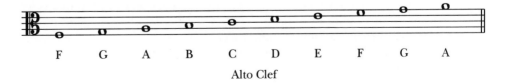

F G A B C D E F G A

Alto Clef

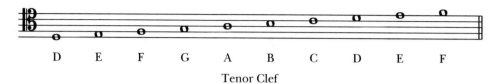

D   E   F   G   A   B   C   D   E   F

Tenor Clef

In the following passage, several different clefs are employed in the vocal parts.

Although a knowledge of all movable C-clefs is necessary for the study of music before about 1800, only two of the clefs are widely used today. The viola reads its music entirely in the alto clef. The bassoon, the cello, and the trombone often read their parts in the tenor clef.

Some instructors feel that a study of the alto and tenor clefs should be reserved for a music theory course. For those who wish to include these skills among the fundamentals of music, however, the following exercises will be useful.

exercise 2–8 Fundamental Skills
Notation in Alto and Tenor Clefs

Write pitch names for the notes shown.

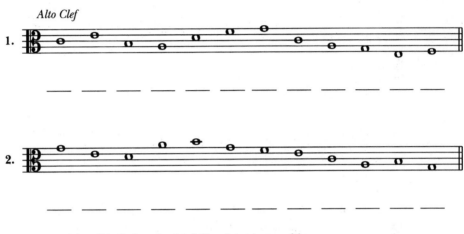

Identify pitches in the following compositions.

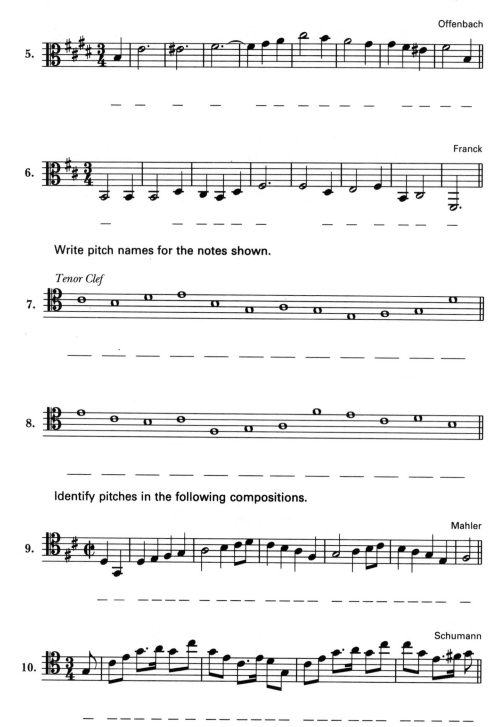

Write pitch names for the notes shown.

Tenor Clef

Identify pitches in the following compositions.

von Weber

Mendelssohn

SELF-TEST

1. In the spaces provided, write the clef and note specified. Write the note in two different staff locations.

a. Treble clef: B quarter note
b. Tenor clef: C eighth note
c. Bass clef: F sixteenth note
d. Bass clef: G half note
e. Treble clef: A whole note
f. Alto clef: D eighth note

a.   b.   c.   d.   e.   f.

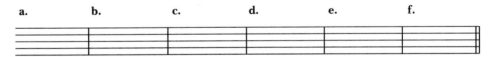

2. By letter name, identify the following notes.

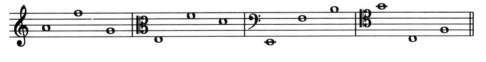

3. Circle pairs of notes that are *not* an octave apart.

4. Using the octave sign, rewrite this passage so that there are *no* ledger lines. Identify all pitches.

Mozart

5. Identify the following terms:

    a. Grand staff

    b. *Loco*

    c. Interval

    d. Clef

    e. *Bassa*

SUPPLEMENTARY EXERCISES

1. The following composition is a chant dating from before A.D. 800 and representing some of the earliest Western music. On the staff provided, rewrite the chant in modern notation, using eighth notes. Beam the notes as suggested by the brackets on the original staff. Stems should go in the correct direction for the majority of notes. Single eighth notes should have flags.

The treble clef used indicates pitches sounding an octave lower. In your revised version, use the bass clef and write the pitches as they will actually sound.

2. The following composition is by Carl Philipp Emanuel Bach, son of Johann Sebastian Bach (1685–1750). Rewrite the passage given in the treble clef and sounding an octave higher. *Do not* use an octave sign, but employ ledger lines as necessary.

C.P.E. Bach

3. By letter name, identify the pitches where blanks occur in the following compositions. Ignore the accidental symbols in identifying pitch names.

4. Write thirty-second notes an octave above those given (do *not* use the octave sign). Identify all notes by name.

a.

— — — — — — — — — — — — — — — —

b.

— — — — — — — — — — — — — — — —

Without using the octave sign, write quarter notes an octave below those given. Identify all notes by name.

a.

— — — — — — — — — — — — — — — —

b.

— — — — — — — — — — — — — — — —

5. Write the actual sounding pitches that will result from the notations below. Name each note.

Bizet

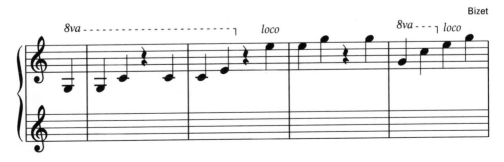

6. Return to Skill Exercise 2-3 on page 26. Rewrite line 3 (originally in the treble clef) in the same octaves, but in the alto clef. Rewrite line 5 (notated in the bass clef) to appear in the same octaves in the tenor clef. Use the staves below for your revisions.

a.

b.

The Keyboard

ESSENTIAL TERMS

- *accidental*
- *double flat*
- *double sharp*
- *enharmonic*
- *flat*
- *half step*
- *natural*
- *octave designation*
- *sharp*
- *whole step*

As you learned in the previous chapter, Western music is based on the octave—the most simple and natural interval. In our system, the octave is divided into twelve equal smaller intervals, called HALF STEPS. The half step is the smallest interval in Western music. A convenient way to illustrate the half step is to refer to the piano keyboard, which is constructed so that the interval from one key to the next closest key above or below is a half step. The distance from a given key to the closest key above or below is a half step regardless of whether the key in question is black or white. See left-hand illustration at the top of page 46.

> ***Whole Steps.*** Two half steps combine to make a WHOLE STEP—another of the basic intervals in traditional music. The distance from any one key to the *second* closest key above or below is a whole step. See right-hand illustration at the top of page 46.

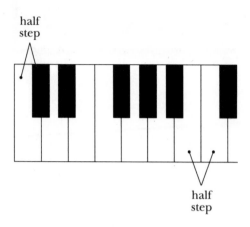

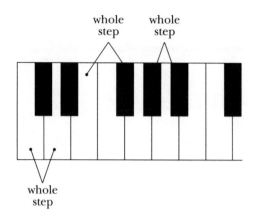

THE KEYBOARD

From the center of the keyboard, pitches of increasingly low frequency are found to the left; to the right are pitches of higher frequency.[1] The standard keyboard is based on the seven basic pitches, A B C D E F and G. These are the white keys; the black keys fall in between. Observe, however, that black keys do not fall between *every* pair of white keys. Looking at the black keys alone, notice that within any octave, they fall from left to right (lower to higher pitch on the keyboard) in groups of two, then three.

The arrangement of black keys serves as a reference in identifying the notes on the keyboard. The note C is always the white key just below the first (lower) of the *two* black keys. The note F is the white key to the left of the lowest of the *three* black keys. This arrangement is the same in every octave.

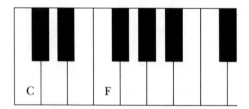

The notes A B C D E F and G are sequential over adjacent white keys. As is the case with the staff, once any one note is located on the keyboard, the keys that produce the other pitches are easily determined as well.

---

[1] Frequency and other acoustical terms are discussed in Appendix A.

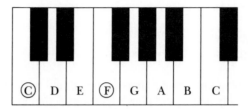

Half Steps and Whole Steps. The intervals between basic pitches are not the same. Although most basic pitches are separated by a whole step, half steps occur between B and C and between E and F (the two points where black keys do not appear).

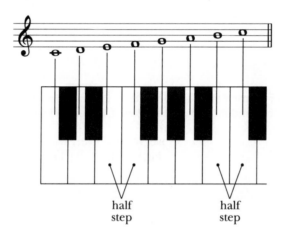

Octave Placement. The standard keyboard includes over seven octaves, allowing the performer to choose a high, middle, or low register; the names and locations of the notes *within each octave*, however, are exactly the same. So that the performer will know from written music exactly which octave the composer intends, the notations on the staff vary. Notice in the following example that although the positions of the notes on the keyboard within each octave are identical, the notation on the staff is different.

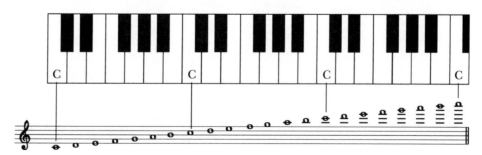

exercise 3–1 *Musicianship Skills*
KEYBOARD: Locating Pitches

A. Seated at the keyboard, play each of the lines below. Begin with "middle C," in the center of the keyboard; then, locate and play the pitches C that are one, two, and three octaves higher. Repeat the octaves from high to low. Remember: C is always the white key to the left of the two adjacent black keys.

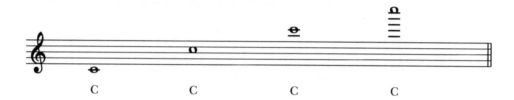

C   C   C   C

Locate the pitch F immediately above middle C. Play this pitch; then, play the pitches F that fall one, two, and three octaves below it. Repeat the octaves in ascending order.

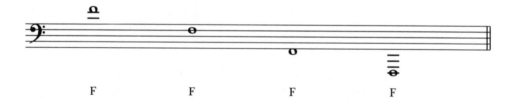

F   F   F   F

B. The following exercise consists of stepwise patterns of eight notes each. Begin by writing the name of each pitch in the blank below it. Refer to this chart of right- and left-hand fingering patterns. Thumbs are numbered "1"; little fingers, "5."

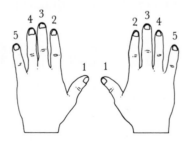

Play in turn the first pitch of each ascending series with your right thumb. When you have located all the starting pitches, return to the first set and play all eight pitches using a standard fingering pattern. Use the thumb, index finger, and third finger for the first, second, and third pitches, respectively. For the fourth pitch, turn the thumb under the third finger. Play the fifth through the eighth pitches with the remaining fingers of the right hand.

Right Hand Fingering Pattern: Ascending

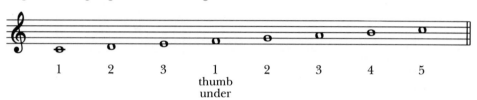

1   2   3   1   2   3   4   5
              thumb
              under

1.   **2.**

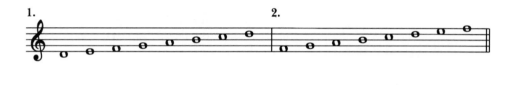

3.   **4.**

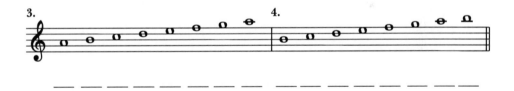

5.   **6.**

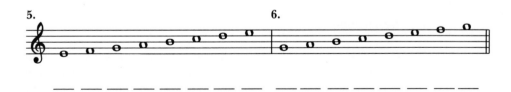

Identify each pitch notated in the bass clef by writing the note name in the blank. Locate and play the first pitch of each ascending series with the left thumb. Turn the third finger over the thumb for the sixth pitch.

Left Hand Fingering Pattern: Ascending

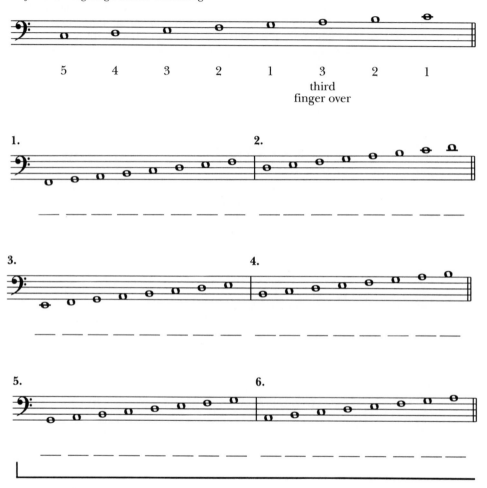

<table>
<tbody>
<tr><td>5</td><td>4</td><td>3</td><td>2</td><td>1</td><td>3</td><td>2</td><td>1</td></tr>
</tbody>
</table>

third
finger over

1.   2.

3.   4.

5.   6.

Octave Designation

Each pitch name appears in several different places on the keyboard; these pitches are one or more octaves apart. To avoid the confusion that might result from different notes having exactly the same letter name, a system of OCTAVE DESIGNATION is used to specify an exact location.

The lowest pitch in each octave is C. "Middle C," at the center of the piano keyboard, is identified as c^1 (a lowercase letter *c* and a superscript *1*). Other pitches in the same octave are identified in the same way.

c^1 d^1 e^1 f^1 g^1 a^1 b^1

In an ascending series after the pitch b^1, the next higher pitch is c^2—the lowest note in the next octave. Octaves above c^2 are identified as c^3, c^4, and c^5, respectively.

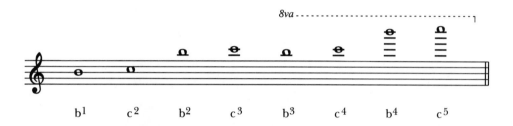

b^1 c^2 b^2 c^3 b^3 c^4 b^4 c^5

When speaking about octaves above middle C, musicians usually say "C-one" (c^1) or "B-three" (b^3), for example. In written form, use lowercase letters for the octaves above middle C. Pitches below middle C are identified using uppercase or lowercase letters *without* superscripted numbers. In descending order, the octaves below c^1 are called *small, great,* and *contra.* The identifying symbols for these octaves are a single lowercase letter (without superscript) for the *small octave,* a single uppercase letter for the *great octave,* and two uppercase letters for the *contra octave.*

Octave designation:	c	C	CC
Octave name:	*small*	*great*	*contra*

The pitch C is the lowest in each octave. Observe on the table of octave designations on page 52 that the two white keys below contra C (CC) on the standard piano keyboard are in the *subcontra* octave and are identified with three uppercase letters.

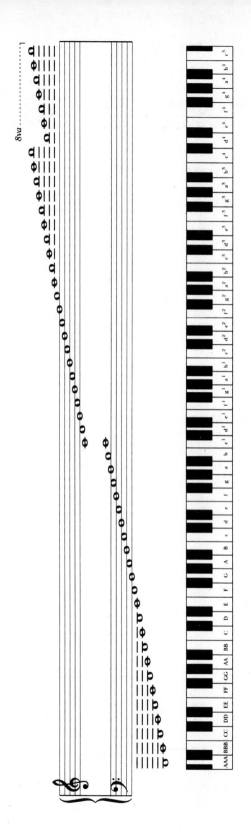

exercise 3–2   Fundamental Skills
Octave Designations

Identify the pitches by letter name and octave designation.

1.

2.
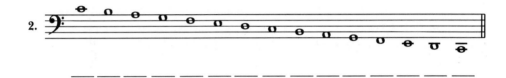

3.
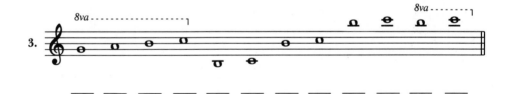

4.
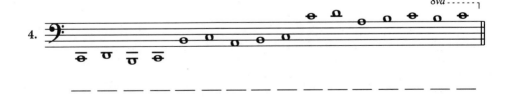

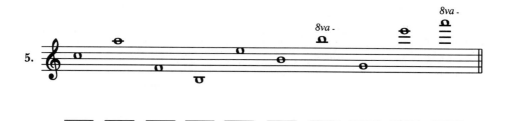

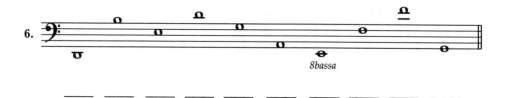

In the following composition, identify the letter names and octave designations of all pitches.

Identify only the pitches where blanks appear. Provide pitch name and octave designation.

8.   Chant

9.   Handel

exercise 3–3 *Fundamental Skills*
Notation in Specific Octaves

Write eighth notes as indicated by pitch name and octave designation. Use the clef
specified, and write the pitch with ledger lines if necessary. Check for proper stem
direction and flag placement.

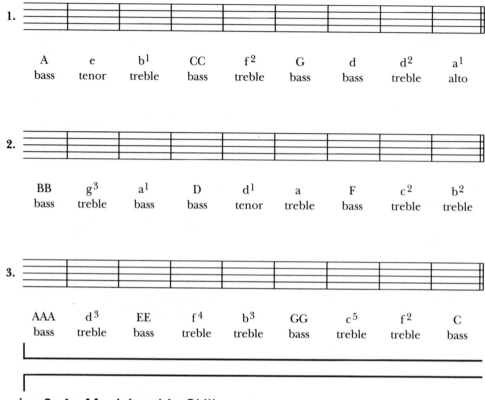

1.

A	e	b^1	CC	f^2	G	d	d^2	a^1
bass	tenor	treble	bass	treble	bass	bass	treble	alto

2.

BB	g^3	a^1	D	d^1	a	F	c^2	b^2
bass	treble	bass	bass	tenor	treble	bass	treble	treble

3.

AAA	d^3	EE	f^4	b^3	GG	c^5	f^2	C
bass	treble	bass	treble	treble	bass	treble	treble	bass

exercise 3–4 *Musicianship Skills*
KEYBOARD: Octaves

Locate and play at the keyboard each pitch in Skill Exercise 3–3. Do not play all pitches with the same finger; use different fingers and alternate left and right hands.

ACCIDENTALS

Sharp, flat, and natural signs are known as ACCIDENTALS. These are signs that appear before the note itself and indicate a raising or lowering of pitch.

The Sharp

The SHARP sign (♯) indicates that a pitch is to be *raised* one half step. If a pitch one half step higher than the basic pitch C is desired, it will be produced by the black key a half step above C; the name of this note is C-sharp (C♯). Notice that the sharp sign (♯) appears *before* a note on the staff, but *after* the letter name.

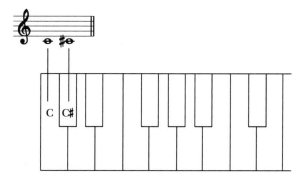

Observe that the pitches C and C-sharp represent two completely different sounds (frequencies). If a piano or another keyboard instrument is available, play these two notes and experience the difference in *sound*. Play the pitches C and C-sharp; this interval is a half step. Next, play C and D to hear a whole step. The note D is the white key above C; the black key above D is D-sharp. Likewise, the black keys above F, G, and A are F-sharp, G-sharp, and A-sharp, respectively.

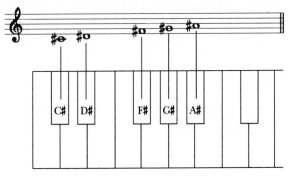

The Flat

The FLAT SIGN (♭) indicates that a pitch is to be *lowered* one half step. The note D is played with the white key just above C. The note D-sharp is produced by the black key above D. Finally, D-flat (D♭) is the black key a half step *below* D.

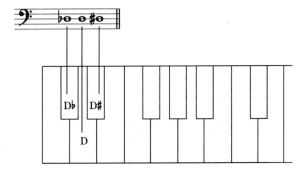

The Natural Sign

The term *natural* in music usually refers to one of the seven basic pitches. The NATURAL sign (♮) is an accidental that *cancels* a previous flat or sharp and indicates a return to the original basic pitch.

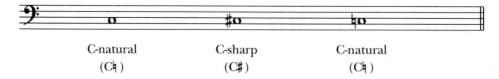

C-natural	C-sharp	C-natural
(C♮)	(C♯)	(C♮)

Measures.   The vertical lines that appear on the staff are called *barlines*. These symbols help a performer separate beats into strong and weak patterns called *measures* (discussed in the next chapter).

Once an accidental appears, it remains in effect *throughout the measure* and is not repeated for subsequent notes of the same pitch. In the following passage, the first pitch in the second measure is D-sharp—a half step higher than the previous pitch, D. The next occurrence of the pitch D is in measure 3 and is therefore D-natural. The barline cancels the sharp sign used earlier. The sharp sign is again necessary, however, to make the following pitch D-sharp.

Franck

Octave Designations with Accidentals.   Specify the octave of a sharp, flat, or natural pitch as you would for the basic pitch itself. The pitch that lies one half step above f^1, for example, is f♯^{1}. The note a half step below C is C♭.

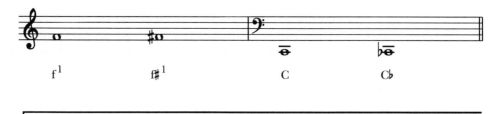

f^1	f♯^{1}	C	C♭

---

exercise 3–5 *Fundamental Skills*
Identifying Half Steps and Whole Steps

For each line, identify the interval as a half step or a whole step (use "H" for "half" and "W" for "whole").

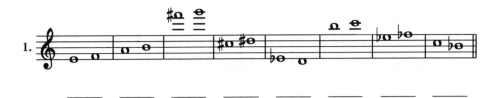

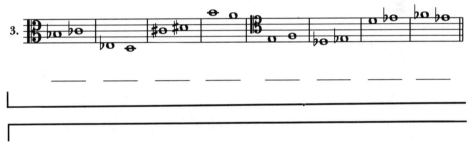

exercise 3–6 *Fundamental Skills*
Notating Half Steps and Whole Steps

As directed, write half steps or whole steps *above* the given pitches. In the blank, identify both pitches with their octave designation.

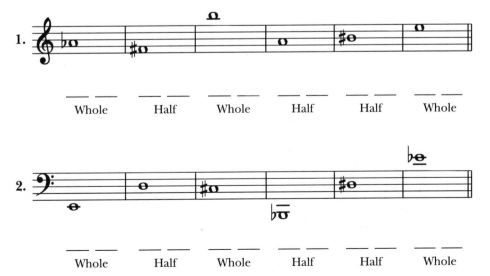

Write whole steps or half steps *below* the given pitch.

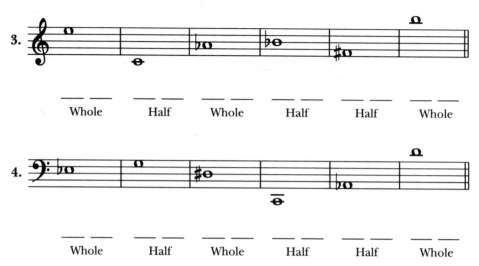

In the following compositions, identify the circled intervals as whole steps or half steps.

exercise 3–7 *Musicianship Skills*
KEYBOARD: Half Steps and Whole Steps

Locate the two pitches of each whole step or half step in Skill Exercise 3-5. Perform each interval at the keyboard. If the first pitch is a white key, use the right thumb and forefinger ascending and the left thumb and forefinger descending. If the first pitch is a black key, use the right or left third and index fingers ascending or descending.

▶ *RECORDED EXAMPLE 3*

(See Exercise 3-8.)

exercise 3–8 *Musicianship Skills*
EAR TRAINING: Hearing Whole Steps and Half Steps

A. A series of whole steps and half steps will be played (either recorded or through a live performance). Identify the interval by writing either "H" or "W" in the blank. Each line begins with three half steps; other intervals are also predominantly half steps, but with whole steps heard occasionally for comparison.

Half Steps

1. _H_   _H_   _H_   ____ ____ ____ ____ ____

2. _H_   _H_   _H_   ____ ____ ____ ____ ____

B. These lines center on the whole step. The first three intervals of each line are whole steps, but thereafter, half steps also occur. Identify the interval by writing the appropriate letter in the blank.

Whole Steps

1. _W_   _W_   _W_   ____ ____ ____ ____ ____

2. _W_   _W_   _W_   ____ ____ ____ ____ ____

C. The final interval set includes both whole steps and half steps. Identify the interval heard.

Whole Steps and Half Steps

1. ____   ____   ____   ____   ____   ____   ____   ____

2. ____   ____   ____   ____   ____   ____   ____   ____

Enharmonic Equivalents

Although the pitches D, D-sharp, and D-flat all produce different sounds, the *same* sound can be notated on the staff in a number of ways. Notice, for example, that D-flat is produced by the same key earlier labeled C-sharp. Obviously, since the two pitches employ the same key, the sounds are identical.

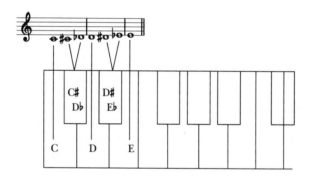

Pitches like C-sharp and D-flat, which *sound* the same but are *notated* differently, are known as ENHARMONICS. Another pair of enharmonic equivalents, F-sharp and G-flat, is identified below. These two pitches are the same in sound but are notated in different places on the staff.

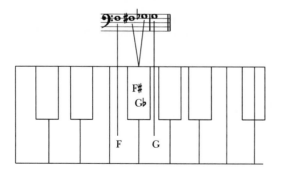

The pitch F-sharp is produced by the black key just above F; F-flat, however, is a white key—the one just below F, which was identified earlier as the note E. The pitches E and F-flat, therefore, are enharmonics. Similarly, E-sharp and F are enharmonics.

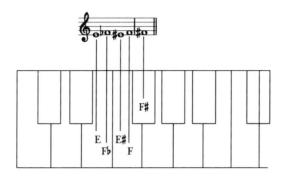

---

exercise 3–9 *Fundamental Skills*
Enharmonic Equivalents

For each pitch given, provide one enharmonic equivalent. In some cases, more than one answer will be correct. Use the blanks to identify both the letter name and the octave designation of the two pitches.

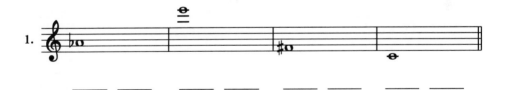

1. ___ ___ ___ ___ ___ ___ ___ ___ ___ ___ ___ ___

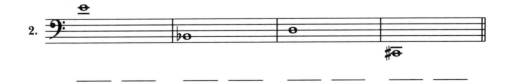

2. ___ ___ ___ ___ ___ ___ ___ ___ ___ ___ ___ ___

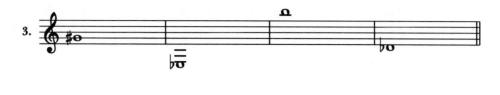

exercise 3–10   *Fundamental Skills*
Recognizing Enharmonic Equivalents

Some of the pairs of pitches below are enharmonic equivalents; others are not. Circle pairs that are enharmonic; then, identify the name and the octave of every pitch in the line.

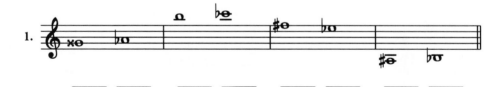

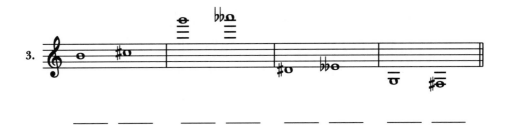

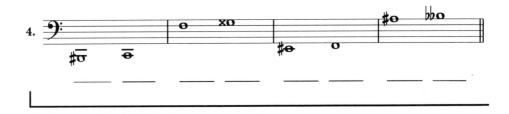

Double Sharps and Double Flats

Through the use of the DOUBLE SHARP (x) or the DOUBLE FLAT (♭♭) signs, basic pitches can be raised or lowered a *whole step*. Whereas C-sharp is played with the black key above C, C–double sharp (C x) lies yet another half step higher—the same key used for D. The pitches C x and D are, therefore, enharmonic equivalents.

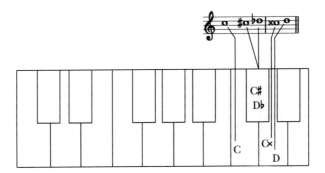

The pitch C-flat is produced by the white key below C (the same one used for B); C–double flat (C ♭♭) is found another half step lower—the black key also used for B-flat. The pitches C–double flat and B-flat are enharmonics. Notice also that there is a *third* enharmonic in this case: A-sharp.

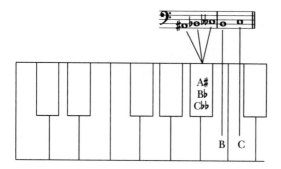

---

exercise 3–11 *Musicianship Skills*
KEYBOARD: Descending Patterns

In Skill Exercise 3-1, you learned and practiced ascending stepwise keyboard patterns. Now reverse the process and descend, beginning with the right little finger (5) and using the fourth (4), third (3), and second (2) fingers for the second, third, and fourth pitches, respectively. When you have played the fifth pitch with your thumb (1), turn your third finger over the thumb to play the last three pitches (3–1).

Right Hand Fingering Pattern: Descending

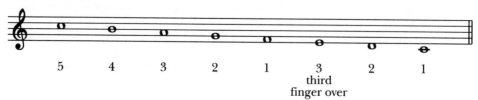

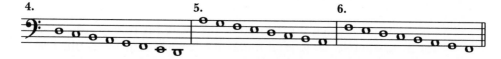

Follow a similar pattern to descend with the left hand, beginning with the thumb (1). After you use the third finger (3) for the third pitch, turn the thumb under the third finger to complete the series with fingers 1–5.

Left Hand Fingering Pattern: Descending

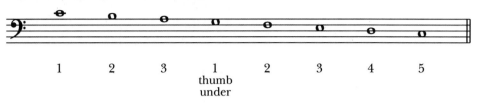

1	2	3	1	2	3	4	5
			thumb under				

7.   8.   9.

10.   11.   12.

exercise 3–12   *Musicianship Skills*
SIGHT SINGING: Whole Steps,
Half Steps, and Octaves

Play the first note of the interval at the keyboard; match this pitch vocally on a neutral syllable (*la*, perhaps); then, sing the complete interval. Play both pitches to check your accuracy, and repeat the performance several times if necessary. Continue to the second interval and perform it as before. You may need to sing an octave or two higher or lower than the pitches actually notated.

Octaves

1.

2.

Half Steps

3.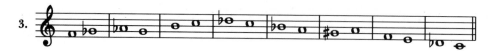

4.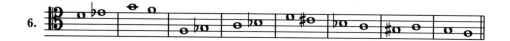

5.

6.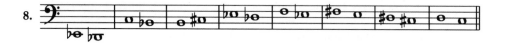

Whole Steps

7.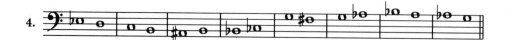

8.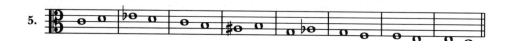

9.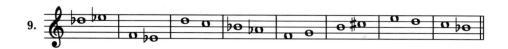

10.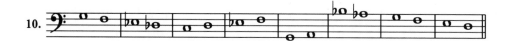

Whole Steps and Half Steps

11.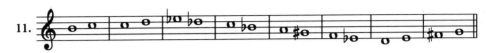

12.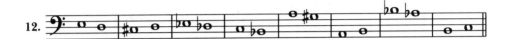

13.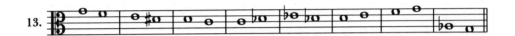

14.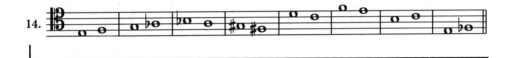

SELF-TEST

1. Write the pitch indicated in its specific octave range. Use the octave sign to avoid ledger lines.

   a. A half step above d^2
   b. A whole step below E♭
   c. A half step below g♯^{1}
   d. An enharmonic equivalent for the pitch A
   e. A whole step above B
   f. An enharmonic equivalent for GG♯
   g. A half step above a♯^{3}
   h. A whole step below d^2
   i. A half step below b
   j. An octave above C

2. Add an accidental to the second pitch to make the given interval correct.

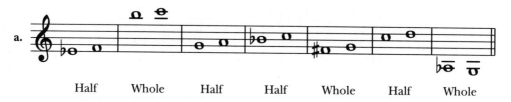

Half   Whole   Half   Half   Whole   Half   Whole

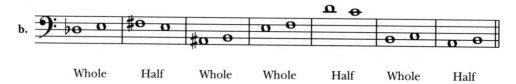

Whole   Half   Whole   Whole   Half   Whole   Half

3. Circle the pitch in each group of three that is *not* an enharmonic equivalent of the first pitch.

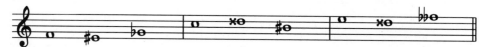

4. Locate the given pitches on the keyboard by writing the pitch name on the appropriate key.

1. D
2. F𝄪
3. G♯

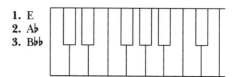

1. E
2. A♭
3. B♭♭

5. Identify the following terms and symbols:

   a. Double sharp

   b. Accidental

   c. ♯

   d. Enharmonic

   e. Natural

SUPPLEMENTARY EXERCISES

1. Determining the kind of intervals present in a melody can often tell you a great deal about the music itself. The following melodies include whole steps, half steps, and other intervals that will be discussed later. Locate pitches that lie a half step or a whole step apart, and mark them appropriately. Leave other intervals unmarked; then, total intervals in the three categories: "Whole step," "Half step," and "Other."

Whole: _____
Half: _____
Other: _____

Whole: _____
Half: _____
Other: _____

Whole: _____
Half: _____
Other: _____

2. Identify the marked intervals as either whole steps (W) or half steps (H).

Mozart

b.

Strauss

c.

Wagner

d.

3. Write an eighth note that is a half step above the given pitch. If the given pitch includes an accidental, remember that it may be necessary to employ the natural or another sign to produce the desired interval.

a.

b.

4. Musical ANALYSIS is one of the most important aspects of music theory. By analyzing various facets of a composition, students learn why the music of different eras and composers within those eras sounds the way it does.

The following melodies represent three style periods in the history of Western music. Undertake an analysis of each melody. First, make a list of each different pitch name used; then, count the number of pitches in each category (C, C-sharp, D, and so on). Determine which pitch is used most frequently. Which pitch or pitches are *not* used? Next, count the number of intervals in each of three categories: whole steps, half steps, and "other" intervals (those that are neither half steps nor whole steps). Determine which interval category is most prevalent in each line. Finally, look at the melodies as a graphic display of ascending and descending motion. Draw curved lines that represent the melodic contour of each melody and compare them in these terms. If directed to do so, write a short paper comparing the three melodies based on your analysis.

César Franck
(1822 - 1890)

Guillaume Dufay
(1400 - 1474)

W. A. Mozart
(1756 - 1791)

Simple Meters

BASIC METRIC PATTERNS

In Chapter 1, we observed that notes receive one, two, three, or more beats. You may have gotten the impression that all beats are of equal importance. Actually, all beats are *not* equal; some have a more important role than others. Just as the word "not" was italicized in the previous sentence so that you would give it more stress when reading, some beats in music are emphasized, or *accented*. An ACCENT is a musical stress. There are several different types of accent, but the most important in rhythm is the *metric* accent.

Metric Accent

Traditional Western music is based on recurring patterns of strong and weak beats called METER. The accents that create different meters are called METRIC ACCENTS. In the song "America," for example, we would not normally give each word equal stress. Sing or rhythmically speak the words, putting stress on the capitalized words:

MY coun-try, **'TIS** of thee, **SWEET** land of **LIB**-er-ty, **OF** thee I **SING** – –.

Triple Meter. The metric pulse of "America" is a three-beat (strong–weak–weak) pattern known as TRIPLE METER. Below, accented syllables are identified with the accent sign (<); unaccented syllables are marked with the symbol ˇ.

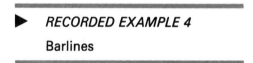

MY coun-try, **'TIS**   of thee, **SWEET** land of **LIB**-   er-ty, **OF** thee I **SING**.

Another familiar tune in triple meter is "My Bonnie Lies over the Ocean." This song begins with an incomplete pattern, having the first accent on the syllable "Bon-." An incomplete pattern that begins a composition is called an ANACRUSIS or a PICKUP.

My **BON**-nie lies **O**-ver the **O**-cean. My **BON**-nie lies **O**-ver the **Se**a.

Instead of capitalizing or italicizing certain words to indicate accents, we place a symbol called a BARLINE before the accented note. Any note or word falling immediately after the barline is accented. A DOUBLE BARLINE occurs at the end of a composition or major section.

▶ *RECORDED EXAMPLE 4*

Barlines

My BON-nie lies O-ver the O-cean.__ My BON-nie lies O-ver the Sea.___

If a composition begins with an anacrusis, the last measure contains the missing portion of the first (incomplete) measure. In addition to the anacrusis that begins with "My," there are eight complete triple metric patterns in the preceding passage. Each of these complete patterns is called a MEASURE; there are eight complete measures in the passage.

exercise 4–1 Fundamental Skills
Triple Meter

A. Study the following series of notes; then, use barlines to divide each line into measures of three beats each. The quarter note has the value of one beat in the first three lines. In some cases, rests appear at the end of a line where in the actual composition, notes beginning the next phrase would be found. If the first barline is provided, the composition begins with an anacrusis. In this event, the final measure will also be incomplete.

Continue as before, but value the eighth note at one beat.

Telemann

5.

Strauss

6.

B. One or more measures in each line of triple meter is incomplete. Given the eighth note as the beat, supply *one note* (simple or dotted) that will complete any measure with fewer than three beats.

Continue as before, but give the quarter note the value of one beat.

Duple Meter. Although many popular songs and traditional compositions are written in triple meter, others have a strong–weak, or DUPLE, pattern. Duple and triple are the two basic meters of traditional rhythmic structure. In both, the first pulse of each group is accented.

Sing or play the following series of eighth notes with no accents at all. Perform them a second time with accents as in triple meter (strong–weak–weak). Finally, accent every other beat to create a duple, or strong–weak, pattern.

The tune "Grandfather's Clock" is in duple meter. Notice that some of the syllables are sung to notes shorter than a beat, and that the first word ("My") is unaccented (an anacrusis).

▶ **RECORDED EXAMPLE 5**

Duple Meter

My   GRAND-fa-ther's CLOCK was too   LARGE for the   SHELF, so   it

STOOD nine-ty   YEARS   on   the   FLOOR _   _

Quadruple Meter. Although the two basic metric patterns are duple (strong–weak) and triple (strong–weak–weak), some melodies are written in QUAD-RUPLE METER—one in which there are four beats in each measure. The difference between two duple patterns and one quadruple pattern is subtle but important. The third quarter note of the duple pattern shown below has exactly the same accent as the first. In the quadruple pattern, however, the third quarter note is emphasized more than the second and the fourth, but *less* than the first. The symbol (–) is used to indicate this semistrong accent on the third beat of a quadruple meter.

The tune we know as "Twinkle, Twinkle, Little Star" might be written in either duple or quadruple meter. Sing the melody both ways, performing the accents very carefully to feel the differences between the two versions.

♩ = 1 beat

Duple

TWINK-le, TWINK-le,   LIT-tle STAR_ , HOW I   WON-der WHATyou ARE_ .

♩ = 1 beat

Quadruple

TWINK-le, TWINK-le, *LIT* - tle STAR_ , *HOW* I WON-der *WHAT* you ARE_ .

exercise 4–2   *Fundamental Skills*
Duple and Quadruple Meters

DUPLE METER

A. Study the following series of notes; then, use barlines to divide each line into measures of two beats each. The quarter note has the value of one beat.

♩ = 1 beat
Smetana

1.

Brahms

2.

Mendelssohn

3.

Continue as before but with the half note valued at one beat.

♩ = 1 beat
Sibelius

4.

Chausson

5.

Schumann

6.

QUADRUPLE METER

Divide these notes into measures of four beats. The quarter note is the beat unit.

♩ = 1 beat

Beethoven

7.

Mozart

8.

Elgar

9.

Continue as before but with the eighth note valued at one beat.

♪ = 1 beat

Elgar

10.

Handel

11.

Schubert

12.

DUPLE METER

B. One or more measures in each line of duple meter is incomplete. Given the half note as the beat, supply *one note* (simple or dotted) that will complete any measure with fewer than two beats.

The quarter note has the beat in the next lines.

QUADRUPLE METER

Add one rest (simple or dotted) that will complete any incomplete measures of quadruple meter. The quarter note is the beat.

 = 1 beat

The eighth note is the beat in the following lines.

♪ = 1 beat

12.

---

exercise 4–3 *Musicianship Skills*
EAR TRAINING: Differentiating
between Duple and Triple Meters

Your instructor will play a number of melodies that are either duple or triple in accent pattern. In the blank, write the word "duple" or "triple" as appropriate. Because differentiating between duple and quadruple meters is a more advanced activity, it is not included in this exercise.

1. _____   2. _____

3. _____   4. _____

5. _____   6. _____

7. _____   8. _____

9. _____   10. _____

11. _____   12. _____

Simple Time Signatures

Composers must give the performer a good deal of information about the rhythmic structure of a composition: the note that gets one beat, for example, and the number of beats in a measure. This information is conveyed through the TIME (or METER) SIGNATURE, which consists of two numerals placed at the beginning of the composition.

time signature

J. Strauss

The time signature is made up of an upper and a lower numeral. The upper numeral reveals the metric pattern (duple, triple, quadruple, and so on); the lower numeral indicates the note that is to receive one beat. If the quarter note gets one beat, the lower numeral is 4; if an eighth-note or a half-note beat is desired, the lower numerals are 8 and 2, respectively.

Observe the information conveyed by the following time signatures.

2 = Duple meter   **3** = Triple meter   **4** = Quadruple meter
4 = Quarter note beat   **8** = Eighth note beat   **2** = Half note beat

---

exercise 4–4   Fundamental Skills
Simple Time Signatures

A. For each time signature shown, write a word representing the accent pattern (duple, triple, or quadruple) in the first blank. In the second blank, write the actual note that will receive one beat.

1. $\frac{3}{4}$ _____ ____   2. $\frac{2}{2}$ _____ ____

3. $\frac{3}{8}$ _____ ____   4. $\frac{2}{4}$ _____ ____

5. $\frac{4}{4}$ _____ ____   6. $\frac{2}{16}$ _____ ____

7. $\frac{4}{8}$ _____ ____   8. $\frac{3}{2}$ _____ ____

B. Write a time signature that corresponds to the accent pattern and unit of beat given.

1. _____ Triple meter   2. _____ Duple meter
          Eighth-note beat   Quarter-note beat

3. _____ Triple meter   4. _____ Quadruple meter
          Half-note beat   Sixteenth-note beat

5. _____ Duple meter   6. _____ Quadruple meter
          Quarter-note beat   Eighth-note beat

Simple Beat Division

When composers use notes shorter than one beat, they must divide the beat. In SIMPLE BEAT DIVISION, the beat divides into two equal parts. A quarter-note beat, for example, divides into two equal eighth notes.

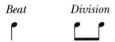

The song "Grandfather's Clock" features a division of the quarter-note beat in a duple meter. The word "Grand" receives a full beat; the syllables "fa-" and "-ther's," however, share an equally divided beat.

If the half note is assigned the value of one beat, the simple division is into two quarter notes.

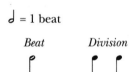

Just as effectively, "Grandfather's Clock" could be written using a half-note beat with a division of quarter notes. When a composition is rewritten from one mode of notation to another without a change in the sounds themselves (like simply changing from $\frac{3}{4}$ to $\frac{3}{2}$), the music is said to be *transcribed* and the resulting notation is a *transcription*.

Finally, note the *appearance* of the rhythms when the eighth note is assigned the value of one beat and the sixteenth note is the division.

My Grand - fa- ther's Clock was too large for the shelf,

Beat Subdivision

If notes smaller than the beat division are desired, the division itself can be SUBDIVIDED into two equal parts. If the quarter note is the beat, for example, the beat division is two eighth notes; the eighth notes *subdivide* into four sixteenth notes.

The same principle applies when other notes receive the beat. Notice here the simple division and subdivision with the whole-note and eighth-note beats.

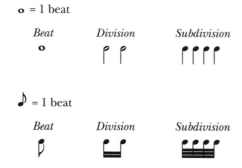

The folk song "Old MacDonald Had a Farm" features an interesting mixture of beat, divided beat, and subdivided beat units. The meter is duple, and in the version given here, the quarter note receives one beat (Recorded Example 6).

▶ *RECORDED EXAMPLE 6*

Beat Subdivision

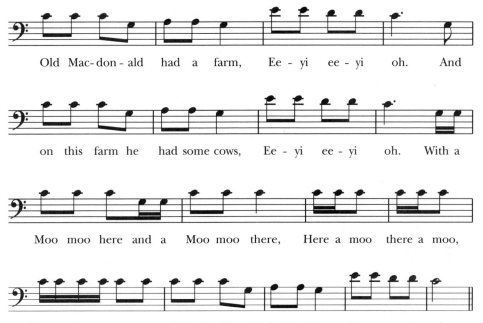

Old Mac- don- ald had a farm, Ee - yi ee - yi oh. And

on this farm he had some cows, Ee - yi ee - yi oh. With a

Moo moo here and a Moo moo there, Here a moo there a moo,

Ev- ery where a moo moo Old Mac- don- ald had a farm, Ee - yi ee- yi oh.

exercise 4–5 *Fundamental Skills*
Beat, Division, and Subdivision

For each meter given, provide the note that receives the beat, the two notes that constitute the beat division, and the four notes constituting the beat subdivision. Indicate also the accent pattern—that is, whether the meter is duple, triple, or quadruple.

	Meter	Beat	Division	Subdivision	Accent Pattern
1.	$\frac{3}{4}$	_____	_____	_____	_____
2.	$\frac{4}{2}$	_____	_____	_____	_____
3.	$\frac{2}{16}$	_____	_____	_____	_____
4.	$\frac{2}{4}$	_____	_____	_____	_____
5.	$\frac{3}{2}$	_____	_____	_____	_____

Meter	Beat	Division	Subdivision	Accent Pattern
6. $\frac{4}{8}$	_____	_____	_____	_____
7. $\frac{3}{1}$	_____	_____	_____	_____
8. $\frac{4}{4}$	_____	_____	_____	_____

Classification of Simple Meters

Meters are classified according to the accent pattern and the manner of beat division. The meter represented by the time signature $\frac{2}{4}$, for example, would be classified as *duple-simple*, since the accent pattern is duple and the beat division is simple. A meter such as $\frac{3}{8}$ would be classified as *triple-simple*, and $\frac{4}{2}$ would be *quadruple-simple*.

Alla Breve *and Common Time.* Sometimes, symbols are used to represent certain meters. The meter $\frac{2}{2}$, for example, is often designated by the symbol ¢; this meter is termed *alla breve* (or, less formally, "cut time"). The letter **C**, referring to *common time*, is often used to designate the time signature $\frac{4}{4}$.

Beaming in Simple Meters

The purpose of beaming is to clarify beat groups for the performer. Although beaming often depends on factors other than note values (phrasing, for instance), conventional notation includes many general guidelines.

In simple meters, groups of twos and fours are most often beamed together when the notes have equal value.

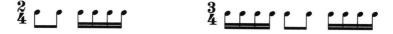

When groups of twos or fours do not begin on a strong beat, however, they should never be beamed.

Incorrect   Correct   Incorrect   Correct

Groups of three that make up a complete beat can be correctly beamed together.

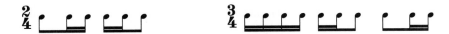

But three *equal* notes are rarely beamed in simple meters (see Chapter 5 for an exception). When a rest precedes or follows a group of three equal notes, however, beaming the three notes together is usually correct.

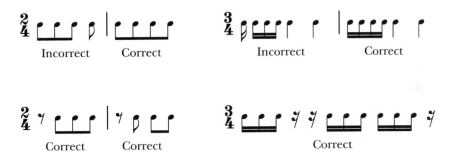

In a triple meter, a group of six notes that constitutes an entire measure may be beamed.

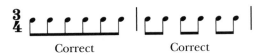

Groups of less than one beat are rarely beamed together unless a dotted note is involved.

Whether to use a single group of four or two groups of two may be a purely editorial decision.

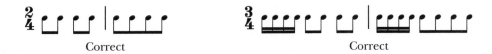

Performing Simple Meters

Conducting. Traditional conducting patterns are helpful in performing rhythms. You should conduct with your right hand and keep the beat relatively high—usually no lower than chest level. The first beat of any metric pattern is down; other motions depend on the accent pattern. The process of arm motion (whether smooth or more jerky, for example) depends upon the style of the music. Study the following conducting patterns and practice them until they are familiar.

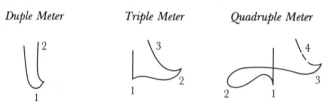

Duple Meter   *Triple Meter*   *Quadruple Meter*

Counting. Another aid in rhythmic performance is a verbal system of counting durational values. Several counting systems are available, but the one suggested here has many advantages. Notes that fall on the beat are counted according to the corresponding number in the accent pattern (Recorded Example 7).[1]

▶ *RECORDED EXAMPLE 7*

Counting the Beat

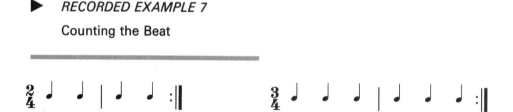

If a note lasts for more than one beat, if it is tied across the barline, or if a rest falls on the beat, the counting is silent.

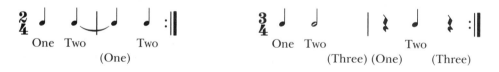

---

[1] The symbol :‖ indicates that material is to be repeated.

One   Three   Two   Three
      (Two)   (Four) (One)   (Four)

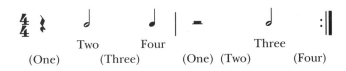

       Two   Four   Three
(One)   (Three)   (One) (Two)   (Four)

For a divided beat, use the beat number for the first half and the syllable "te" for the second. Again, rests are counted silently.

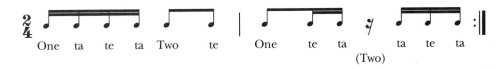

One Two   One te Two te   One Two   te One Two te Three te
                                        (Three)

The syllable "ta" can be added to count the beat subdivision.

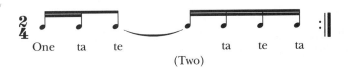

One   ta   te   ta Two   te   One   te   ta   ta   te   ta
                                                (Two)

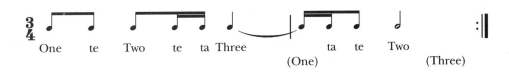

One   ta   te   ta   te   ta
          (Two)

One   te   Two   te   ta Three   ta   te   Two
                                  (One)   (Three)

exercise 4–6 Musicianship Skills
RHYTHMIC READING: Simple Meters

TRIPLE METER

Sing each line of music using counting syllables. Conduct as you perform. This may seem awkward at first, so choose a slow tempo and increase the speed gradually.

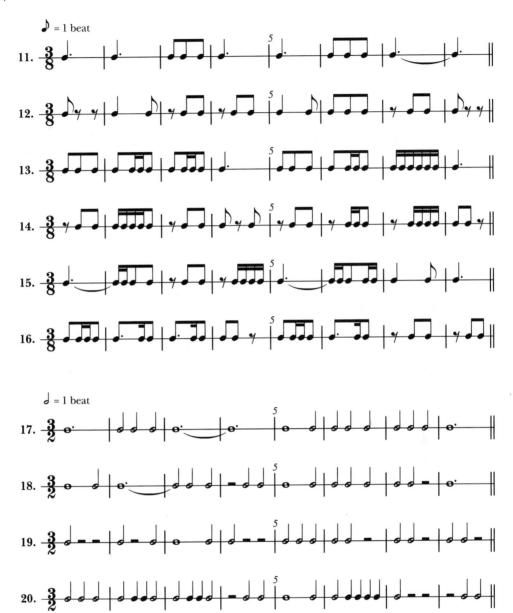

DUPLE METER

QUADRUPLE METER

STUDIES

Most of the rhythmic studies in this text are reductions from actual compositions representing various periods of music literature. They include tempo and expression indications (added editorially to the music if not specified by the composer). Consult Appendix D for a discussion of tempo, expression, and dynamic terms and markings.

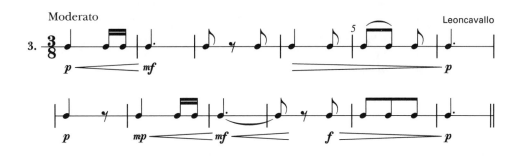

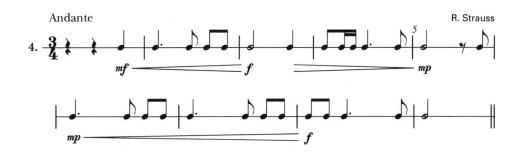

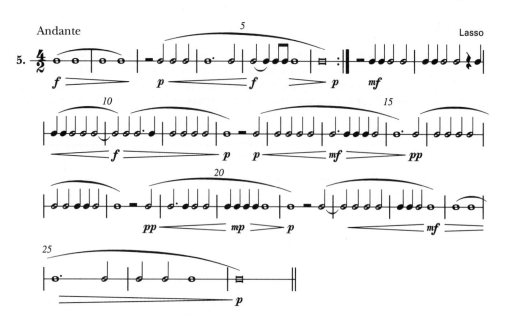

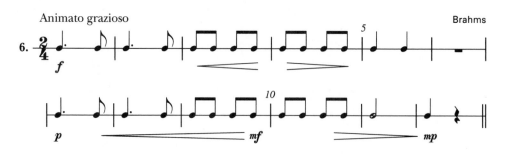

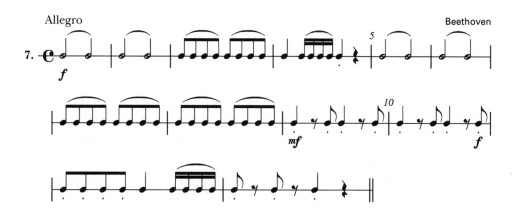

ENSEMBLES

Ensemble performance poses problems completely different from those encountered when you sing or play alone. The following exercises are intended to be performed by individuals or groups (or perhaps one or more soloists accompanied by a group). There are no tempo or other performance directions, so feel free to add your own.

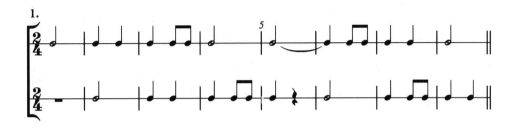

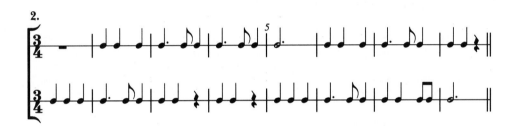

4.

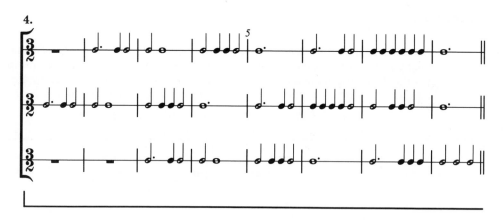

exercise 4–7   Musicianship Skills
EAR TRAINING: Identifying Meter

A. Your instructor will play a number of melodies. In the blank, write "duple," "triple," or "quadruple" to identify the meter of the music.

1. _____   2. _____

3. _____   4. _____

5. _____   6. _____

7. _____   8. _____

B. Sing the following tunes to yourself and identify the meter as before. If you do not know one or more of these melodies, choose another that you do know and identify that meter instead.

1. *The Star-Spangled Banner* _____

2. *Mary Had a Little Lamb* _____

3. *God Bless America* _____

4. *Moon River* _____

5. *New York, New York* _____

6. *The Marines' Hymn* _____

SYNCOPATION

When composers select an accent pattern and make other choices about metric structure, they still must achieve variety in rhythm. One means of varying the rhythmic element is through SYNCOPATION—the intentional misplacement of accents.

In a quadruple-simple meter, for example, there is a strong accent on the first beat, a lesser one on the third beat. These are the natural metric accents. If the emphasis is suddenly shifted to the second and fourth beats, however, the effect is startling.

> ONE   two   *THREE*   four   one   *TWO*   three   *FOUR*

The misplacement of accents that creates a syncopated effect can be accomplished in any one of several ways, including note length.

Note Length.   When a longer note appears between shorter ones (especially if the longer note is *twice* the value of the shorter ones), the natural metric accents are disrupted. The following patterns are some of those most often associated with the term *syncopation*.

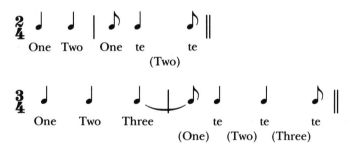

The song "You're a Grand Old Flag" (Recorded Example 8) includes a typical syncopation figure on the words "high FLY-ing flag." The tune begins with an anacrusis.

▶ *RECORDED EXAMPLE 8*

Syncopation

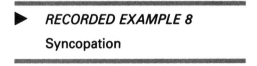

Cohan

> You're a   *GRAND*   old   FLAG   you're a   HIGH *FLY* - ing FLAG

Had the composer chosen natural metric accents, he might have written the passage as notated in the second line.

You're a   *GRAND*   old   FLAG   you're a   *HIGH*   FLY - ing   FLAG

Without the syncopated "kick" of the original rhythm, however, "You're a Grand Old Flag" is limp and predictable. Skillful composers use strategically placed devices like syncopation to create interest within a traditional meter.

exercise 4–8 Musicianship Skills
RHYTHMIC READING: Syncopation

Sing each line of music using counting syllables. Conduct as you perform. This may seem awkward at first, so choose a slow tempo.

STUDIES

Menuetto — Haydn

Andante — Wagner

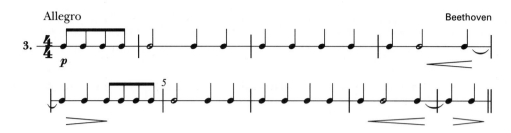

ENSEMBLES

SELF-TEST

1. What are the two basic accent patterns? _____ _____

2. Identify the following terms:

    a. Accent

    b. Barline

    c. Anacrusis

    d. Triple-simple

3. Write the note that receives one beat in each of the following meters.

$\underline{\qquad} \frac{2}{2} \quad \underline{\qquad} \frac{3}{4} \quad \underline{\qquad} \frac{4}{1} \quad \underline{\qquad} \frac{2}{8} \quad \underline{\qquad} \frac{3}{16}$

4. Given the following meters, write the beat, the beat division, and the beat subdivision.

	Beat	*Division*	*Subdivision*
$\frac{3}{8}$	___	_____	_____
$\frac{4}{2}$	___	_____	_____

5. Add one rest (dotted if necessary) to complete each measure.

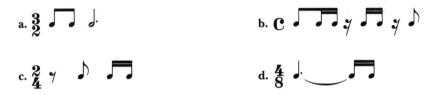

6. Add barlines where necessary.

SUPPLEMENTARY EXERCISES

1. The following composition is notated in $\frac{3}{2}$ meter. Transcribe the time signature to $\frac{3}{8}$ in the first line and $\frac{3}{4}$ in the second line. Revise the notation as necessary. The first measures have been completed as an example.

Handel

The next composition is in $\frac{4}{4}$. Transcribe the music to $\frac{4}{2}$ and to $\frac{4}{8}$.

2. Compose a rhythmic duet in $\frac{3}{4}$ meter by continuing the ideas in the first two measures. Consider using the repetition and variation of these ideas rather than constantly new material.

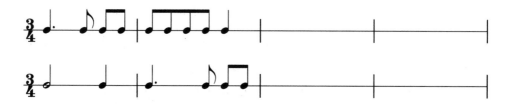

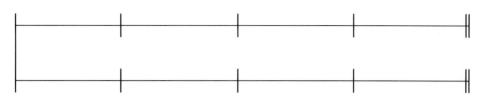

Compose other ensembles, using your own rhythmic ideas. Remember that the alternation of familiar and new material is usually more successful as an organizational technique than constantly providing new material alone. Be aware, too, that more complex ideas, especially as developed by inexperienced composers, are often less successful than very simple ones. Obviously, less complicated rhythms are also easier to perform.

3. In the blank below each time signature, write the note that receives one beat.

$$\frac{4}{4} \qquad \frac{3}{2} \qquad \frac{4}{8} \qquad \frac{2}{16} \qquad \frac{3}{1} \qquad \frac{2}{4} \qquad \frac{3}{8}$$

——— ——— ——— ——— ——— ——— ———

4. Give an example of two different meters that conform to the given classification.

    a. ——— ——— duple-simple

    b. ——— ——— quadruple-simple

    c. ——— ——— triple-simple

5. For each beat given, write the two notes representing the division and the four notes representing the subdivision.

♩ ——— —————— ♩ ——— —————— ♪ ——— ——————

6. In the time signatures given, provide the values (in beats) of the notes and rests shown.

a. $\frac{3}{4}$ ¼· —— ⅞ —— ♩ —— ♩ —— ♩·· —— ⅞· —— |

b. $\frac{4}{2}$ ▫ —— ▬· —— ¼ —— ♩· —— ▬ —— o —— |

c. $\frac{2}{8}$ ♩ —— ⅞ —— ♩ —— ♩· —— ¼ —— ⅞· —— |

7. For the given passages, add barlines as appropriate. All the lines end with a full measure and none of them begins with an anacrusis.

Compound Meters and Borrowed Division

COMPOUND METER

A COMPOUND METER is one in which the beat divides into three equal parts. In a simple meter, the beat is always a simple (undotted) note; in a compound meter, on the other hand, the note representing one beat is always a *dotted* note.

Beat Division

The beat in simple meters (an undotted, or simple, note) divides into two parts. As we discussed earlier, the quarter-note beat divides into two eighth notes; the sixteenth-note beat divides into two thirty-second notes.

Beat   *Division*   *Beat*   *Division*

Recall, however, that the dot adds one-half the original value to a note or a rest. Whereas the quarter note divides into two eighth notes, the *dotted quarter note* has half again the original value, permitting a three-part division.

A dotted note can be divided evenly into three parts; similarly, three simple notes can be tied together to make one note with three times their single value. The dotted half note, for example, divides into three quarter notes; the dotted eighth note divides into three sixteenths.

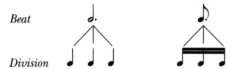

Simple and Compound Meters. Simple and compound meters are differentiated easily through a simple rule and a single exception.

Rule: *If the upper numeral of the time signature is* not *divisible by 3, the meter is* simple *and the beat divides into two equal parts.*

Exception: The numeral 3 itself indicates a simple meter with a two-part beat division.

Any meter that is not simple is compound (there are no other possibilities in traditional music). The upper numeral of a compound time signature will *always* be divisible by 3 (except 3 itself—the exception). Compound time signatures are represented principally by the upper numerals 6, 9, and 12.

exercise 5–1   Fundamental Skills
Simple and Compound Time Signatures

A number of meter signatures are given. Determine whether the meter is simple or compound by applying the rule and the exception just discussed. Use the blank for your answer.

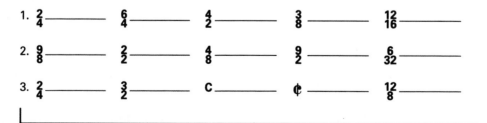

1. $\frac{2}{4}$_____ $\frac{6}{4}$_____ $\frac{4}{2}$_____ $\frac{3}{8}$_____ $\frac{12}{16}$_____

2. $\frac{9}{8}$_____ $\frac{2}{2}$_____ $\frac{4}{8}$_____ $\frac{9}{2}$_____ $\frac{6}{32}$_____

3. $\frac{2}{4}$_____ $\frac{3}{2}$_____   C_____   ₵_____ $\frac{12}{8}$_____

The Beat in Compound Meters. In a compound meter, the dotted note serves as the unit of beat because it divides naturally into three equal parts. Metric plans in simple and compound meters, however, are identical. Compound meters have two, three, and four beats per measure just as simple meters do. Compound meters are classified principally as duple-compound, triple-compound, and quadruple-compound.

The song "Three Blind Mice" offers an example of duple-compound meter: There are two beats per measure, with the beat divided into three parts. The dotted quarter note is given as the unit of beat in the following passage, although a number of other dotted notes could fulfill this role (Recorded Example 9).

▶ *RECORDED EXAMPLE 9*

Compound Meter

"Three Blind Mice" can also be notated using a dotted eighth- or a dotted half-note beat. Compare the notations below with the notation of the first line of the preceding version. Assuming that the *tempo* remains the same, these two transcriptions will sound exactly alike. The symbol :‖: indicates that the material within the dots is to be repeated.

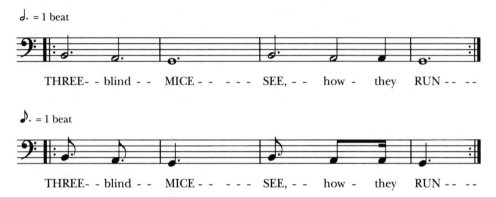

THREE- - blind - -   MICE - -   - - -   SEE, - -   how -   they   RUN -- - -

THREE- - blind - -   MICE - -   - - -   SEE, - -   how -   they   RUN -- - -

Beat Subdivision

Although the beat in a compound meter divides into three parts, the subdivision of the beat is still simple—into two parts. If the beat is the dotted half note, for example, it divides into three quarter notes; the subdivision is six eighth notes.

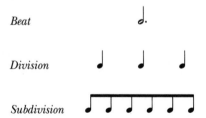

Other compound beats subdivide in a similar manner. The dotted-quarter-note beat divides into three eighths and subdivides into six sixteenth notes. The dotted-eighth-note beat divides into sixteenths and subdivides into thirty-second notes.

exercise 5–2 *Fundamental Skills*
Understanding the Compound Beat

For each meter given, provide the note that receives one beat, the three that make up the division, and the six that make up the subdivision.

	Meter	Beat	Division	Subdivision
1.	$\frac{6}{8}$	_____	_____	_____
2.	$\frac{9}{4}$	_____	_____	_____
3.	$\frac{6}{16}$	_____	_____	_____
4.	$\frac{12}{4}$	_____	_____	_____
5.	$\frac{9}{8}$	_____	_____	_____
6.	$\frac{6}{2}$	_____	_____	_____
7.	$\frac{9}{16}$	_____	_____	_____
8.	$\frac{12}{8}$	_____	_____	_____

Note Values in Compound Meters

In compound meters, notes receiving more than one beat are valued as they are in simple time (twice the beat, four times the beat, and so on). If the beat is a dotted quarter note, the dotted half note or rest receives two beats; the dotted whole, four beats.

♩. = 1 beat

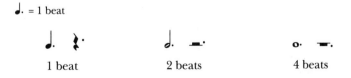

| 1 beat | 2 beats | 4 beats |

There is no single symbol, however, to represent a unit of three beats in a compound meter. Whereas a single dotted note can stand for three beats in a simple meter, tied notes or consecutive rests are necessary in compound meters.

3 beats   3 beats*

* A whole rest is acceptable for an entire measure of rest in any meter.

Divisions and Subdivisions. Whereas the beat division and subdivision in a simple meter are one-half and one-quarter the beat's value, respectively, smaller values in compound meters are more often thirds and sixths of a beat. If the beat is a dotted quarter note, a single eighth note or rest is one-third of a beat. An undotted quarter note or rest receives two-thirds of a beat.

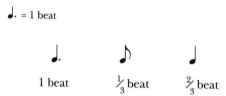

1 beat   ⅓ beat   ⅔ beat

If the dotted half note is the beat, the symbols are different, but the values are the same.

♩. = 1 beat

1 beat   ⅓ beat   ⅔ beat

---

exercise 5–3 *Fundamental Skills*
Note Values in Compound Meters

A. Write the value of the notes and rests shown. The dotted quarter note is the beat.

♩. = 1 beat

If the dotted *eighth* note is the beat, compute the values of the notes and rests shown.

♪. = 1 beat

1. ♩. _____   2. ♩. _____

3. 𝄾 _____   4. ♩ _____

5. 𝄾· _____   6. 𝄽· _____

With a dotted-half-note beat, write the values of the notes and rests given.

♩. = 1 beat

1. ▬· _____   2. ♩ _____

3. 𝄽 _____   4. ♩. _____

5. o· _____   6. ♩ _____

B. Several series of notes are shown. Considering the beat specified, compute the total value of each series in beats or fractions of a beat.

Dotted-Quarter-Note Beat

♩. = 1 beat

1. ♩. ♩ ♪ ♩. _____   2. ♩ ♪ o.⌣♩ ♪ _____

3. ♩ 𝄾 ♩. ♫♫ _____   4. ♩. ♩. 𝄽 ♪ ♩ _____

5. ♩ ♪♪𝄽 ♩. _____   6. ♫♫ 𝄾♩ 𝄾♩ 𝄾 _____

7. ♩. ♩ ♪♩ ♩. _____   8. 𝄽 ♪𝄾♩ ♩. ♩ _____

Dotted-Half-Note Beat

♩. = 1 beat

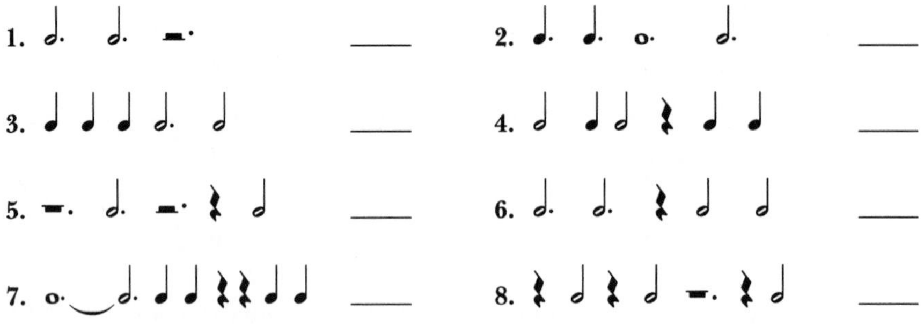

1. _____   2. _____

3. _____   4. _____

5. _____   6. _____

7. _____   8. _____

Dotted-Eighth-Note Beat

♪. = 1 beat

1. _____   2. _____

3. _____   4. _____

5. _____   6. _____

7. _____   8. _____

Compound Time Signatures

As we discussed earlier, the upper numeral of the time signature in simple meters indicates the accent pattern, and the lower numeral represents the unit of beat. In compound meters, however, the information given in the time signature is not as direct. Whereas in a simple meter, the lower numeral represents a specific note (4 = quarter note, for instance), there is no number understood to represent a dotted note.

$$\frac{2}{\text{♩}} = \frac{2}{4} \qquad \frac{2}{\text{♩.}} = \frac{2}{?}$$

Since a number that can represent a dotted note in a time signature is unavailable, composers indicate with the lower numeral not the beat but the *beat division*. The beat division is always a simple note, which can be indicated by a familiar numeral—1, 2, 4, 8, 16, or 32. If the beat is the dotted half note, for example, the lower numeral of the time signature is 4, because the quarter note is the beat division. In a compound time signature, therefore, a lower numeral of 4 indicates not a quarter note but a *dotted-half-note* beat.

Triple-Simple   *Triple-Compound*

3   9
4   4

Beat:

Because in a compound meter, the lower numeral represents not the beat but the *beat division*, the upper numeral of the time signature must be adjusted as well. If we want a time signature that will reflect three dotted-half-note beats in a measure (triple-compound meter), the number 4 is used as the lower numeral (the beat division) and the number 9 appears as the upper numeral. The number 9 indicates that there are nine quarter notes in the measure, but since we know that the meter is *compound*, we know that the number 4 refers not to the beat but to the beat division. Furthermore, we know that the number 9 is *three times* the number of beats in a measure.

In a duple meter, there are two beats in a measure (strong–weak). If the meter is duple-simple and a quarter-note beat is desired, the upper numeral of the time signature is 2; the lower numeral is 4. If the meter is duple-*compound*, however, the upper numeral will be not 2 but *6* (three times the number of beats in a measure). The lower numeral will vary depending on the unit of beat; if a dotted-quarter-note beat is desired, the lower numeral will be 8, because the dotted quarter note (which cannot be represented by a number) divides into three eighth notes.

Duple-Simple   *Duple-Compound*

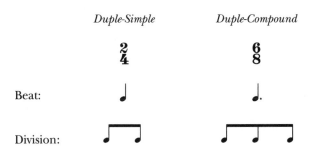

If a duple-compound meter with a dotted-eighth-note beat is desired, the upper numeral will still be 6, but the lower numeral will now be 16 to reflect the *division* of the dotted-eighth-note beat. The time signature $\frac{6}{4}$ designates a duple-compound meter with a dotted-half-note beat.

If a meter is compound, the information given in the time signature concerning beat and accent pattern is the same as for simple meters, but one must first "decode" the numbers.

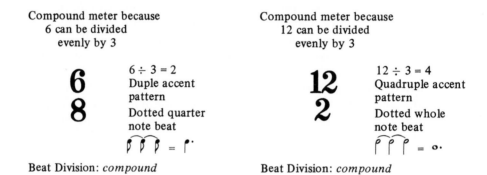

---

exercise 5–4   *Fundamental Skills*
Compound Meter Signatures

A. The meter signatures given are all compound. First, write the note represented by the lower numeral. This is the beat division. Next, write a dotted note with three times this value. The dotted note is the unit of beat. Finally, determine the accent pattern by dividing the upper numeral by 3.

Meter Signature	Note Represented by Lower Numeral	Dotted Note with Three Times This Value	Accent Pattern
1. $\frac{6}{8}$	_____	_____	_____
2. $\frac{9}{8}$	_____	_____	_____

3. $\frac{6}{4}$ ___ ___ ___

4. $\frac{9}{4}$ ___ ___ ___

5. $\frac{12}{4}$ ___ ___ ___

6. $\frac{9}{16}$ ___ ___ ___

7. $\frac{6}{2}$ ___ ___ ___

8. $\frac{12}{8}$ ___ ___ ___

B. Supply meter signatures that conform to the accent pattern, beat unit, and beat division specified. Some meters are simple; others are compound.

	Accent Pattern	Beat Unit	Beat Division
1. ___	Triple	♩	♩ ♩
2. ___	Duple	♩.	♬♬♬
3. ___	Triple	♩.	♩ ♩ ♩
4. ___	Quadruple	♩.	♪♪♪
5. ___	Duple	♩	♬♬
6. ___	Triple	♩.	♪♪♪

exercise 5–5 *Fundamental Skills*
Using Barlines in Compound Meters

A. The lines below represent compound meters. Supply barlines as indicated by the time signatures. If the first barline is supplied, the line begins with an anacrusis. In that case, remember that the final measure will be incomplete.

B. Some of these measures are incomplete. Supply one note (simple or dotted) that will complete any incomplete measures.

2.

3.

Beaming in Compound Meters

Whereas groups of two and four equal notes are usually beamed together in simple meters, three and six like values are more often beamed in compound meters.

The first patterns below are readable, but the beaming suggests a simple meter like $\frac{3}{4}$ rather than a compound meter. In the second example, the beaming corresponds to the three-part division of a compound meter like $\frac{6}{8}$.

Poor   Correct

Depending on the values employed, *many correct beaming combinations exist in compound meters.* As always, however, *groups of less than or more than one beat beamed together often constitute incorrect notation.*

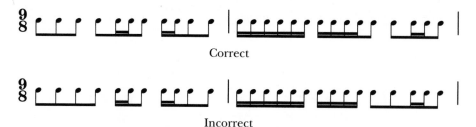

Correct

Incorrect

As in simple meters, complete beat groups can usually be beamed together, regardless of the number of notes involved.

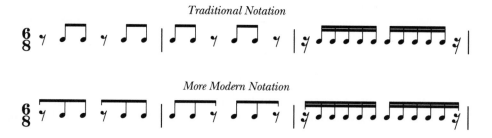

Correct

When rests occur, complete beat groups are still beamed together, despite the occurrence of rests.

Traditional Notation

More Modern Notation

Performing Compound Meters

Counting.   In a compound meter, notes or rests on the beat are counted with the beat number just as they are in simple meters (Recorded Example 10). Because the compound beat divides into three parts, however, the counting syllables "la" and "li" are used for the second and third divisions, respectively.

▶   *RECORDED EXAMPLE 10*

Counting the Compound Beat

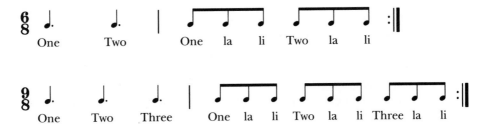

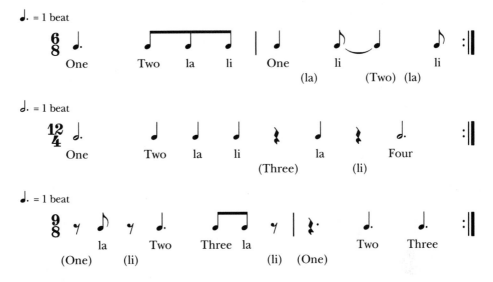

As in simple meters, rests and ties are counted silently.

Subdivision. The beat division may be subdivided into two parts in both simple and compound meters. Accordingly, the same syllable, "ta," is used for the subdivision in compound meters.

Conducting in Compound Meters. Because accent patterns in compound meters are the same basic three employed in simple meters, use the two-, three-, and four-beat patterns shown on page 92 for duple-compound, triple-compound, and quadruple-compound meters, respectively.

exercise 5–6   Musicianship Skills
RHYTHMIC READING: Compound Meters

The following exercises employ typical rhythms in compound meters. Study and "decode" the time signature; then, set a comfortable tempo for the beat. You may find it helpful to write in the counting below the notes themselves. Remember to conduct while you perform.

DUPLE METER

11. 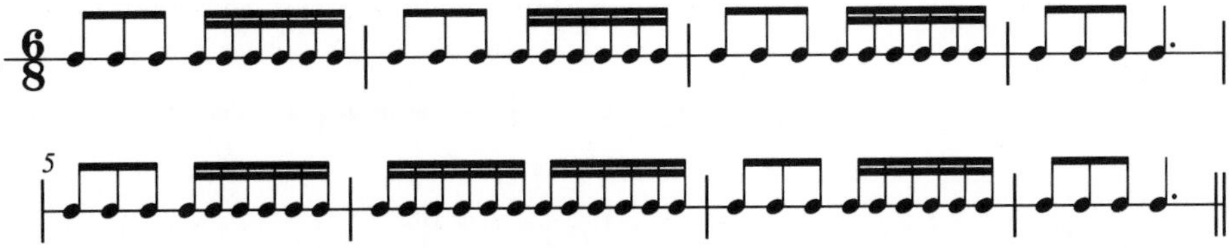

12. 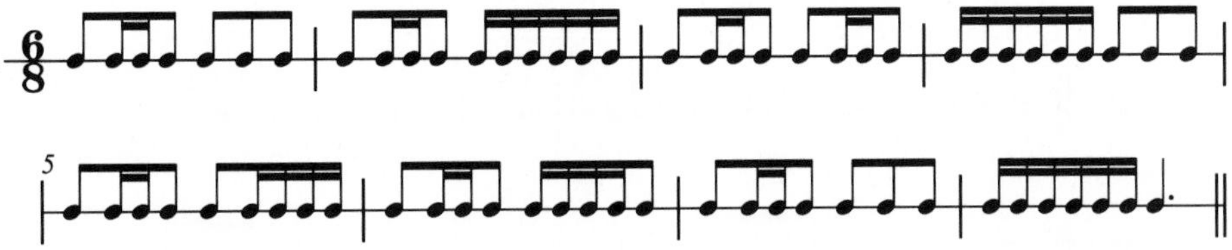

13. 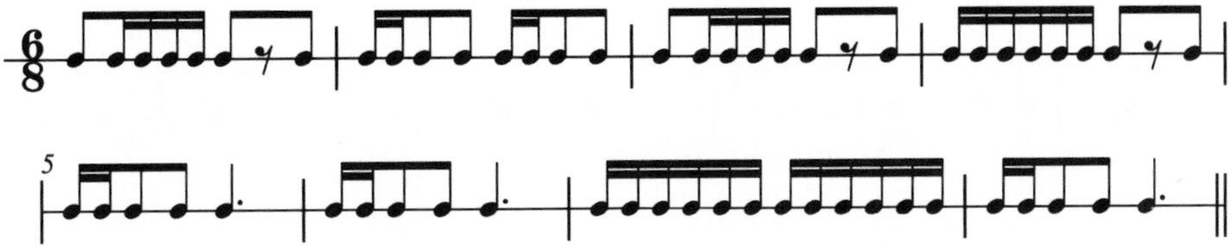

14. 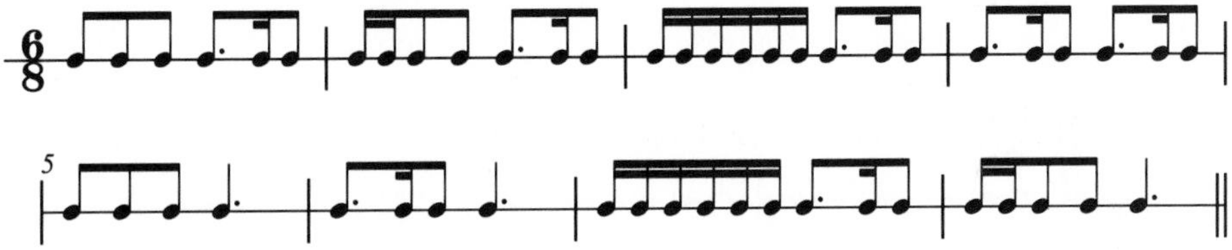

♪. = 1 beat

15. 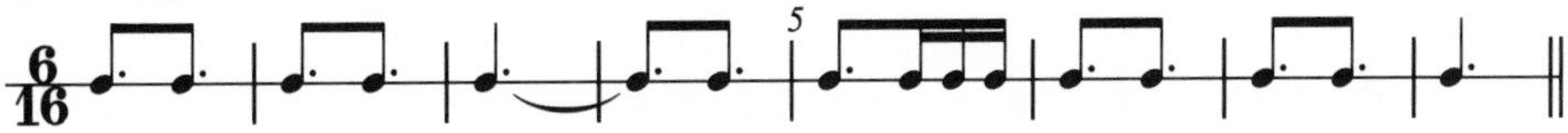

16. 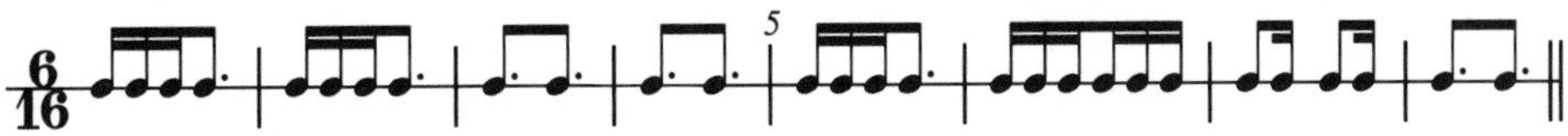

17. 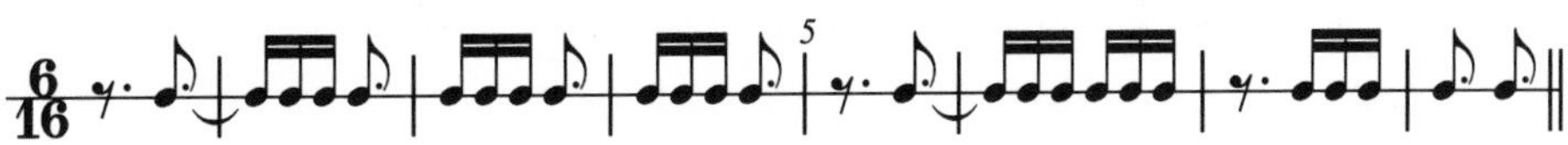

18. 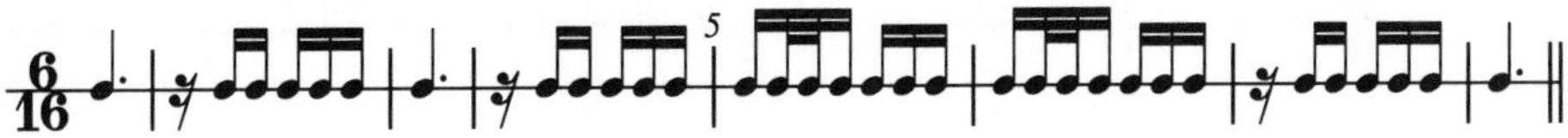

TRIPLE METER

QUADRUPLE METER

STUDIES

Allegro

Handel

4.

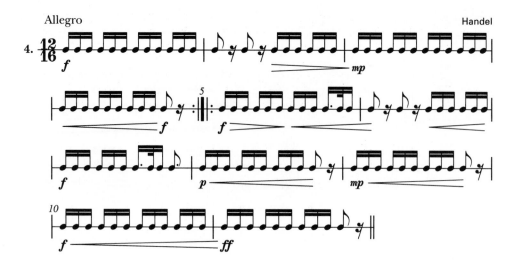

ENSEMBLES

1.

2.

3.

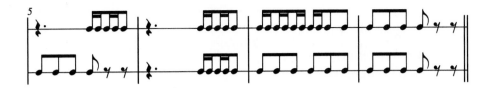

exercise 5–7 Musicianship Skills
EAR TRAINING: Identifying Simple
and Compound Meters

A. Your instructor will play several melodies. First, determine the accent pattern (duple or triple) and write that word in the first blank. Next, listen for the beat division and write the word "simple" or "compound" in the second blank as appropriate. Finally, choose a meter signature that could be used for the melody you hear, and write that in the third blank (several time signatures will be correct in each case).

1. _____ _____ ____   2. _____ _____ ____

3. _____ _____ ____   4. _____ _____ ____

5. _____ _____ ____   6. _____ _____ ____

7. _____ _____ ____   8. _____ _____ ____

B. On your own, determine the accent pattern and manner of beat division to the following tunes. Write the accent pattern in the first blank and the word "simple" or "compound" in the second blank. If you do not know one or more of the songs, choose others to identify.

1. *The Impossible Dream*   _____ _____

2. *Hey, Jude*   _____ _____

3. *Hail! Hail! The Gang's All Here* _____ _____

4. *America the Beautiful*   _____ _____

5. *Rock-A-Bye Baby*   _____ _____

6. *Down in the Valley*   _____ _____

7. *Stars and Stripes Forever*   _____ _____

8. *For He's a Jolly Good Fellow* _____ _____

BORROWED DIVISION

Using traditional musical notation, a composer must choose either a two-part or a three-part beat division. Once the time signature is in place, the performer will interpret the rhythmic symbols accordingly. Although the composer may want either a two-part or a three-part beat division *primarily*, however, there may be occasions when the contrasting division is desired. If the meter is $\frac{6}{8}$, the beat will divide naturally into three parts.

Beat

Division

In addition to the natural beat division in a meter like $\frac{6}{8}$, the composer may temporarily want a beat divided into *two* equal parts. Traditional rhythmic notation includes a method of indicating the alternative beat division—the "borrowing" of a two-part division for use in a compound meter or a three-part division for use in a simple meter. The beat division specified in the time signature is termed the NATURAL DIVISION; the contrasting beat division is known as the BORROWED DIVISION.

The Triplet. If the meter is simple—$\frac{3}{4}$, for instance—the beat is a quarter note, which divides naturally into two eighth notes. For a three-part division, however, the composer marks the notes in question with the numeral 3 to indicate a TRIPLET figure—three notes in the time of two. Since the three eighth notes are all played on one beat, the eighth notes of the triplet are played *faster* than those of the natural division.

Natural Division   *Borrowed Division*

1 Beat   1 Beat

In other meters, the triplet looks different but is performed in the same way. In $\frac{4}{2}$, for example, the beat divides naturally into two quarter notes; the borrowed division is a quarter-note triplet. In $\frac{3}{8}$, the natural division is two sixteenth notes, with three sixteenths constituting the triplet.

Natural Division   *Borrowed Division*

1 Beat   1½ Beats   1 Beat

A familiar tune that utilizes a triplet figure is the "Air Force Song" (Recorded Example 11). There is no anacrusis, and the triplets occur in the second and sixth measures.

▶ *RECORDED EXAMPLE 11*

Borrowed Division

Off we go - IN-to the WILD blue YON-der, FLY-ing high - IN-to the SUN.

"The U.S. Air Force." By Robert Crawford. Copyright © 1939, 1942, 1951 by Carl Fischer, Inc., New York.
Copyright renewed. All rights reserved. Used by permission.

The eighth-note triplet is certainly the most common, but in other meters, the quarter- and sixteenth-note triplets are performed the same way.

Off we go   -   IN-to the WILD blue   YON- der,

Off we go   -   IN-to the WILD blue   YON- der,

Off we go   -   IN-to the WILD blue   YON- der,

The Duplet.   The DUPLET is a borrowed division that provides a two-part beat division for use in compound meters. The natural division of the beat in $\frac{9}{8}$ is three eighth notes, and two eighth notes alone do not have a full beat's value. Placing the numeral 2 above or below two eighth notes, however, indicates that they are a duplet and should be performed in one beat—the time normally occupied by three eighth notes.

Natural Division   *Borrowed Division*

1 Beat   ⅔ Beat   1 Beat

Counting the Borrowed Division. Syllables for counting the triplet in a simple meter correspond to those for the natural division in a compound meter (Recorded Example 12).

▶ *RECORDED EXAMPLE 12*

Counting the Borrowed Division

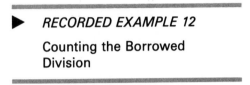

Natural Division   *Borrowed Division*

One Two   One te Two te   One   Two   One la li Two la li

Likewise, the counting for the duplet in a compound meter is the syllable "te," as used for the natural divided beat in a simple meter. The use of different syllables for the beat division in simple and compound meters accentuates the inherent differences between the meters.

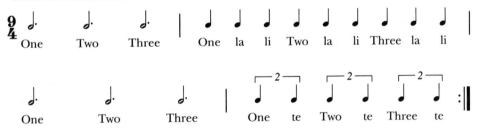

One   Two   Three   One   la   li   Two   la   li Three la   li

One   Two   Three   One   te   Two   te   Three   te

exercise 5–8 *Fundamental Skills*
Understanding Borrowed Division

A. A borrowed division is written with the same durational value as the natural division. For triplets, however, there are three notes on one beat where two occur in the natural division. Duplets are the reverse: two notes where three occur in the natural division. Complete the following table to include the natural and borrowed division of the beat. The first has been done as an example.

Meter Example: $\frac{4}{8}$	Beat	Division	Borrowed Division	Subdivision
1. $\frac{3}{4}$	_____	_____	_____	_____
2. $\frac{6}{8}$	_____	_____	_____	_____
3. $\frac{3}{8}$	_____	_____	_____	_____
4. $\frac{4}{4}$	_____	_____	_____	_____
5. $\frac{9}{16}$	_____	_____	_____	_____
6. $\frac{12}{8}$	_____	_____	_____	_____
7. $\frac{2}{2}$	_____	_____	_____	_____
8. $\frac{6}{2}$	_____	_____	_____	_____

B. Provide barlines for the following passages. If the first barline is supplied, the line begins with an anacrusis. In this case, remember that the final measure will be incomplete.

exercise 5–9   Musicianship Skills
RHYTHMIC READING: Borrowed Division

The following exercises include borrowed divisions in some of the simpler and more frequent patterns. As always, study the meter signature; then, determine the value of all rhythmic symbols.

TRIPLET PATTERNS

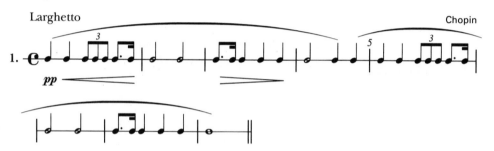

Studies

Larghetto   Chopin

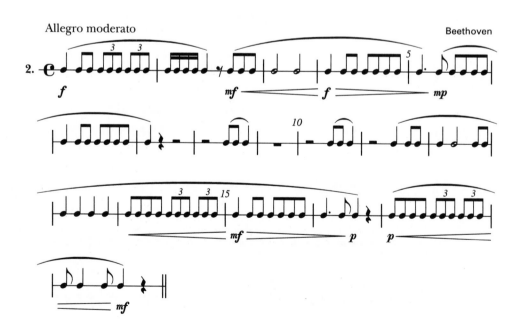

Allegro moderato   Beethoven

Ensembles

DUPLET PATTERNS

SELF-TEST

1. Circle meters that are duple-compound.

$$\frac{4}{2} \qquad \frac{6}{4} \qquad \frac{3}{4} \qquad \frac{2}{8} \qquad \frac{6}{16} \qquad \frac{9}{8}$$

2. Write meter signatures that conform to the given specification. Provide the note that receives one beat.

Meter	Classification	Beat
a. ____	triple-simple	____
b. ____	quadruple-compound	____
c. ____	duple-simple	____

3. For the given meters, write the beat, the division, and the subdivision.

	Beat	Division	Subdivision
a. $\frac{3}{2}$	____	_____	_____
b. $\frac{9}{4}$	____	_____	_____

4. In beats (or fractional parts), write the values of the given note(s) or rest(s).

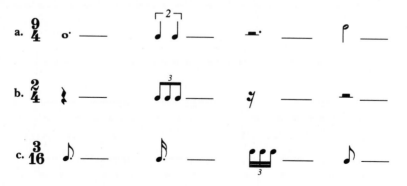

5. Provide barlines for the following passages.

Tchaikovsky

a.

Brahms

b.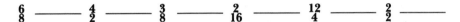

6. Explain the difference between the natural and the borrowed division.

7. For the meters given, write the notes that constitute the borrowed division.

$\frac{6}{8}$ ——— $\frac{4}{2}$ ——— $\frac{3}{8}$ ——— $\frac{2}{16}$ ——— $\frac{12}{4}$ ——— $\frac{2}{2}$ ———

8. Some of the measures in the following passages have too many or too few beats. Circle inappropriate measures and *correct* the error by adding a note or a rest, indicating a duplet or a triplet, or perhaps by decreasing the value of a single note or rest. Write any new notes immediately above or below the original notation. Several different notations are possible.

a.

b.

c.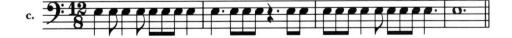

SUPPLEMENTARY EXERCISES

1. Write a short rhythmic duet using one of the motives suggested. Use repetition and variation rather than new material to extend the composition.

Possible Motives:

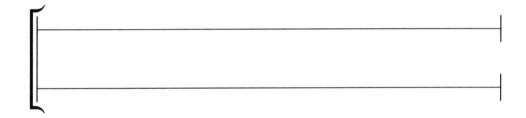

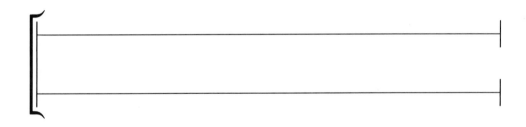

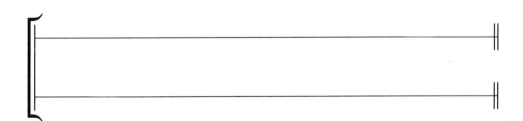

2. The following composition is notated in $\frac{3}{2}$ meter. Transcribe the notation to $\frac{3}{8}$.

a.

M-305A

b.

3. For each meter listed, circle *s* if the meter is simple, *c* if it is compound.

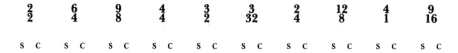

$\frac{2}{2}$ $\frac{6}{4}$ $\frac{9}{8}$ $\frac{4}{4}$ $\frac{3}{2}$ $\frac{3}{32}$ $\frac{2}{4}$ $\frac{12}{8}$ $\frac{4}{1}$ $\frac{9}{16}$

s c   s c   s c   s c   s c   s c   s c   s c   s c   s c

4. The following meters are compound. Determine the accent pattern of each.

$\frac{9}{8}$

_____-Compound

$\frac{12}{4}$

_____-Compound

$\frac{6}{16}$

_____-Compound

$\frac{6}{2}$

_____-Compound

5. Classify the following meters, first, according to accent pattern and, second, indicating whether they are simple or compound.

a. $\frac{3}{4}$ $\frac{4}{8}$

_____-_____   _____-_____

$\frac{12}{8}$ $\frac{2}{2}$

_____-_____   _____-_____

b. $\frac{9}{4}$ $\frac{3}{1}$

_____-_____   _____-_____

$\frac{2}{16}$ $\frac{6}{8}$

_____-_____   _____-_____

6. Write the note that receives one beat in the following compound meters. Remember that the lower numeral is the beat *division*.

$\frac{6}{8}$ —— $\frac{6}{4}$ —— $\frac{9}{16}$ —— $\frac{12}{4}$ —— $\frac{6}{32}$ —— $\frac{9}{8}$ —— $\frac{12}{16}$ ——

7. For the following simple and compound meters, write the note receiving one beat, the notes that constitute the beat division and beat subdivision, and, finally, the metric classification.

	Meter	Beat	Division	Subdivision	Classification
a.	$\frac{6}{8}$	——	——	—————	—————-—————
b.	$\frac{2}{2}$	——	——	—————	—————-—————
c.	$\frac{3}{2}$	——	——	—————	—————-—————
d.	$\frac{12}{16}$	——	——	—————	—————-—————
e.	$\frac{4}{4}$	——	——	—————	—————-—————

8. Add barlines to the following passages. Some feature borrowed divisions.

Major Scales and Keys

ESSENTIAL TERMS

- *chromatic half step*
- *diatonic half step*
- *dominant*
- *key*
- *key signature*
- *leading tone*
- *mediant*
- *scale*
- *scale degree*
- *solfège*
- *subdominant*
- *submediant*
- *supertonic*
- *tonic*
- *transposition*

THE MAJOR SCALE

Composers in the Common Practice Period (ca. 1600–1900) were especially careful to organize music so that the listener could follow various transformations of the rhythm, melody, harmony, and form throughout the course of a work. They organized melody primarily by making pitches conform to those of either a major or a minor *scale*. A SCALE is an organized series of pitches that represents the actual or the potential melodic inventory of a composition. *Major* scales and keys will be studied in the present chapter; the counterpart, minor scales and keys, will be covered in Chapter 7.

The keyboard is based on a major scale beginning on the pitch C; the pitches of this scale correspond to the white keys beginning (and ending) on the pitch C (Recorded Example 13).

▶ *RECORDED EXAMPLE 13*

Major Scale and Melody

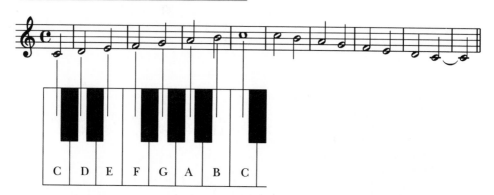

Few melodies consist entirely of scales. Handel's "Joy to the World," however, begins with a complete descending major scale.

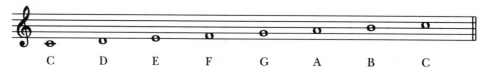

Joy   to   the   world   the   Lord   is   come.

The Tonic. The first pitch of a scale is important from a melodic standpoint because it indicates the central tone in the composition (or section), to which the other pitches are related. The first pitch of a scale is called the TONIC (from the Greek word for "weight"). In the following scale, C is the tonic; notice that this pitch is repeated an octave higher to end the scale. Scales are also named for their tonics. The tonic of the C major scale is C; G is the tonic of a major scale beginning on G.

C   D   E   F   G   A   B   C

Scales can be written and practiced both in ascending and in descending forms.

Ascending   *Descending*

Scale Degrees

Because *order* is so important in scales, each pitch is assigned a SCALE DEGREE NUMBER to designate its relationship to the tonic pitch. The tonic is the first scale degree. The second scale degree is the second pitch of the ascending scale; the fourth scale degree is the fourth pitch; and so on.

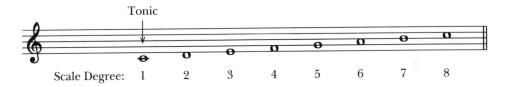

Tonic

Scale Degree: 1   2   3   4   5   6   7   8

Different types of scales are distinguished primarily by the *intervals* between pitches. The major scale comprises chiefly whole steps; half steps lie between the third and fourth and between the seventh and eighth scale degrees.

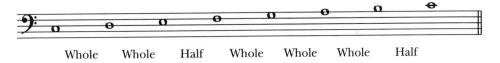

Whole   Whole   Half   Whole   Whole   Whole   Half

Scale Degree Names.   Just as the first scale degree is also known as the tonic, other scale degrees have names as well. Shown below, these names refer to a pitch's relationship to the tonic. Both scale degree numbers and scale degree names should be learned thoroughly.

Tonic   Supertonic   Mediant   Subdominant   Dominant   Submediant   Leading Tone

Diatonic and Chromatic Half Steps

Two categories of half steps occur in traditional music. If the half step comprises pitches with *different* letter names (F-sharp and G, for example), the half step is termed DIATONIC. A CHROMATIC half step, on the other hand, is one involving pitches with the *same* letter name (F and F-sharp, for example). All the intervals below are half steps; note the important difference between those labeled diatonic and those designated as chromatic.

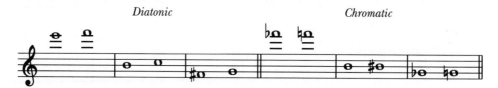

Although both diatonic and chromatic half steps appear in many melodies, chromatic half steps are *never* used in writing major scales. No traditional scale, for example, has two consecutive pitches named G (even if one is G and the other is G-sharp).

exercise 6–1 *Fundamental Skills*
Diatonic and Chromatic Half Steps

A. Several half steps are shown. In the blank, write "D" if the half step is diatonic and "C" if it is chromatic. Write "N" if the interval is not a half step.

B. Write diatonic or chromatic half steps as directed *above* the given pitch.

Above

1.

Diatonic   Chromatic   Chromatic   Diatonic   Chromatic   Diatonic   Chromatic

Above

2.

Diatonic   Chromatic   Chromatic   Diatonic   Chromatic   Diatonic   Chromatic

Write diatonic or chromatic half steps as directed *below* the given pitch.

Below

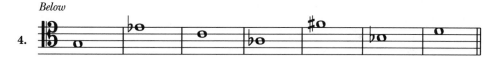

3.

Diatonic   Chromatic   Chromatic   Diatonic   Chromatic   Diatonic   Chromatic

Below

4.

Diatonic   Chromatic   Chromatic   Diatonic   Chromatic   Diatonic   Chromatic

C. Write the pitches indicated from the C major scale as well as a diatonic or a chromatic half step above or below as directed. The scale degree name tells you which pitch to write first; then, above or below that pitch, write the second. Begin by completing a C major scale; then, fill in the remaining triad names. Use this scale as a reference when completing the exercise.

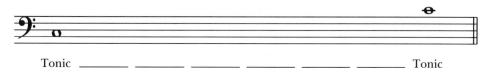

Tonic _____ _____ _____ _____ _____ _____ Tonic

1. A diatonic half step above the dominant pitch
2. A diatonic half step below the mediant pitch
3. A chromatic half step above the tonic pitch

4. A chromatic half step below the leading-tone pitch
5. A diatonic half step above the supertonic pitch
6. A chromatic half step below the subdominant pitch
7. A diatonic half step above the submediant pitch
8. A chromatic half step below the dominant pitch

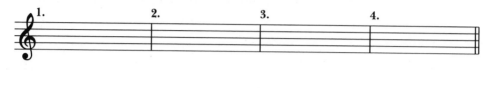

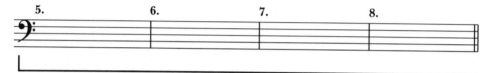

The Major "Effect"

An essential difference between major and minor concerns the interval between the first and third scale degrees. This interval imparts much of the characteristic major or minor "flavor" to a melody. The major "effect," heard in Recorded Example 14, is created when the interval between the first and third scale degrees is *two whole steps*.

▶ *RECORDED EXAMPLE 14*

Major and Minor "Effects"

The minor effect (which will be studied in detail in the next chapter) results when the interval between the first and third scale degrees is a whole step plus a *diatonic* half step.

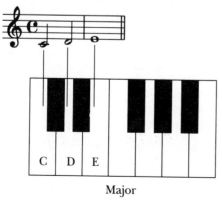

Major

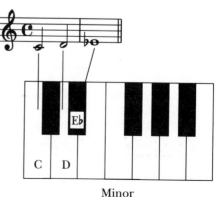

Minor

Major

Are you sleep-ing, Are you sleep-ing, Broth-er John, Broth-er John?

Minor

Are you sleep-ing, Are you sleep-ing, Broth-er John, Broth-er John?

In identifying a given scale, remember that the distance between the first and third scale degrees differentiates between major and minor. If the distance is two whole steps, the scale is major; if the span is a whole step plus a diatonic half step, the scale is minor.[1]

▶ *RECORDED EXAMPLE 15*

(See Exercise 6-2.)

exercise 6–2   *Musicianship Skills*
EAR TRAINING: Major and Minor

A. You will hear sixteen pitch patterns. Each begins on the tonic and contains seven additional pitches. Listen for the first, second, and third scale degrees. These are the first pitches heard in lines 1–2, but later, they may occur at another point in the series. Determine whether the effect is major or minor, and write the answer in the blank. Four different patterns will be heard in each line.

1. _____ _____ _____ _____

2. _____ _____ _____ _____

3. _____ _____ _____ _____

4. _____ _____ _____ _____

[1] In music before about 1600 and after about 1875, there are other possibilities besides major and minor.

B. (Not Recorded) Listen to the melodies played by your instructor and identify them as major or minor in effect.

1. _____ _____ _____ _____

2. _____ _____ _____ _____

3. _____ _____ _____ _____

4. _____ _____ _____ _____

Transposition

If a traditional composition is based on the C major scale, the work will be constructed so that the listener hears the pitch C as more important than any of the other pitches. TRANSPOSITION is the process of moving a series of pitches (a major scale in this case) so that it centers on another tonic, but *without changing the original pattern of intervals between pitches*.

If we want to *transpose* the C major scale to begin on the pitch D, for example, D will be the new tonic. Although a series of basic pitches beginning on D includes two half steps, these do not occur between the third and fourth and between the seventh and eighth scale degrees as they do in a major scale. Unless the original order of intervals is maintained, the transposition is not complete.

C Major Scale   D Major Scale?

To transpose the C major scale to begin on D, first write the basic pitches from D to D, as shown above. To complete the transposition, however, you must add *accidentals* to duplicate the intervallic pattern for the major scale.

The second scale degree (E) is a whole step above D; this interval conforms to the major scale pattern, and no accidental is added to the basic pitch E. The third scale degree (F), however, is not a whole step but a half step above the second. Because the major scale pattern calls for a whole step between the second and third scale degrees, the F must be made F-sharp.

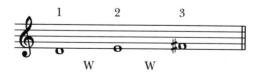

The interval between F-sharp and G is a half step, and since that interval corresponds to the major scale pattern, we will leave the G-natural. Likewise, the fifth and sixth pitches (A and B) need no accidental.

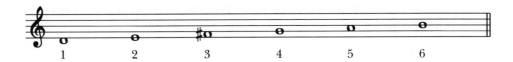

The seventh pitch of the scale, C, lies not a whole step but a half step above B (the sixth scale degree). To conform to the major scale pattern, the C must be made C-sharp (because the interval between the sixth and seventh scale degrees in a major scale must be a whole step); this accidental also creates the necessary half step between the seventh and eighth scale degrees. The D major scale is now complete and includes two accidentals—F-sharp and C-sharp.

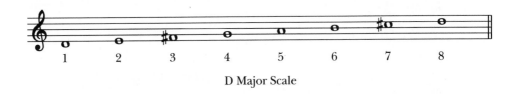

D Major Scale

If the C major scale is transposed to begin on E-flat, three flats are necessary to reproduce the intervallic pattern.

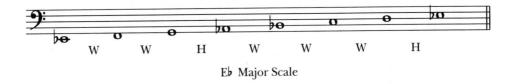

E♭ Major Scale

Five of the basic pitches must be sharped in a B major scale.

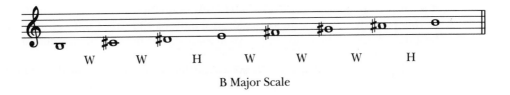

B Major Scale

exercise 6–3   *Fundamental Skills*
Major Scale Pattern

Some of these scales are major; some are other types, to be discussed later. Identify the intervals in the scales as whole step ("W") or half step ("H"). Circle scales that are major.

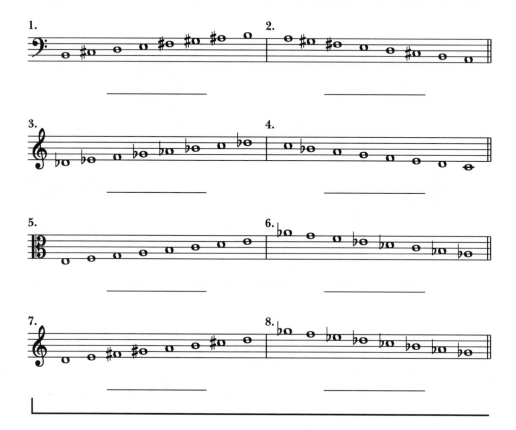

Construction of Major Scales

The construction of major scales is dependent on the recall of the whole- and half-step pattern: W W H W W W H. Any sequence of intervals that conforms to this pattern will be a major scale; any pattern that does not conform *cannot* be a major scale. The following steps are suggested in constructing major scales:

   1. Beginning with the tonic, write in basic pitches up to and including the octave above the tonic.

2. Write the whole- and half-step pattern between pitches. (If this pattern can be *visualized* and not written, all the better.)

3. Add accidentals as necessary to make interval sequence conform to the major scale pattern.

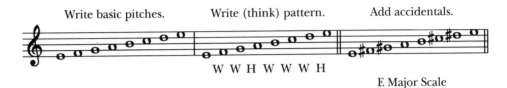

Write basic pitches.   Write (think) pattern.   Add accidentals.

W W H W W W H

E Major Scale

Half steps occur between the third and fourth and between the seventh and eighth scale degrees in the major scale. After the scale is complete, these points should be checked to make certain that the interval is a diatonic half step.

Descending Scales. To write a descending major scale, simply reverse the interval pattern: Half, Whole, Whole, Whole, Half, Whole, Whole.

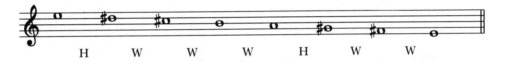

H   W   W   W   H   W   W

Another (and perhaps better) approach to writing descending scales is to think through or sketch the scale in its ascending pattern, then write the pitches in reverse order.

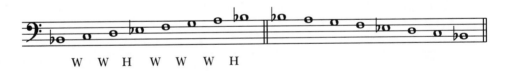

W   W   H   W   W   W   H

exercise 6–4 *Fundamental Skills*
Writing Major Scales

A. Write ascending scales on the tonics shown. Begin with basic pitches up to and including an octave above the tonic. (If the tonic has an accidental, remember to add this accidental to the octave as well.) Next, write "whole" or "half" between pitches as appropriate. Finally, add accidentals to match the interval pattern.

1.   **2.**

3.   **4.**

5.   **6.**

7.   **8.**

B. Write descending major scales beginning with the tonics given. Proceed as in exercise A, but reverse the interval pattern (H W W W H W W). Be sure that all half steps are diatonic.

1.   **2.**

3.   **4.**

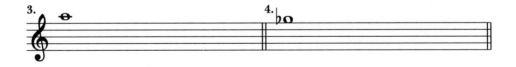

5.   **6.**

7.   **8.**

C. *Letter Names.* In addition to notating scales on a staff, you should be able to write scales using pitch names. The process is the same:

1. Write the E major scale with basic pitches.

E	F	G	A	B	C	D	E

2. Apply the interval pattern.

E	F	G	A	B	C	D	E
W	W	H	W	W	W	H	

3. Add accidentals as needed.

E	F♯	G♯	A	B	C♯	D♯	E
W	W	H	W	W	W	H	

Complete major scales beginning on the tonics shown.

1. D ___ ___ ___ ___ ___ ___ ___

2. B♭ ___ ___ ___ ___ ___ ___ ___

3. A ___ ___ ___ ___ ___ ___ ___

4. F ___ ___ ___ ___ ___ ___ ___

5. D♭ ___ ___ ___ ___ ___ ___ ___

6. B ___ ___ ___ ___ ___ ___ ___

7. G ___ ___ ___ ___ ___ ___ ___

8. C ___ ___ ___ ___ ___ ___ ___

9. E♭ ___ ___ ___ ___ ___ ___ ___

10. F♯ ___ ___ ___ ___ ___ ___ ___

exercise 6–5 *Musicianship Skills*
SIGHT SINGING: Major Scale Patterns

A. Using the method specified by your instructor, sing the following scale patterns. Play the first note on the piano; then, sing the scale both ascending and descending. Try not to let pitch go flat as you sing; this is a natural tendency for most beginners. After you have sung the passage, play the tonic on the keyboard to see if you ended on the correct pitch.

This exercise centers on scale degrees 1–5.

1.   2.

3.   4.

5.   6.

B. These exercises center on complete major scales. First, write out the scales, including any necessary accidentals. Next, sound the tonic pitch on the keyboard and sing the scale ascending and descending. Check your final pitch again on the keyboard. You may need to sing an octave above or below the notated pitches.

1.   2.

3.   4.

exercise 6–6 *Musicianship Skills*
KEYBOARD: Ascending Major Scales

At the keyboard, play the twelve major scales in the second part of Skill Exercise 6–5. You need not use specific fingerings, but do not use the same finger for each note. Avoid using the thumb on a black key.

MAJOR KEYS

The term *key* is difficult to define because it refers not to a specific technique or set of conditions but, rather, to the "feeling" that one pitch is more important than all the others in the scale. The skilled composer organizes a melody so that the listener *hears* one pitch as the most important in a given section or complete composition. A study of the techniques through which a feeling for key is created is one of the most important aspects of music theory. For present purposes, however, KEY can be defined as an effect produced when pitches of a melody are arranged so that the tonic of a scale is heard as the most important pitch. If the scale in question is G major, the *key* is G major; if the key is D minor, the pitches of the D minor scale will be predominant in the melody, and the pitch D itself will be heard as the most important of these.

If a composer wants to create a feeling for the key of E major, the pitches of that scale will be predominant in the melody. As shown below, the E major scale employs four accidentals: F-sharp, C-sharp, G-sharp, and D-sharp.

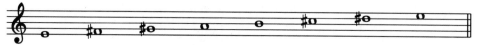

E Major Scale

If the E major scale is to be used extensively, *every* F will be sharp; *every* C will be sharp; and so on. Rather than writing in the accidentals every time these pitches are used, composers identify the accidentals associated with a given scale at the beginning of a composition in the *key signature*.

Key Signatures

As the name suggests, a KEY SIGNATURE is a list of the accidentals associated with a given key. If the key is E major, the accidentals are those from the E major scale: F-sharp, C-sharp, G-sharp, and D-sharp. These accidentals are listed at the beginning of a composition between the clef and the time signature, and they are *always* in effect unless marked otherwise (with a natural sign, for example). The following melody is in the key of E major; the four sharps of the E major scale are given in the key signature and are not repeated thereafter. *Every* F, C, G, and D, however, is played *sharp*.

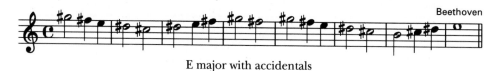

E major with accidentals

E major with key signature

If an F-natural rather than an F-sharp were desired in the third measure, the composer would add the natural sign to cancel the effect of the sharps in the key signature. The natural sign would affect every F in that measure; in the next measure, however, unless the natural sign were repeated, each F would again be played sharp.

Order of Sharps and Flats

If the scale that produces the effect of a certain key has one sharp, that sharp will be F-sharp. If the scale has two sharps, they will be F-sharp and C-sharp. There is no major or minor scale or key whose two sharps are named G-sharp and D-sharp, for example. With flats, the sequence of appearance is just as rigid; one flat will always be B-flat; two will be B-flat and E-flat; and so on.

The order of flats spells out the word "BEAD," with the additional flats being "GCF." The sharps occur in the *reverse* of this order. Learning the order of the flats, therefore, produces the order of the sharps if the sequence can be written (or visualized) backward.

Order of Flats: *Bb Eb Ab Db Gb Cb Fb*

Order of Sharps: *F♯ C♯ G♯ D♯ A♯ E♯ B♯*

When sharps or flats are written on the staff as a key signature, they appear left to right in the order given above—generally alternating between higher and lower choices of octave. The B major scale includes five sharps; notice the placement and order of these sharps when written as a key signature.

B Major Scale   Key Signature: B Major

The key of C major has no accidentals; this fact is reflected in the key signature, which contains *no* sharps or flats.

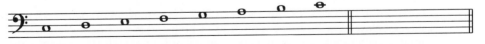

C Major Scale   Key Signature: C Major

The key of C major has no sharps or flats; the key of C-sharp major has all seven sharps in its scale and key signature. Notice the placement of the seven sharps on the grand staff.

C♯ Major Scale

Key Signature: C♯ Major

The key of C-flat major has all seven flats in its key signature. Note the correct placement of these flats on the grand staff.

C♭ Major Scale

Key Signature: C♭ Major

The positions of the sharps and flats on the staff are traditional; deviations constitute notational inaccuracies.

Correct   Incorrect   Correct   Incorrect

exercise 6–7 *Fundamental Skills*
Key Signatures

A. Return to the twelve major scales in Skill Exercise 6–5B on page 164, and use the staves below to write a key signature in both treble and bass clefs based on the accidentals present. Be sure to use the correct order and staff placement for the sharps or flats. Use the blank to identify each major key.

1.   2.   3.   4.   5.   6.

7.   8.   9.   10.   11.   12.

Major Key Signatures

Enharmonic duplications (B = C♭, D♭ = C♯, and G♭ = F♯) create fifteen, rather than twelve, different major keys. Study these keys and memorize their key signatures.

C major   G major   D major   A major   E major   B major   F♯ major   C♯ major

F major   B♭ major   E♭ major   A♭ major   D♭ major   G♭ major   C♭ major

The Circle of Fifths.   As will be discussed in a later chapter, a PERFECT FIFTH is an interval made up of seven half steps (from C to G, for example, or from B to F-sharp).

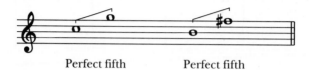

Perfect fifth   Perfect fifth

You can remember key signatures easily through a series of perfect-fifth progressions. Beginning with the key of C (no sharps or flats), for example, a perfect fifth above this tonic is G—a key with one sharp. A perfect fifth above G is D major, which has two sharps; above D, the key of A major with three

MAJOR KEYS

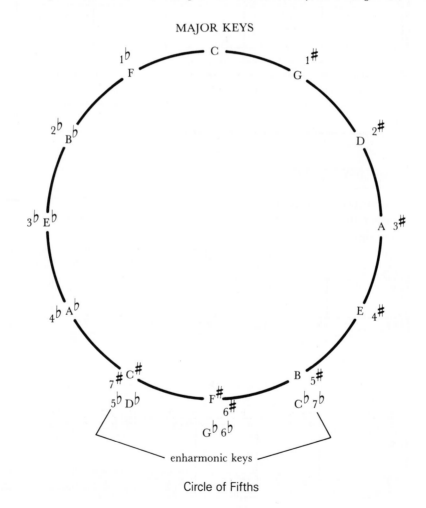

Circle of Fifths

sharps; and so on. The same process can be used to remember the flat keys. Beginning again with the key of C major, a perfect fifth below this tonic is F— the major key with one flat. A perfect fifth below F is B-flat major, which has two flats, and so on. This series of key relationships is called the CIRCLE OF FIFTHS. Note the three enharmonic keys. (See page 170.)

exercise 6–8 *Fundamental Skills*
Scale Degrees in Major Keys

A. The ability to name or identify a particular scale degree within a given key— especially without first constructing the entire scale—is an important skill. Asked to name the fourth scale degree of F major, for example, you would respond "B-flat." The pitch B is the fourth basic pitch above F, and since the key of F major has one flat, the fourth scale degree is B-flat. The sixth scale degree of G-flat major is E-flat; the second scale degree of D major is E.

Write the pitches indicated. Be sure to include any necessary accidental. Write the scale degree name (tonic, submediant, and so on) in the blank.

	G major	B♭ major	E major	C major	D♭ major	F major	A♭ major
1.	2	5	6	5	6	3	7

_____   _____   _____   _____   _____   _____   _____

	D major	B major	F major	C♯ major	A major	G major	G♭ major
2.	3	7	2	4	6	2	5

_____   _____   _____   _____   _____   _____   _____

	C major	E♭ major	F♯ major	D major	C♭ major	E major	A♭ major
3.	2	3	5	7	4	6	4

_____   _____   _____   _____   _____   _____   _____

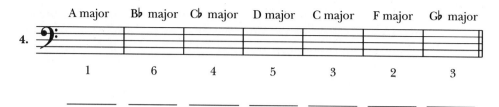

4.

A major	Bb major	Cb major	D major	C major	F major	Gb major
1	6	4	5	3	2	3

_____   _____   _____   _____   _____   _____   _____

B. This exercise centers on scale degree names. Write the appropriate letter name, including any accidental.

1. G major, supertonic   _____   2. F major, dominant   _____

3. E-flat major, leading tone   _____   4. A major, subdominant   _____

5. B major, mediant   _____   6. A-flat major, tonic   _____

7. D major, submediant   _____   8. E major, leading tone   _____

9. D-flat major, subdominant   _____   10. C major, dominant   _____

11. F major, mediant   _____   12. B-flat major, supertonic   _____

C. When you are given a pitch and asked to identify it relative to the tonic of a given key, the task is simpler. The pitch B is the third scale degree in G major and the fifth scale degree in E major. In these exercises, you may assume that the given pitch actually appears in the specified key.

In the first blank, write the scale degree number that identifies the given pitch in the specified key. In the second blank, write the scale degree name (tonic, supertonic, and so on).

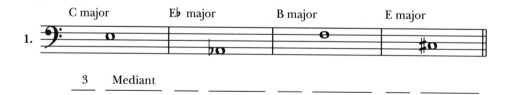

1.

3   Mediant   ___   ___   ___   ___   ___   ___

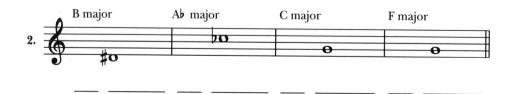

2.

___   ___   ___   ___   ___   ___

Bb major   G major   D major   Db major

3.

_____ _____ _____ _____

Ab major   Cb major   F major   E major

4.

_____ _____ _____ _____

D. A single pitch serves various roles, depending on the key. For each pitch below, name three different major keys that contain that pitch. Identify the scale degree position of the pitch in the second blank.

1.

Major key	Scale degree	Major key	Scale degree	Major key	Scale degree
A	1	____	____	____	____
C	6	____	____	____	____
E	4	____	____	____	____

2.

Major key	Scale degree	Major key	Scale degree	Major key	Scale degree
____	____	____	____	____	____
____	____	____	____	____	____
____	____	____	____	____	____

3.

Major key	Scale degree	Major key	Scale degree	Major key	Scale degree
____	____	____	____	____	____
____	____	____	____	____	____
____	____	____	____	____	____

exercise 6–9 Musicianship Skills
SIGHT SINGING: Stepwise Patterns

A. The following patterns are stepwise but ascend and descend in various contours. As before, play the first note on an instrument, sing the pattern using the method suggested by your instructor, and check the final pitch when you have finished.

1.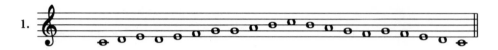

2.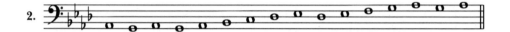

3.

4.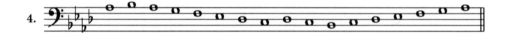

5.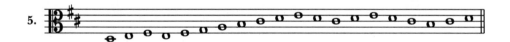

6.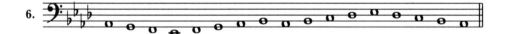

7.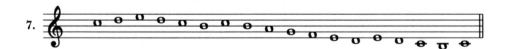

8.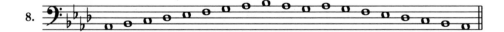

9.

10.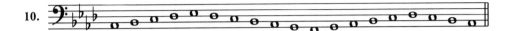

11.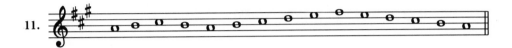

12.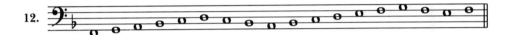

B. The following melodies, based on the patterns above, are stepwise. First, practice the rhythm on a neutral syllable. When you can perform the rhythm accurately and without breaking the tempo, sing the melody.

ADDITIONAL MELODIES FOR SIGHT SINGING

STEPWISE PHRASES FROM MUSIC LITERATURE

Beethoven

11.

D major

Farnaby

12.

G major

Handel

13.

D major

Humperdinck

14.

C major

ENSEMBLES

15.

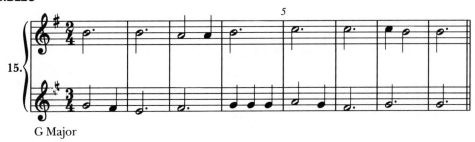

G Major

16.

B♭ Major

SELF-TEST

1. Supply the following:

    a. The interval pattern for major scales: ____ ____ ____ ____ ____

    ____ ____ .

    b. The order of sharps: ____ ____ ____ ____ ____ ____ ____

    c. The order of flats: ____ ____ ____ ____ ____ ____ ____

    d. The scale degree names for the G major scale:

2. Identify the "effect" of the following scale fragments (first, second, and third scale degrees) as either major or minor.

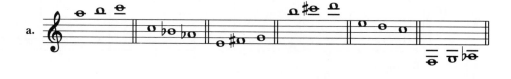

    _____ _____ _____

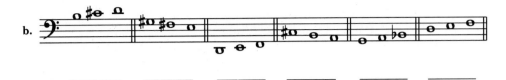

b.

——　　——　　——　　　　——　　——　　——

3. Write major scales beginning on the given tonics.

a.

b.

c.

4. Identify the scale degree name and number for each of the pitches given. Put the number in the first blank and the name in the second.

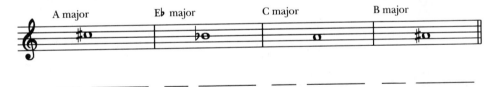

——　——　　　　——　——　　　　——　——　　　　——　——

5. Write the letter name (and accidental, if any) that appears as the specified scale degree in the key indicated.

　　a. B major, subdominant ————

　　b. E-flat major, dominant ————

　　c. F-sharp major, leading tone ————

　　d. A major, mediant ————

6. Identify the following intervals as whole step (W), diatonic half step (D), chromatic half step (C), or "none of the above" (N).

___   ___   ___   ___   ___   ___   ___   ___   ___   ___

7. Using accidentals, write the major scale indicated. To the right of the scale, make a key signature from the accidentals. Be sure to write the accidentals in their correct position in the key signature (consult the text if necessary).

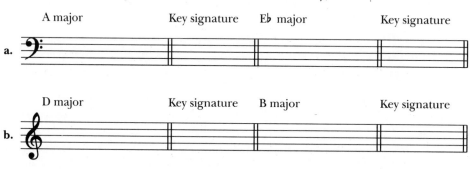

8. Write key signatures for the indicated major keys.

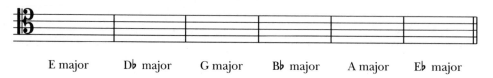

9. Identify the following terms:

    a. Key

    b. Transposition

    c. Tonic

    d. Key signature

    e. Scale

1. Shown below are several melodic fragments, consisting of *four* pitches each. Some of these fragments could belong to several major keys; others conform to only one key. Study the fragments and list *all* possible keys.

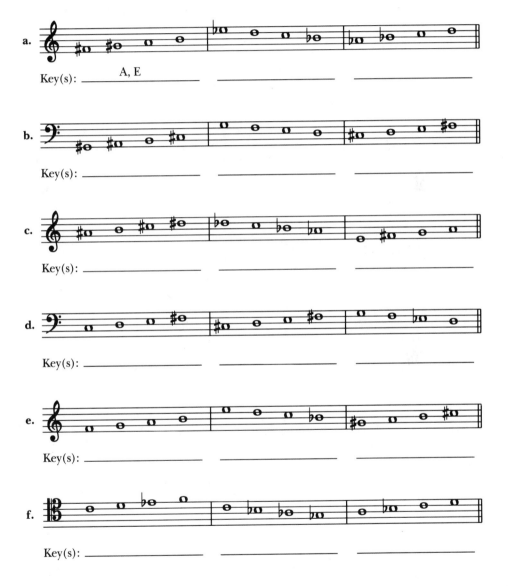

a. Key(s): _____ A, E _____ _____ _____

b. Key(s): _____ _____ _____

c. Key(s): _____ _____ _____

d. Key(s): _____ _____ _____

e. Key(s): _____ _____ _____

f. Key(s): _____ _____ _____

2. Write major scales beginning on the specific pitches. Choose an appropriate clef and write in the accidentals. Use the octave sign if necessary to avoid ledger lines.

Write major scales:

    a.   Beginning on CC
    b.   Beginning on B$\flat^2$
    c.   Beginning on a
    d.   Beginning on D
    e.   Beginning on f^1
    f.   Beginning on e^2
    g.   Beginning on E$\flat$
    h.   Beginning on c$\sharp$

a.   b.

c.   d.

e.   f.

g.   h.

3. Each of the following melodies and phrases is based on one of the fifteen major keys but is notated with accidentals rather than a key signature. Determine the key of each melody by building a key signature from the accidentals involved. Write the key signature in the blank staff preceding the melody, and write the name of the key in the blank. Be aware that some compositions begin, and even end, on pitches other than the tonic. Finally, remember that unless cancelled by a natural sign, an accidental is in force for an entire measure.

a.   Mozart

b.   Schumann

c.   Mozart

4. As directed, choose one or more of the preceding melodies and analyze the pitch content. Begin by writing the appropriate major scale using letter names. Next, tally the number of occurrences of each pitch. Count the total number of pitches in the melody and determine how often each pitch is used. Which, if any, pitches are not used at all? Comment on which pitches seem most and least important in the construction of the melody. As you did in an earlier chapter, analyze the melodic contour and draw a graphic representation showing relative ascending and descending motion.

Minor Scales and Keys

In most traditional Western music, there are two possibilities for the melodic structure of a composition: major and minor. Although a number of other scale systems existed (and were exploited before and after the Common Practice Period), composers between about 1600 and 1900 limited themselves to two "modes" of melodic composition. As you learned in the previous chapter, an essential difference between major and minor is the interval between the first and third scale degrees. In major, this interval is two whole steps; in minor, the first and third scale degrees are separated by a whole step plus a diatonic half step.

Major   Minor

THE MINOR SCALE

Whereas the major scale spans the white keys of the keyboard from C to C, the MINOR SCALE is found on the white keys beginning on the pitch A (Recorded Example 16).

▶ *RECORDED EXAMPLE 16*

Minor Scale on A

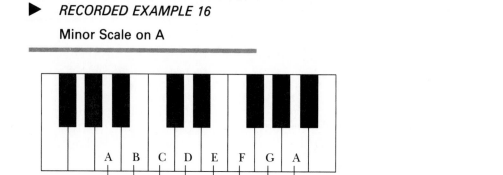

Like the major scale, the minor scale has a definite pattern of intervals, which you should memorize:

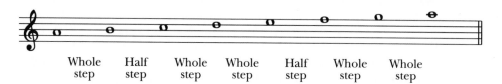

| Whole step | Half step | Whole step | Whole step | Half step | Whole step | Whole step |

If the scale descends, of course, the pattern is reversed (W W H W W H W).

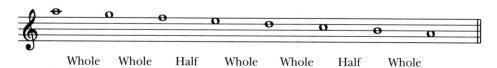

| Whole | Whole | Half | Whole | Whole | Half | Whole |

Study the differences between the C major and C minor scales, and between the A major and A minor scales as shown below. Whereas the two half steps lie between the third and fourth and between the seventh and eighth scale degrees in a major scale, half steps fall between the second and third and between the fifth and sixth degrees of the minor scale.

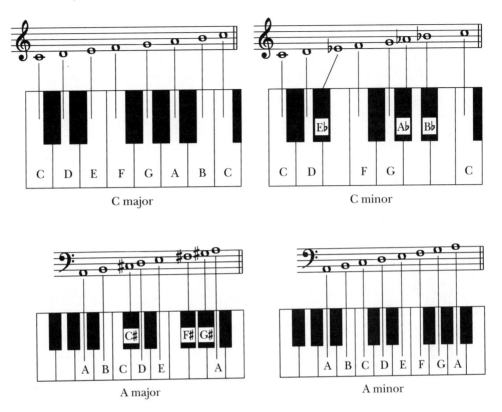

Minor scales are transposed exactly as major scales are: Begin with the given tonic, write basic pitches up to and including the octave above the tonic, and then add accidentals as necessary to duplicate the minor scale pattern: W H W W H W W. Beginning on D, for example, a B-flat must be added to duplicate the pattern.

If the tonic is B, two sharps are necessary to create a minor scale.

Minor Key Signatures.   The signatures for minor keys are formed exactly as they are for major keys: an inventory of the accidentals necessary to duplicate the interval pattern. The order of sharps and flats and their placement on the staff are also identical to those of major keys. Signatures for the fifteen minor keys are shown below.

A minor   E minor   B minor   F♯ minor C♯ minor G♯ minor D♯ minor A♯ minor

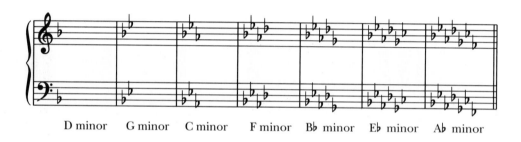

D minor   G minor   C minor   F minor   B♭ minor   E♭ minor   A♭ minor

exercise 7–1   *Fundamental Skills*
Minor Scales

A. Duplicate the minor scale pattern to begin on the given tonics. Mark the half steps and add accidentals as necessary.

B. Using letter names, spell the ascending minor scales.

Tonic

1. B   ___ ___ ___ ___ ___ ___ ___

2. E   ___ ___ ___ ___ ___ ___ ___

3. C   ___ ___ ___ ___ ___ ___ ___

4. F♯ ___ ___ ___ ___ ___ ___ ___

5. D   ___ ___ ___ ___ ___ ___ ___

6. G   ___ ___ ___ ___ ___ ___ ___

7. B♭ ___ ___ ___ ___ ___ ___ ___

8. F   ___ ___ ___ ___ ___ ___ ___

exercise 7–2 Musicianship Skills
KEYBOARD: Minor Scales

There are definite fingering patterns for minor scales, but for the time being, you may practice them on the keyboard with any convenient fingering pattern. Do not use the same finger for every note, however, and as always, avoid using the thumb on a black key. Beginning in the specific octave designated, write ascending and descending minor scales. Use the octave sign to avoid ledger lines. Next, practice the scales at the keyboard.

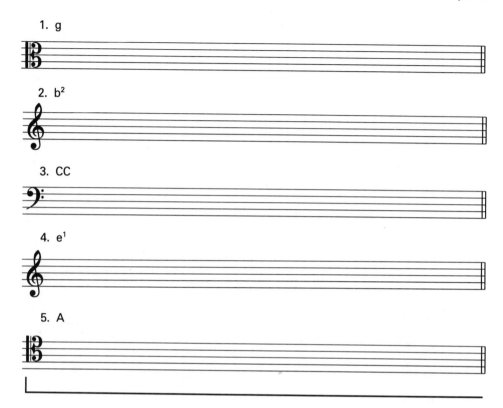

1. g

2. b²

3. CC

4. e¹

5. A

VARIATIONS IN MINOR

Unlike the major scale, which remains more or less unaltered, the minor scale has three distinct forms: *natural*, *harmonic*, and *melodic*. These forms are not arbitrary but are designed to reflect the choices made most often by composers. Performers study the three forms of minor through scales to become familiar with typical melodic patterns. In actual composition, however, the three forms are adhered to less rigidly.

Natural (Pure) Minor

The form of minor derived from the application of the intervallic formula learned earlier (W H W W H W W) is known as *natural minor*. The NATURAL MINOR SCALE takes its unique sound from this whole-step–half-step pattern. The D natural minor scale, for example, was given earlier; a B-flat is necessary to duplicate the interval pattern. The resulting scale is known as *D natural minor* (Recorded Example 17).

▶ *RECORDED EXAMPLE 17*

Minor Scales

D Natural Minor Scale

Leading Tone and Subtonic.   In addition to the interval between the first and third scale degrees, an important difference between major and natural minor scales concerns the seventh scale degree. In major, a half step lies between the seventh and eighth scale degrees. In the natural minor scale, however, a whole step separates these same pitches. As we discussed in the last chapter, the leading tone is the seventh scale degree that lies a diatonic half step below the tonic; major scales always have a leading tone. Another possibility exists in minor, however. A SUBTONIC is a seventh scale degree that lies a whole step below the tonic; natural minor scales have a subtonic (Recorded Example 18).

▶ *RECORDED EXAMPLE 18*

Leading Tone and Subtonic

C major   C minor

If pitches conform to the natural minor pattern given earlier, the seventh degree is a whole step below the tonic. In the F natural minor scale, for example, the seventh degree, E-flat, is a whole step below the tonic and therefore termed a subtonic.

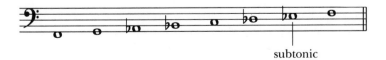

subtonic

Harmonic Minor

Because composers of the Common Practice Period liked the sound of the leading tone associated with major, they often chose to employ it even when writing in minor. Create a leading tone in minor by raising the seventh degree of the natural minor scale a half step. This new scale is known as HARMONIC MINOR (Recorded Example 19). In natural minor, the seventh degree is a subtonic; in harmonic minor, the seventh degree is a *leading tone*.

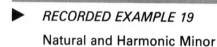

▶ RECORDED EXAMPLE 19

Natural and Harmonic Minor

A natural minor

A harmonic minor

Construct a harmonic minor scale by beginning with natural minor (from the intervallic pattern), then raising the seventh degree a half step. If the seventh degree is naturally flat, it will become natural in harmonic minor; if it is natural, it will become sharp; if it is sharp, it will become double sharp. The following examples are written both with accidentals and with a key signature. Notice that the key signature is always that of natural minor; the raised seventh appears as an accidental.

C natural minor   C harmonic minor

G natural minor   G harmonic minor

D♯ natural minor   D♯ harmonic minor

Like major and natural minor scales, the harmonic minor scale is written the same ascending and descending.

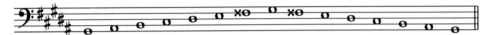

G♯ Harmonic Minor Scale

exercise 7–3   *Fundamental Skills*
Harmonic Minor Scales

A. In the space provided, use accidentals to complete natural minor scales on the given tonics. Next, compile a key signature from the accidentals and use that to construct a harmonic minor scale in the second space. In addition to the key signature, you will need to use an accidental to raise the seventh degree. Follow the example given.

Example:

B. Given below are pitches from natural or harmonic minor scales with the scale degree name given. From the information provided, complete the ascending scale using accidentals. If the mediant pitch is given, for example, and that pitch is D, the scale must be B minor. If D were identified as the dominant pitch, on the other hand, the scale would be G minor. Make the first four scales natural minor and the second four harmonic minor.

Natural Minor

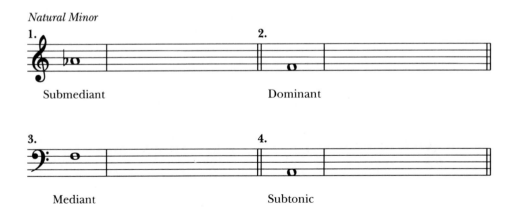

Harmonic Minor

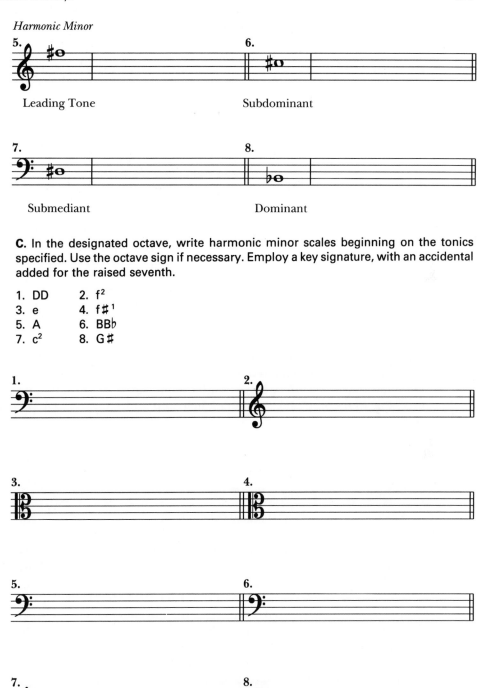

5.

Leading Tone

6.

Subdominant

7.

Submediant

8.

Dominant

C. In the designated octave, write harmonic minor scales beginning on the tonics specified. Use the octave sign if necessary. Employ a key signature, with an accidental added for the raised seventh.

1. DD   2. f^2
3. e   4. f♯^{1}
5. A   6. BB♭
7. c^2 8. G♯

1.

2.

3.

4.

5.

6.

7.

8.

D. Use letter names to complete these harmonic minor scales.

    Tonic

1. A   ____   ____   ____   ____   ____   ____   ____

2. C♯   ____   ____   ____   ____   ____   ____   ____

3. E   ____   ____   ____   ____   ____   ____   ____

4. D♯   ____   ____   ____   ____   ____   ____   ____

5. B   ____   ____   ____   ____   ____   ____   ____

6. F   ____   ____   ____   ____   ____   ____   ____

7. D   ____   ____   ____   ____   ____   ____   ____

8. G♯   ____   ____   ____   ____   ____   ____   ____

Melodic Minor

Although the raised seventh degree in harmonic minor provided a leading tone, sometimes it also created a stylistic problem: the *augmented second*. Between the sixth and raised seventh degrees of a harmonic minor scale is an interval comprising a whole step and a *chromatic* half step and known as the AUGMENTED SECOND.

C Harmonic Minor Scale

Traditional composers avoided the augmented second in a melodic context. The practice that evolved from this preference resulted in the third form of minor: *melodic*. In a MELODIC MINOR SCALE (Recorded Example 20), the sixth and seventh degrees are *both* raised a half step from the natural minor pattern. Since the seventh degree is raised a half step, the melodic minor scale has a leading tone; the raised sixth degree that characterizes melodic minor eliminates the augmented second.

▶ *RECORDED EXAMPLE 20*

Harmonic and Melodic
Minor Scales

A harmonic minor

A melodic minor

Descending Melodic Minor.   Whereas major scales as well as natural and harmonic minor scales are written the same in ascending and descending forms, melodic minor has two forms. Ascending melodic minor, with raised sixth and seventh degrees, has already been discussed. The traditional descending form of melodic minor is the same as that of natural minor. Where the sixth and seventh degrees are raised ascending, they return to their natural state descending (Recorded Example 21).

▶ *RECORDED EXAMPLE 21*

Ascending and Descending Melodic Minor

Ascending   Descending

G melodic minor

exercise 7–4   *Fundamental Skills*
Melodic Minor Scales

A. Write ascending and descending melodic minor scales on the specified tonics. Use the octave designated and use accidentals as necessary to alter the sixth and seventh scale degrees. Write also the solfège syllables if instructed to do so.

1. B   2. e♭¹
3. F   4. a
5. a♯¹   6. G

1. 𝄢

2. 𝄞

3. 𝄡

4. 𝄞

5. 𝄡

6. 𝄢

B. Use letter names to write ascending and descending melodic minor scales.

		Ascending	*Descending*
	Tonic		
1.	C	___ ___ ___ ___ ___ ___ ___ ___	___ ___ ___ ___ ___ ___ ___
2.	G	___ ___ ___ ___ ___ ___ ___ ___	___ ___ ___ ___ ___ ___ ___
3.	F♯	___ ___ ___ ___ ___ ___ ___ ___	___ ___ ___ ___ ___ ___ ___
4.	E♭	___ ___ ___ ___ ___ ___ ___ ___	___ ___ ___ ___ ___ ___ ___
5.	G♯	___ ___ ___ ___ ___ ___ ___ ___	___ ___ ___ ___ ___ ___ ___
6.	A	___ ___ ___ ___ ___ ___ ___ ___	___ ___ ___ ___ ___ ___ ___

7. C♯ __ __ __ __ __ __ __   __ __ __ __ __ __ __

8. B   __ __ __ __ __ __ __   __ __ __ __ __ __ __

C. The names of scale degrees are the same in major and minor. Write the pitch specified by the minor key and scale degree name. Add an accidental if necessary.

1.

| B minor | F minor | D minor | A minor |
| Subtonic | Raised submediant | Leading tone | Subtonic |

| E minor | F♯ minor | G minor | C minor |
| Dominant | Leading tone | Mediant | Supertonic |

2.

| E minor | D minor | D♯ minor | F♯ minor |
| Raised submediant | Raised submediant | Subtonic | Subtonic |

| B♭ minor | E♭ minor | G♯ minor | C♯ minor |
| Subdominant | Leading tone | Submediant | Subtonic |

3.

| G♯ minor | C minor | F minor | E minor |
| Leading tone | Raised submediant | Raised submediant | Subtonic |

| A♭ minor | G minor | F♯ minor | B minor |
| Dominant | Leading tone | Mediant | Supertonic |

D. The following pitches belong to a natural, harmonic, or melodic minor scale on the specified tonic. Identify the given pitch by scale degree name. If the pitch is altered (a raised sixth or seventh, for example), include that information in your answer as well.

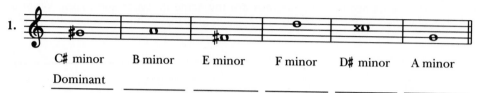

1.

C# minor	B minor	E minor	F minor	D# minor	A minor
Dominant					
___	___	___	___	___	___

2.

Eb minor	C minor	F# minor	B minor	Bb minor	G# minor
___	___	___	___	___	___

3.

Bb minor	C# minor	A minor	E minor	C minor	Ab minor
___	___	___	___	___	___

4.

B minor	G minor	F minor	Eb minor	G# minor	A minor
___	___	___	___	___	___

exercise 7–5 Fundamental Skills
Recognizing Scales

A. Study each ascending scale. Determine whether it is major or one of the three forms of minor; then, write the appropriate identification in the blank.

B. The following melodies are constructed from a major scale or from one of the three forms of minor. Analyze the scale with the given tonic; then, identify the scale type in the blank. One of the melodies employs two different forms of minor. Locate this melody and speculate on why the composer used the two different forms.

6. Tonic   Mozart

7. Tonic   Franck

8. Tonic   Schubert

▶ *RECORDED EXAMPLE 22*

(See Exercise 7–6)

exercise 7–6   Musicianship Skills
EAR TRAINING: Hearing Major and Minor

A. Considering the first five scale degrees, the only difference between major and minor is the mediant (third scale degree). Several ascending major or minor patterns will be played. In the first set, scale degrees fall in order: 1 2 3 4 5. In the second set, all five scale degrees appear but in various orders, and some pitches will be heard more than once. For both sets, write the word "major" or "minor" in the blank as appropriate. You will hear two different patterns in each line.

Set I: Ordered Scale Degrees 1–5

1. _____   _____

2. _____   _____

3. _____   _____

4. _____   _____

Set II: Unordered Scale Degrees 1–5

1. _____   _____

2. _____   _____

3. _____   _____

4. _____   _____

B. Eight scales will be played—both ascending and descending. Write "major" if the scale is major, or write the form of minor ("natural," "harmonic," or "melodic").

1. _____   _____

2. _____   _____

3. _____   _____

4. _____   _____

C. (Not Recorded) Your instructor will play several melodies. Identify the basic scale material as major or minor.

1. _____   _____

2. _____   _____

3. _____   _____

4. _____   _____

KEY RELATIONSHIPS

As we discussed earlier, the keys (and scales) of C major and A minor have the same key signature: no sharps or flats. The two keys are related in that they contain the same *pitches*. The keys of C major and C minor have *different* key signatures and several different pitches; the relationship between these two keys centers on their having the same *tonic pitch*. These two close relationships—of key signature and tonic pitch—are important in traditional music.

The Parallel Relationship

When major and minor keys have the same tonic, the relationship is termed PARALLEL. The parallel relationship is complementary; C major is the parallel major of C minor, just as C minor is the parallel minor of C major. Parallel major and minor keys always have the same tonic pitch. The key of G minor, therefore, is the parallel minor of G major; F-sharp minor is the parallel minor of F-sharp major. Although parallel major and minor keys have the same tonic, they have different key signatures.

C major   C minor   G major   G minor

The Relative Relationship

The keys of C major and A minor have different tonics but the same key signature. Major and minor keys with the same key signature share a complementary REL-ATIVE RELATIONSHIP. The key of C major is the relative major of A minor; A minor is the relative minor of C major.

Determining Relative Minor Keys. Relative major and minor keys *do not* have the same tonic. The tonic of the relative minor of a given major key will always be the sixth scale degree of that major scale. The relative minor of C major, for example, is A minor; the pitch A is the sixth scale degree of C major.

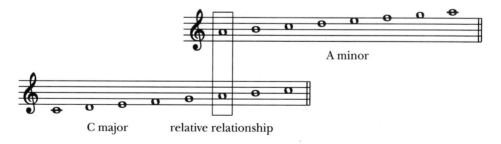

A minor

C major   relative relationship

To find the relative minor of a given major key, find the sixth scale degree of that major key; this pitch will be the tonic of the relative minor. The key signature of this minor key will be the same as that of the relative major. Remember that the sixth degree of a major scale can be determined by counting from the tonic up to the sixth scale degree, but that the same pitch can be determined by beginning on the tonic and counting *down* to the sixth scale degree.

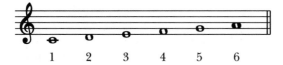

Note carefully that although counting lines and spaces will result in the correct basic pitch, an accidental may be associated with that pitch. When you count up or down from a tonic to find the sixth scale degree (relative minor), be sure to adhere to the major scale interval pattern.

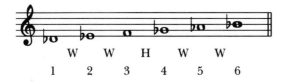

Problem: *Find the relative minor of D major.*

    1. Find the sixth degree of the D major scale. Do this by counting up six pitches or down three. Make certain, however, that the key signature of the major key is applied to the resulting sixth scale degree.

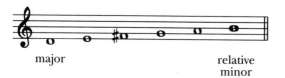

major   relative
                                             minor

major   relative
               minor

    2. When the key signature of the major key is duplicated for a minor key beginning on the sixth scale degree, the natural relative minor will have been formed.

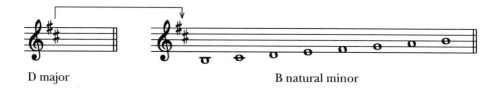

D major   B natural minor

exercise 7–9 *Fundamental Skills*
Relative Minor Keys

A. For the following major keys, determine the relative minor and write the name of that key in the blank. Write the key signature, which is the same for both keys.

Major	*Relative Minor*	*Key Signature*

1. B-flat   _____

2. G   _____

3. F   _____

4. B   _____

Major	Relative Minor	Key Signature

5. C _____

6. A-flat _____

7. F-sharp _____

8. E-flat _____

B. Write the following ascending and descending scales, using the form of minor indicated. Use accidentals as necessary.

1. The relative *natural* minor of E major
2. The relative *harmonic* minor of B-flat major
3. The relative *melodic* minor of D major
4. The relative *harmonic* minor of D-flat major
5. The relative *natural* minor of A major
6. The relative *melodic* minor of B major

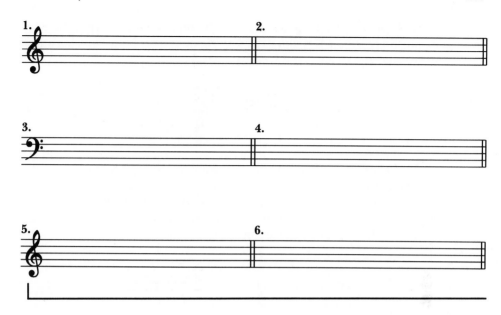

Determining Relative Major Keys.   When you want to reverse the process and find the relative major of a given minor key (to determine the key signature of the minor key, perhaps), employ the tonic of the minor key as the sixth degree of an unknown major scale. Whether ascending or descending, the first step is to determine the tonic of that major scale. To that end, remember that the intervals between sixth, seventh, and eighth scale degrees in major are inflexible.

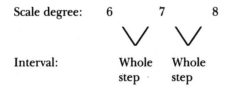

Scale degree:	6	7	8
Interval:	Whole step	Whole step	

If B is the tonic of the given minor key, consider this pitch the sixth scale degree of the relative major. To find the relative major, ascend a whole step to the seventh scale degree, then a diatonic half step higher to find the tonic.

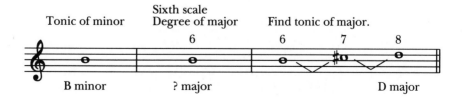

A whole step above B is C-sharp; a half step above C-sharp is D. The relative major, therefore, is D major. The key signature for both D major and B minor is two sharps—F-sharp and C-sharp.

D major   B minor

The correct interval pattern between sixth, seventh, and eighth scale degrees *must* be employed. The relative major of F minor, for example, is not A major, but *A-flat* major. The tonic of the relative major is a whole step plus a diatonic half step above the tonic of the minor. Unless you check the interval pattern carefully, you can easily make mistakes.

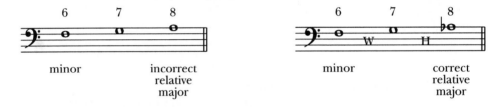

minor   incorrect   minor   correct
                      relative   relative
                      major   major

Problem: *Find the relative major of C-sharp minor.*

  1. Assume the pitch C-sharp as the sixth scale degree of some major scale. Find the tonic of this major scale by calculating the intervals between sixth, seventh, and eighth scale degrees in major.

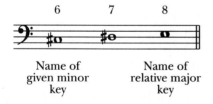

Name of   Name of
given minor   relative major
key   key

  2. The tonic (eighth scale degree) found through this process is the name of the relative major. The minor key will have the same key signature as this relative major key.

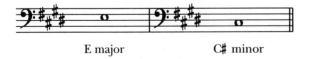

E major   C♯ minor

exercise 7–8 Fundamental Skills
Relative Major Keys

A. Using the formula outlined above, find the relative major of each given minor key; then, produce the key signature that applies to both minor and relative major.

Minor	Relative Major	Key Signature

1. E-flat _____

2. F-sharp _____

3. B _____

4. G _____

Minor	Relative Major	Key Signature

5. C-sharp _____

6. E _____

7. A-flat _____

8. F _____

B. If you need to find the parallel minor of a given major key, you may want first to find the relative major of that minor. This will provide the key signature of the minor key. Remember: In the parallel relationship, two keys have the same tonic; unless you happen to know the key signature, you must still find the relative major to determine the key signature of the parallel minor.

Write the ascending and descending scales as indicated.

1. The parallel major of C major
2. The parallel *harmonic* minor of E major
3. The parallel major of B minor
4. The relative *melodic* minor of E-flat major
5. The relative *natural* minor of B-flat major
6. The relative major of D-sharp minor
7. The parallel *harmonic* minor of A major
8. The relative *harmonic* minor of F major

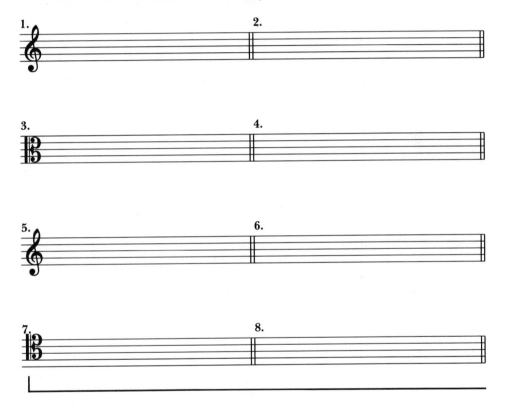

Minor Key Signatures

When composers use minor, the key signature reflects the *natural* form. In traditional music, however, harmonic and melodic forms of minor occur regularly and even simultaneously. When harmonic or melodic minor is employed, the sixth or seventh degree, or both, is altered through accidentals. Notice that the following composition employs two different forms of minor.

M-429

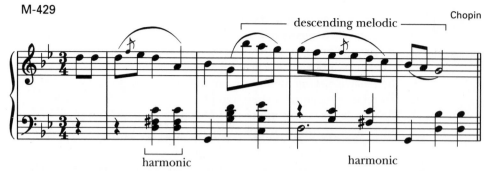

Although a minor key signature can be determined through its relative major, the process is time-consuming and offers the potential for errors. As discussed in the last chapter, the Circle of Fifths (shown in the diagram) represents a convenient way of remembering minor key signatures. The key of A minor, for example, has no sharps or flats. Seven half steps (a perfect fifth) higher is the key of E minor, with a key signature of one sharp; a perfect fifth below A is D, with a key signature of one flat. A perfect fifth above E minor (one sharp) is B minor, with two sharps in the key signature; a perfect fifth below D minor (one flat) is G minor, which employs two flats.

exercise 7–9 *Musicianship Skills*
SIGHT SINGING: Minor Scale Patterns

A. Using the solfège syllables (Appendix E) or another method specified by your instructor, sing the following five-note patterns. Play the first pitch on the keyboard; then, match that pitch and sing the pattern ascending and descending. Be conscious that the only difference between major and minor within the first five scale degrees is the third.

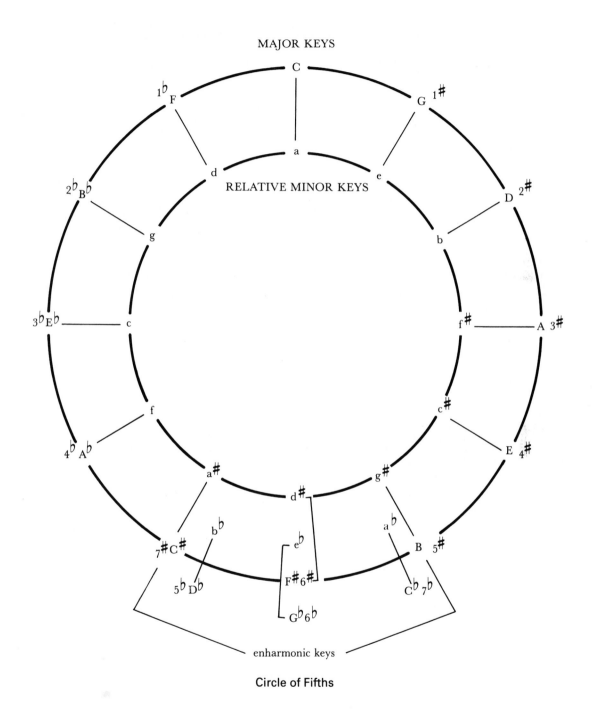

Circle of Fifths

B. Sing complete scales, including the upper pitches that distinguish between the three forms of minor. Sing all scales both ascending and descending, and as always, check your final pitch on the piano after you have sung the pattern. The pitches for F minor are shown here, but you should practice the scales with a variety of tonics throughout your natural range.

1. *Major*   **2.** *Natural minor*

3. *Harmonic minor*   **4.** *Melodic minor*

C. Sing the tunes listed below to yourself and determine whether they are major or minor. If you do not know some of the tunes, think of others and identify their mode. Write "major" or "minor" in the blank as appropriate.

1. *We Three Kings of Orient Are*   _____

2. *Streets of Laredo*   _____

3. *We Are the World*   _____

4. *When Johnny Comes Marching Home* _____

5. *Happy Birthday to You*   _____

6. *God Rest Ye Merry, Gentlemen*   _____

SELF-TEST

1. Write the interval pattern for the natural minor scale.

_____   _____   _____   _____   _____   _____   _____

2. In the space provided, match the letter or letters identifying the scale form or forms that correspond to the given statement.

_____ has a leading tone.

_____ includes an augmented second.

_____ two whole steps between first and third degrees.

_____ has a subtonic.

_____ same ascending and descending.

_____ whole step plus diatonic half step between first and third degrees.

_____ raised sixth degree ascending.

_____ different ascending and descending.

A. Major

B. Natural Minor

C. Harmonic Minor

D. Melodic Minor

3. Identify the tonic pitch, scale type, and form (if minor).

a.

_____   _____   _____

b.

_____   _____   _____

4. Write the scales indicated.

Natural minor   Harmonic minor

a.

Melodic minor (ascending)   Melodic minor (descending)

b.

5. Identify the following terms:

    a. Augmented second

    b. Natural minor

    c. Subtonic

    d. Chromatic half step

    e. Leading tone

1. Review the definitions of a leading tone and a subtonic; then, write the pitches that represent those alternative possibilities in the scales given. Although the subtonic is not customarily associated with a major scale, it is commonly found in music before about 1600 and after about 1875.

	Scale	*Leading Tone*	*Subtonic*
a.	C major	_____	_____
b.	G major	_____	_____
c.	G minor	_____	_____
d.	B major	_____	_____
e.	A-flat major	_____	_____
f.	A minor	_____	_____
g.	F-sharp major	_____	_____
h.	F-sharp minor	_____	_____
i.	B-flat major	_____	_____
j.	E minor	_____	_____

2. Write ascending natural minor scales on the given tonics. Use the octave designated and employ the octave sign if necessary.

a. g **b.** F♯
c. b² **d.** GG♯
e. C♯ **f.** d

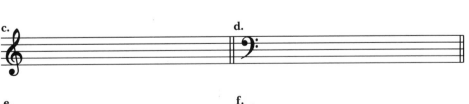

3. Using pitch names, construct ascending harmonic minor scales on the given tonics. Circle the augmented second.

       Tonic

  a. D   ____ ____ ____ ____ ____ ____ ____

  b. E♭   ____ ____ ____ ____ ____ ____ ____

  c. C♯   ____ ____ ____ ____ ____ ____ ____

  d. A   ____ ____ ____ ____ ____ ____ ____

  e. B♭   ____ ____ ____ ____ ____ ____ ____

  f. E   ____ ____ ____ ____ ____ ____ ____

  g. C♭   ____ ____ ____ ____ ____ ____ ____

  h. A♯   ____ ____ ____ ____ ____ ____ ____

4. Write *ascending and descending* melodic minor scales on the given tonics.

5. The following scales are either major or natural, harmonic, or melodic minor. Identify the scale type and form (if minor).

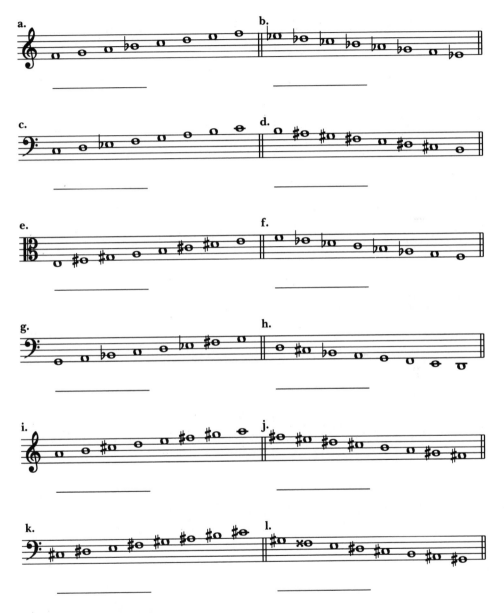

6. The following melodic fragments belong to one *or more* major or minor keys (or both). In the blank, identify all possible keys for each fragment. If the key is minor, be prepared to identify the form.

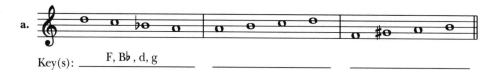

a.

Key(s): ___F, B♭, d, g___   _____   _____

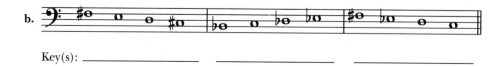

b.

Key(s): _____   _____   _____

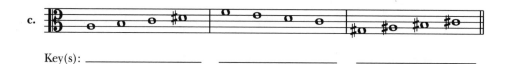

c.

Key(s): _____   _____   _____

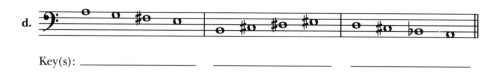

d.

Key(s): _____   _____   _____

7. Analyze the following melodies as you did in a previous chapter. As before, the tonic is given. Your task will be to make an inventory of the pitches present and determine which are used most and least frequently. Some of the melodies are major, others are minor. If the melody is minor, determine the predominant form and if directed to do so, comment on the use of the raised sixth or seventh (or both).

a. Tonic   Legrenzi

8. Using the rhythmic studies on pages 99–100 and 133 as a guide, compose a melody for flute or voice that is major or minor as indicated. Analyze the rhythms first, and consider using melodic patterns that parallel the repetition and variation of the rhythmic content. Remember that the tonic should be the most important pitch in a composition. Consider beginning and ending on this pitch and using it often in important metric positions (the first beat of a measure, for example). Finally, try to balance ascending and descending motion as well as melodic movement by step with occasional leaps. Analyze your own melodies for rhythmic content and compare them with those you studied and analyzed in the previous exercise.

Base your compositions on the following rhythmic studies:

a. Study 4, page 99: F minor, using natural minor throughout.

b. Study 3, page 99: Use the key of D major.

c. Study 7, page 100: Use G melodic minor in its ascending and descending forms as appropriate.

d. Study 1, page 133: Use the key and mode of your choice.

CHAPTER 8

Intervals

ESSENTIAL TERMS

- *augmented interval*
- *diminished interval*
- *harmonic interval*
- *interval inversion*
- *major interval*
- *melodic interval*
- *minor interval*
- *perfect interval*

An INTERVAL is the distance (or difference) between two pitches. In previous chapters, we have discussed several intervals: the octave, the unison, the whole step, the half step, the augmented second, and the perfect fifth. Intervals can be either *harmonic* or *melodic*. A HARMONIC INTERVAL is formed from the simultaneous occurrence of two pitches; MELODIC INTERVALS occur consecutively.

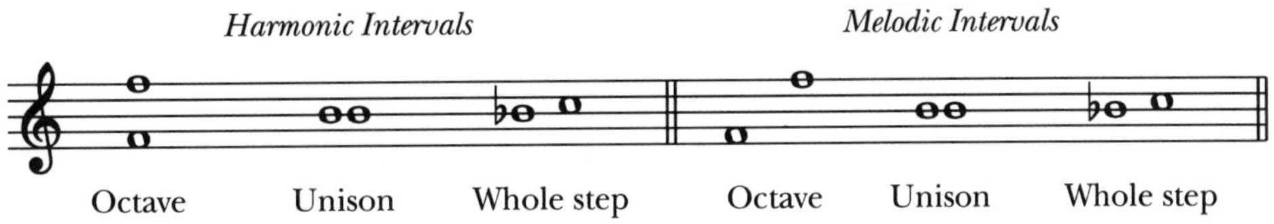

INTERVAL TYPE

Intervals are differentiated by type and quality. The TYPE of an interval is an arithmetic distance determined simply by reckoning the number of steps (lines and spaces) between the two pitches. Begin with the lower pitch; then, count lines and spaces, ending with the upper. If the upper pitch is just one line or space above the lower, the interval is a SECOND. The intervals previously discussed as whole steps and half steps are more accurately termed *seconds*, because the upper pitch lies on the line or the space directly above the lower pitch. Seconds always involve a line *and* a space.

Seconds

A THIRD is an interval formed when two pitches appear on adjacent lines *or* adjacent spaces. Thirds, like those shown below, always involve either lines *or* spaces—not a combination.

Thirds

FOURTHS, like seconds, always involve a line *and* a space. The arithmetic type of the harmonic intervals below is a fourth.

Fourths

A FIFTH is like a third in that both pitches lie on either lines *or* spaces. The intervals below are melodic fifths.

Fifths

SIXTHS and SEVENTHS follow a similar pattern. The upper pitches are six and seven lines or spaces, respectively, above the lower pitch. Sixths are formed by pitches on lines *and* spaces; sevenths occur between pitches on lines *or* spaces.

Sixths   Sevenths

Octaves and Unisons. As we discussed previously, the OCTAVE is the "duplication" of the original pitch name either higher or lower. The UNISON (or PRIME) results from the duplication of exactly the *same* pitch in another voice (or a melodic repetition of the same pitch in the same voice). The following intervals are either octaves or unisons. Octaves are written on lines *and* spaces and, like unisons, are made up of the same pitch name, including any accidental.

           Octaves   Unisons

exercise 8–1 Fundamental Skills
Interval Type

A. Construct melodic intervals of the type indicated above the given pitch. Do not employ accidentals.

1.

   Second Fourth Third Seventh Sixth   Fifth   Octave Second Fifth Seventh

2.

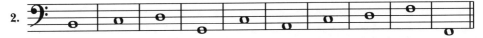

  Octave   Third   Fourth   Sixth Seventh Fifth Unison Sixth   Third Seventh

3.

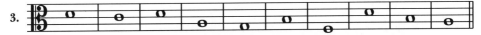

  Second   Third   Sixth   Fifth Second Fourth Octave Third   Fifth Fourth

Write a pitch below the one given that creates the specified interval type. Accidentals are unnecessary.

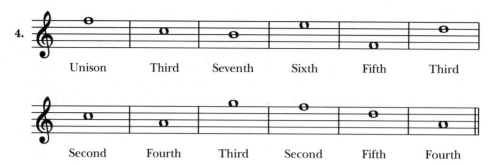

4.

| Unison | Third | Seventh | Sixth | Fifth | Third |

| Second | Fourth | Third | Second | Fifth | Fourth |

5.

| Third | Second | Fourth | Sixth | Seventh |

| Fourth | Fifth | Second | Third | Fourth | Fifth |

6.

| Fifth | Seventh | Second | Third | Octave | Fifth | Unison | Sixth | Octave | Sixth |

B. Identify the arithmetic interval type.

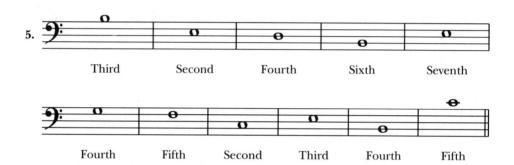

1.

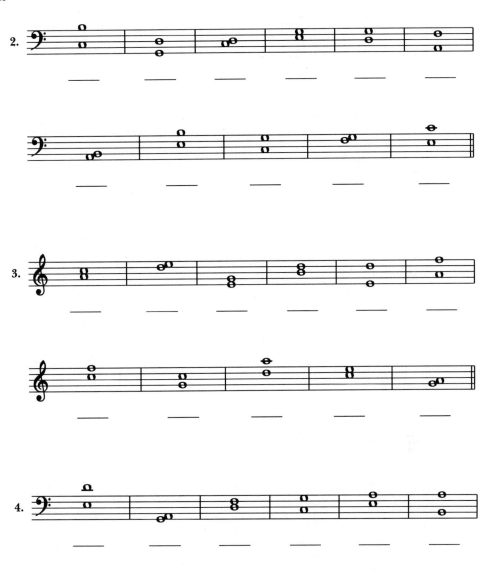

exercise 8–2   Musicianship Skills
KEYBOARD: Interval Type

Use the blank to write the note that makes up the specified interval above the given pitch. At the keyboard, play the first pitch in the octave designated; then, play the second pitch above or below the one given. Since this exercise involves no accidentals, you should use the thumb and second finger for a second, the thumb and third finger for a third, and so on. Use the thumb and fifth finger for the sixth, seventh, and octave. Reverse the fingering pattern for descending intervals. Practice the intervals both harmonically and melodically. Use the left hand for pitches in the contra, great, and small octaves; otherwise, use the right hand.

1. A third above g _____

2. A fourth below C _____

3. A fifth below b^3 _____

4. A seventh above d _____

5. A second above c^1 _____

6. A fourth below e^2 _____

7. An octave above DD _____

8. A sixth above c^1 _____

9. A sixth below C _____

10. A fifth below f^4 _____

11. A seventh below g^2 _____

12. A second above a^1 _____

13. A fifth below GG _____

14. A unison with c^3 _____

15. A seventh above b^2 _____

16. A third below b^1 _____

INTERVAL QUALITY

Arithmetic interval type is a general way of classifying sounds as seconds, sixths, or whatever. In fact, however, many different sounds are classified as the same arithmetic type of interval. The following intervals, for example, have already been discussed: They are all *seconds*; yet, they all have different sounds.

Whole step   Half step   Augmented second

SECONDS

Identifying interval *quality* as well as type permits a much more exact analysis of the sound produced when two pitches occur either simultaneously or consecutively. Two methods of determining interval quality will be presented in this chapter. The first method, based on Half-Step Content, is useful in implanting the concept of interval size. The second method, based on Major-Scale Comparison, is a much faster and more reliable means to the same end. Although the half-step method is explained primarily to serve as a foundation for classifying intervals, the Major-Scale Comparison method will become one of your most important tools for understanding and using music fundamentals.

INTERVAL QUALITY DETERMINED THROUGH HALF-STEP CONTENT

Intervals occur in one of two basic qualities: *major* and *perfect*. Seconds, thirds, sixths, and sevenths can be major in quality; fourths, fifths, unisons, and octaves can be perfect. The number of half steps between the two pitches determines interval quality.

Perfect Intervals

By definition, an octave is *perfect* if there are twelve half steps between upper and lower pitches. PERFECT OCTAVES (abbreviated P8) are seen below. The first and twelfth pitches of a chromatic scale are a perfect octave apart.

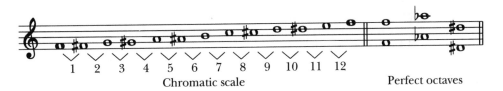

Chromatic scale   Perfect octaves

A UNISON is classified as perfect if the two pitches involved have exactly the same letter name (meaning that there are no half steps between pitches). PERFECT UNISONS (abbreviated P1 or PU) are shown below.

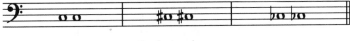

Perfect unisons

Fourths and fifths are perfect if they have five and seven half steps between pitches, respectively. The fourths and fifths below are perfect in quality (abbreviated P4 and P5).

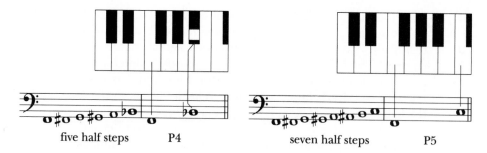

five half steps   P4   seven half steps   P5

Diminished and Augmented Intervals. If an octave, a unison, a fourth, or a fifth is not perfect, it has either more or fewer than the designated number of half steps between pitches. If the interval has one half step fewer, it is classified as a DIMINISHED (d) interval; if it has one half step more, the interval is AUGMENTED (A).

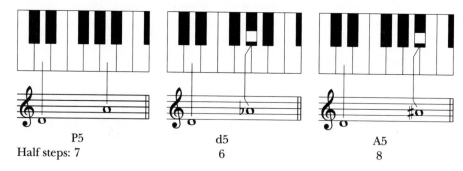

P5   d5   A5
Half steps: 7   6   8

A variety of perfect, augmented, and diminished intervals is heard in Recorded Example 23.

▶ *RECORDED EXAMPLE 23*

Perfect, Augmented,
and Diminished Intervals

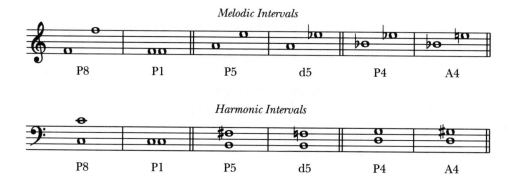

Melodic Intervals

P8   P1   P5   d5   P4   A4

Harmonic Intervals

P8   P1   P5   d5   P4   A4

exercise 8–3 *Fundamental Skills*
Recognizing Intervals

A. Identify the following intervals (they are perfect, diminished, or augmented). In the first blank, write the number of half steps between the two pitches. In the second blank, write the interval type and quality (P4, d4, and so on).

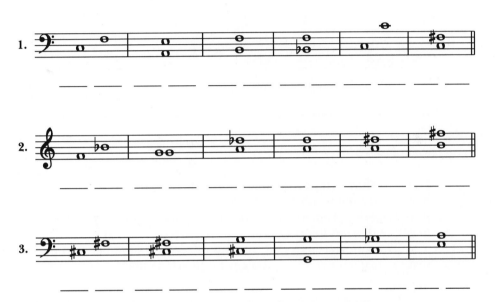

B. If necessary, add an accidental to the *upper* pitch of the following intervals so that their quality corresponds to that designated.

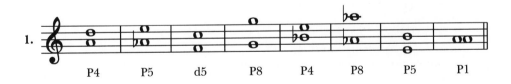

1.   P4   P5   d5   P8   P4   P8   P5   P1

2.   d4   P5   P8   P4   d4   A5   P5   P4

C. Follow the instructions of exercise B, but alter the *lower* pitch if necessary.

1.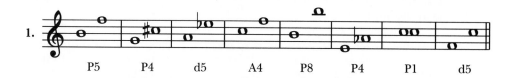

P5   P4   d5   A4   P8   P4   P1   d5

2.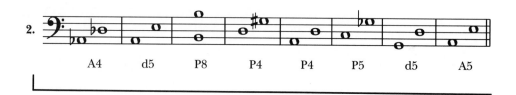

A4   d5   P8   P4   P4   P5   d5   A5

Major Intervals

Fourths, fifths, octaves, and unisons can be classified as perfect in quality. Other intervals (seconds, thirds, sixths, and sevenths) can be *major* in quality. These two categories of intervals are entirely separate; perfect intervals can *never* be major, and major intervals can *never* be perfect.

The MAJOR SECOND (M2) consists of two half steps between pitches. Notice that the major second is equivalent to the whole step.

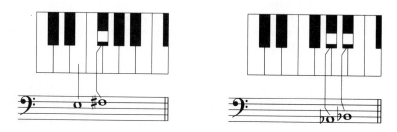

Major seconds

Notating Harmonic Seconds. When seconds are written melodically, any accidentals are placed before the notehead, as usual. When they are written harmonically, however, an accidental associated with the second pitch must appear *before* the notes themselves. If accidentals affect both pitches, those flats, sharps, or naturals are written in order from left to right preceding the notes. The correct placement of accidentals is crucial to avoid errors in reading.

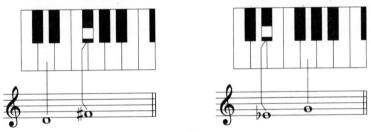

The MAJOR THIRD (M3) includes four half steps between pitches.

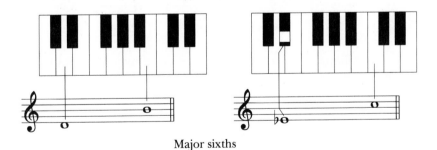

Major thirds

The MAJOR SIXTH (M6) is composed of nine half steps.

Major sixths

A SEVENTH is major (M7) if the upper pitch is separated from the lower pitch by eleven half steps.

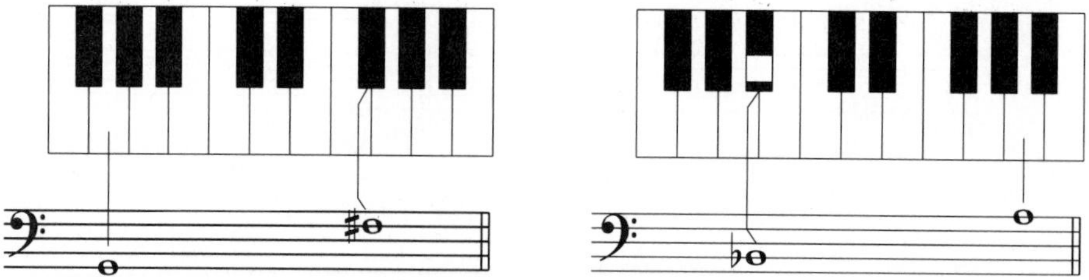

Major sevenths

Minor Intervals. Thirds, sixths, seconds, and sevenths with one half step fewer between pitches than required for classification as *major* are identified as MINOR (abbreviated m2, m3, and so on).

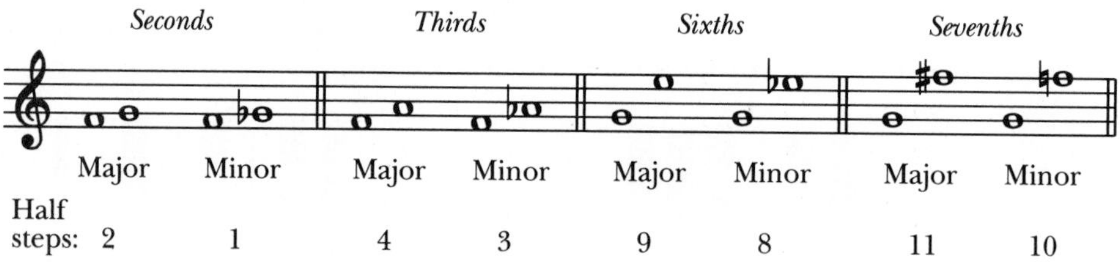
Seconds
Thirds
Sixths
Sevenths
Major
Minor
Major
Minor
Major
Minor
Major
Minor
Half steps: 2
1
4
3
9
8
11
10

When a major interval is decreased a half step, it becomes *minor* in quality. This can be accomplished either by raising the lower pitch or by lowering the upper pitch.

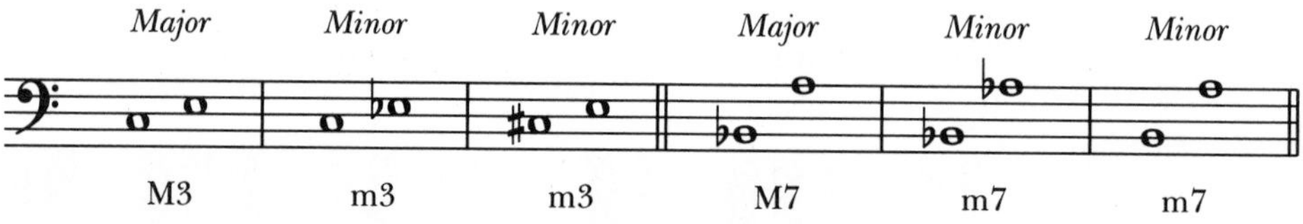
Major
Minor
Minor
Major
Minor
Minor
M3
m3
m3
M7
m7
m7

Similarly, a *minor* interval can be made major either by raising the upper pitch or by lowering the lower pitch a half step.

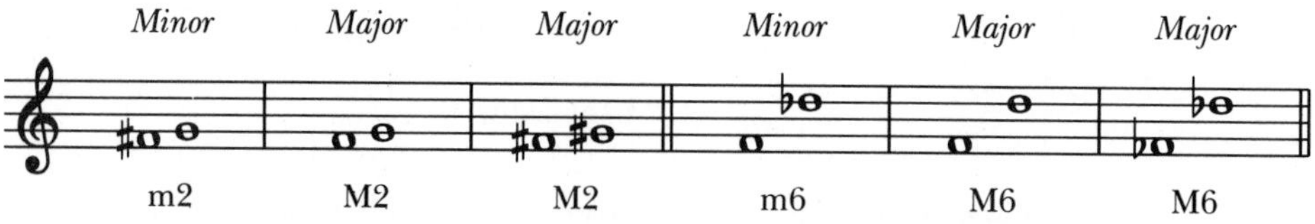
Minor
Major
Major
Minor
Major
Major
m2
M2
M2
m6
M6
M6

Augmented and Diminished Intervals. The only similarity between perfect and major or minor intervals is that they both can be made either augmented or diminished. Decreased a half step, major intervals become minor. Minor intervals decreased a half step become DIMINISHED; increased a half step, major intervals become AUGMENTED. Minor intervals increased a half step, of course, become major.

Major	*Minor*	*Diminished*	*Diminished*	*Minor*	*Major*	*Augmented*	*Augmented*

| M3 | m3 | d3 | d3 | m7 | M7 | A7 | A7 |

Review the changes in interval quality that result from increases and decreases of a half step.

	Increased Half Step Become	*Decreased Half Step Become*
PERFECT INTERVALS	Augmented	Diminished
MAJOR INTERVALS	Augmented	Minor
MINOR INTERVALS	Major	Diminished

Listen to the sounds of the major, minor, diminished, and augmented intervals heard in Recorded Example 24.

► *RECORDED EXAMPLE 24*

Major, Minor, Diminished, and Augmented Intervals

Melodic Intervals

| M3 | m3 | d3 | M6 | A6 | M6 | m6 | d6 |

Harmonic Intervals

| M3 | m3 | d3 | M6 | A6 | M6 | m6 | d6 |

Doubly Augmented and Diminished Intervals. Occasionally, an interval will be even smaller than diminished or larger than augmented. Such intervals are identified as DOUBLY AUGMENTED (AA) or DOUBLY DIMINISHED (dd). The interval

B to F, for example, comprises six half steps and is a diminished fifth; the interval B to F-flat is a doubly diminished fifth (with five half steps). Likewise, C to F-sharp has six half steps and is an augmented fourth; C-flat and F-sharp (with seven half steps) is a doubly augmented fourth.

Enharmonic Spellings

Enharmonic equivalents, you will remember, are pitches that have the same sound but different notations. Intervals can be enharmonic equivalents as well. The interval D to G-sharp, for example, is an augmented fourth (six half steps); another pitch, A-flat, is also six half steps above D. The intervals D to G-sharp and D to A-flat are enharmonic equivalents; they sound exactly the same. In notation, however, the two intervals are completely different. The pitches D to G-sharp constitute an augmented *fourth*, whereas D to A-flat is a diminished *fifth*.

Understanding that intervals are always identified and written according to interval *type* is crucial. The pitch G-sharp would *never* be acceptable as a diminished fifth above D; G-sharp is a fourth above D—not a fifth. Similarly, if you identified the interval D to A-flat as an augmented fourth, your answer would be incorrect; D to A-flat is a diminished fifth.

Compound Intervals

Intervals larger than an octave are termed COMPOUND INTERVALS. An octave plus a second, for example, is known as a NINTH; an octave plus a third is a TENTH, and so on.

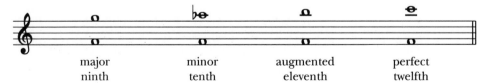

exercise 8–4 *Fundamental Skills*
Major Intervals through Half Steps

A. The following intervals are major, minor, diminished, or augmented. In the first blank, write the number of half steps between the two pitches. In the second blank, write the interval type and quality (M3, m3, and so on).

B. If necessary, add an accidental to the upper pitch of the following intervals so that their quality corresponds to that designated.

1.   m3   M6   m7   M7   M3   m2   m6   M3   M7

2.   M2   m3   m6   M6   M2   M3   M7   m6

C. Follow the instructions of exercise B, but alter the *lower* pitch if necessary.

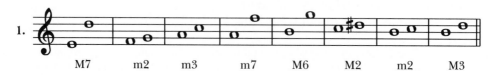

| M7 | m2 | m3 | m7 | M6 | M2 | m2 | M3 |

| M6 | m7 | M3 | m6 | M7 | m3 | M2 | m2 | M7 |

| M7 | m2 | d3 | d7 | A6 | M2 | m2 | A3 |

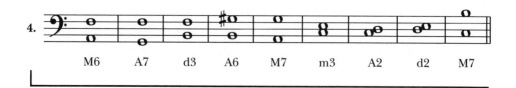

| M6 | A7 | d3 | A6 | M7 | m3 | A2 | d2 | M7 |

INTERVALS THROUGH MAJOR-SCALE COMPARISON

Although any interval can be written and identified by counting half steps, the process is slow and carries a great potential for error. Another method, Major-Scale Comparison, is recommended as the fastest and least complicated means of writing and identifying intervals.

If certain interval qualities are established as "norms" so that differing qualities can be compared with them at a glance, both construction and identification of intervals are easier. Such norms are available in the intervals in the major scale. If each degree of a major scale is written successively above the tonic, the resulting intervals are either perfect or major.

| P1 | M2 | M3 | P4 | P5 | M6 | M7 | P8 |

A major

Diatonic Pitches

Pitches that belong to a given major or minor scale are said to be DIATONIC in that key. In A major, for example, the pitches A B C♯ D E F♯ and G♯ are *diatonic*; all other pitches are *outside* the key and are *not* diatonic (or nondiatonic). Interval construction and identification through key signature is based on a simple principle:

> *The diatonic intervals formed between the tonic pitch of a given major scale and the other pitches of that scale are either* perfect *or* major *in quality.*

If the upper pitch of an interval is diatonic in the key represented by the lower pitch, the quality of the interval *must* be either major or perfect. In the following example, C-natural is diatonic in the E-flat major scale; without counting half steps, you can *immediately* identify the interval as a *major* sixth if you know the key signature of E-flat major.

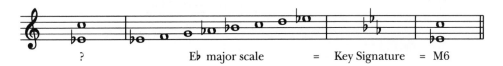

With the Major-Scale Comparison method of constructing and identifying intervals, there is no need to count half steps. If major key signatures are learned thoroughly, the process is fast and accurate.

An additional example of the Major-Scale Comparison method is shown below. If you know the key signature of G major, you can quickly and accurately identify the quality of the fourth. Since C is a diatonic pitch in the key of G major, the interval is a *perfect* fourth. In the second example, the interval from D to C-sharp can be reckoned without counting half steps because C-sharp is diatonic in D major (the key represented by the lower pitch); if a seventh is diatonic, it is major.

exercise 8–5 *Fundamental Skills*
Diatonic Pitches

The following melodies are written with accidentals rather than a key signature. Some of the phrases contain pitches outside the key (nondiatonic pitches). The key is given; circle all *nondiatonic* pitches.

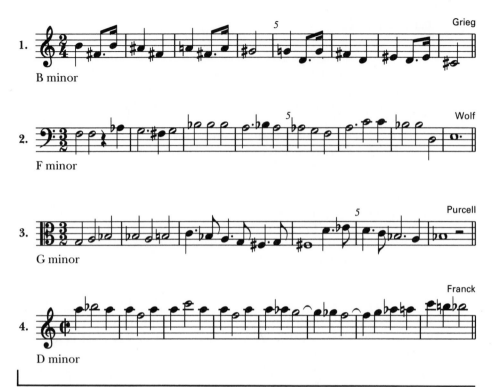

Intervals with Nondiatonic Pitches. If the upper pitch of an interval is *not* diatonic in the key represented by the lower pitch, the quality of the interval is determined by observing the difference between the given (or desired) interval and the diatonic interval. The interval from E-flat to C-sharp, for example, is obviously not a major sixth, because C-sharp does not occur in the E-flat major scale. But since the pitches E-flat to C-natural form a major sixth (because C-natural is diatonic in the key of E-flat major), we can see at a glance that the interval from E-flat to C-sharp is a half step larger than major and therefore *augmented* in quality.

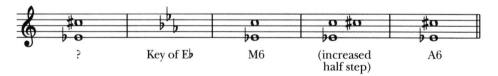

If the pitches in the sixth are E-flat to C-flat, and C-flat is recognized initially as nondiatonic, the interval Eb–Cb is identified as a half step smaller than the diatonic interval Eb–C. Since Eb–C is a major sixth, Eb–Cb must be minor.

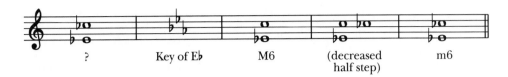

| | Key of E♭ | M6 | (decreased half step) | m6 |

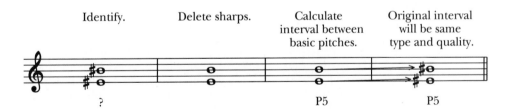

With fourths, fifths, unisons, and octaves, the process of construction and identification through Major-Scale Comparison is exactly the same. The interval from B to F cannot be a perfect fifth because the key of B major has five sharps—one of which is F-sharp. The pitches B to F-sharp, therefore, form a perfect fifth; B to F-natural is a half step smaller than a perfect fifth and is classified as *diminished*.

| | Key of B | (decreased half step) | d5 |

Discounting Accidentals. If the two pitches of the interval are affected by the same accidental (*not* a combination), the accidentals can be ignored in interval identification. For example, if the interval between E-sharp and B-sharp must be identified, the comparison method is less effective, since E-sharp is not one of the fifteen major keys.[1] The interval could be calculated by counting half steps, of course, but because the two pitches are affected by the same accidental, the sharps can simply be ignored. The interval between E and B is calculated through Major-Scale Comparison in the usual way. Since E to B is a perfect fifth, E-sharp to B-sharp is *also* a perfect fifth.

| Identify. | Delete sharps. | Calculate interval between basic pitches. | Original interval will be same type and quality. |

| | | P5 | P5 |

The same situation would exist if the pitches were E–double flat and B–double flat; if basic pitches are altered *in the same way*, the interval type and quality are not changed (the sound, of course, is different).

---

[1] A knowledge of theoretical keys (keys with double flats or double sharps in their key signatures) makes it possible to use the key-signature method of interval construction and identification in every case.

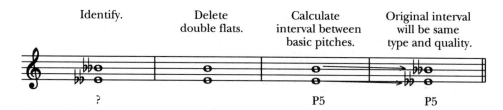

Identify.	Delete double flats.	Calculate interval between basic pitches.	Original interval will be same type and quality.
?		P5	P5

Discounting and Restoring Accidentals.   When the two pitches of an interval are not affected by the same accidental, and the lower pitch does not correspond to one of the major keys, a third approach may be helpful. First, discount the accidental of the lower pitch so that it represents one of the fifteen major keys; next, calculate the quality in the usual way. Finally, *adjust* the result to reflect the accidental discounted earlier. Be careful to note that sharping the lower pitch decreases interval size; if a flat is added to the lower pitch, the interval will be larger.

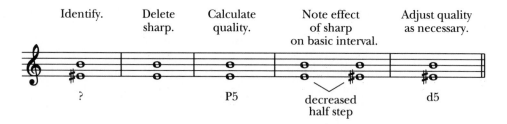

Identify.	Delete sharp.	Calculate quality.	Note effect of sharp on basic interval.	Adjust quality as necessary.
?		P5	decreased half step	d5

---

exercise 8–6   Musicianship Skills
KEYBOARD: Intervals

A. Return to Skill Exercise 8-4 (B and C). Play each interval on the keyboard exactly as notated. Use two different fingers of the same hand for the two pitches. The exact fingering pattern will depend upon the size of the interval and the pitches involved. As in earlier keyboard exercises, use the left hand for the contra, great, and small octaves; use the right hand for the one-line octave and above.

B. Begin by writing the pitch name of the note that forms the specified interval above the note given. At the keyboard, play the first pitch in the octave designated; then, play the second pitch above the one given.

   1. M3 above e _____   2. P4 above C _____

   3. m2 above f^3 _____   4. M7 above d^1 _____

5. P5 above Bb _____

6. m3 above f^1 _____

7. M6 above eb^2 _____

8. P4 above c♯ _____

9. d5 above C _____

10. m6 above e _____

11. A4 above b^1 _____

12. P8 above g♯^{3} _____

13. M3 above ab^1 _____

14. d7 above DD _____

15. P4 above b^2 _____

16. A6 above ab _____

▶ *RECORDED EXAMPLE 25*

(See Exercise 8-7.)

exercise 8–7 Musicianship Skills
EAR TRAINING: Major and Perfect Intervals

A. (Recorded) Ear training centers in part on developing the ability to recognize abstract intervals. To preview this study, you are asked here to identify melodic intervals heard as either perfect (fourths, fifths, unisons, and octaves) or major (seconds, thirds, sixths, and sevenths). Perfect intervals tend to sound "stable" and "open," whereas major intervals are heard either as dissonant (seconds or sevenths) or as "sweet" and consonant. You will hear four different intervals in each line.

Remember: All the intervals will be major or perfect. Write "P" or "M" in the blank as appropriate.

1. _____   _____   _____   _____

2. _____   _____   _____   _____

3. _____   _____   _____   _____

4. _____   _____   _____   _____

5. _____   _____   _____   _____

B. (Not Recorded) Your instructor will play melodic intervals that are perfect fourths, perfect fifths, or perfect octaves. Listen carefully to the interval; then, sing silently from one pitch to another. Write "P5," "P8," or "P4" in the blank as appropriate.

1. _____   _____   _____   _____

2. _____   _____   _____   _____

3. _____   _____   _____   _____

4. _____   _____   _____   _____

5. _____   _____   _____   _____

C. (Not Recorded). These intervals are major or minor seconds or major or minor thirds. You learned the sound of the seconds earlier as whole steps and half steps. The thirds are the intervals that in scales determine the major or minor effect. Listen to the interval; then, write "M2," "m2," "M3," or "m3" in the blank to identify the interval.

1. _____   _____   _____   _____

2. _____   _____   _____   _____

3. _____   _____   _____   _____

4. _____   _____   _____   _____

5. _____   _____   _____   _____

exercise 8–8   Fundamental Skills
Compound and Enharmonic Intervals

A. Write compound intervals as specified above the given pitch. First, reduce the designated interval by an octave (a tenth becomes a third, for example). Next, construct the smaller interval as usual, but write the resulting pitch an octave higher.

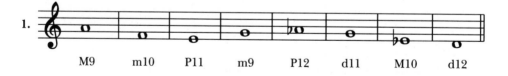

1.   M9   m10   P11   m9   P12   d11   M10   d12

2.   A9   M10   P12   A11   m9   m10   P11   M9   d12

B. The notated intervals below sound the same as the specified interval, but they are written incorrectly as enharmonic equivalents. In the space provided, rewrite the notated interval so that it corresponds to the identification. Change the upper pitch in the first line, the lower pitch in the second line.

Change upper pitch if necessary.

A4   M3   m9   P5

A6   m7   d5   A2

Change lower pitch if necessary.

P8   m6   A4   m10

p5   d7   d3   dd5

exercise 8–9 Fundamental Skills
Constructing and Identifying Intervals

A. Identify the type and quality of the following intervals.

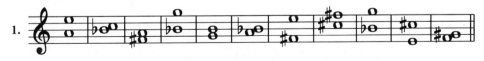

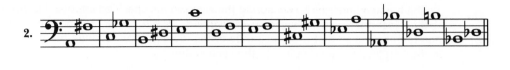

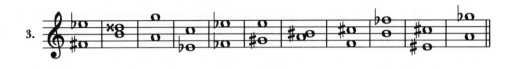

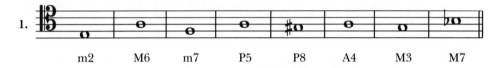

B. Write the designated interval above the given pitch.

INTERVAL INVERSION

The word *inversion* suggests that some change in a relationship has taken place. An inverted pyramid, for example, is one that has been turned upside down and rests on its point.

Similarly, an INVERTED INTERVAL is one in which the original positions of the two pitches have been reversed. Interval inversion can be accomplished in either of two ways: (1) by raising the lower pitch an octave so that it appears above the upper, or (2) by lowering the upper pitch an octave so that it lies below the lower.

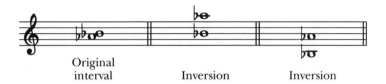

Original   Inversion   Inversion
interval

When intervals are inverted, type and quality usually change. In the preceding example, the major second inverts to a minor seventh. Notice also the following inversions; except when quality is perfect, *both* type and quality change.

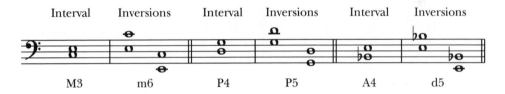

Interval	Inversions	Interval	Inversions	Interval	Inversions
M3	m6	P4	P5	A4	d5

Changes in interval type that result from inversion are predictable. Seconds invert to sevenths; sevenths invert to seconds. Thirds invert to sixths, and sixths invert to thirds. Likewise, fourths and fifths invert. Notice that numerically, a given interval and its inversion add up to nine ($2 + 7 = 9$, $7 + 2 = 9$, and so forth).

Inversion of interval quality is equally straightforward. If the original quality is major, the inverted interval will be minor; likewise, minor intervals inverted become major. The same is true of augmented and diminished intervals: An augmented interval becomes diminished when inverted; diminished intervals become augmented. Inverted perfect intervals, however, remain perfect. Study the table of inversion and the examples shown below.

TYPE		QUALITY	
Inverted	*Become*	*Inverted*	*Becomes*
Seconds	Sevenths	Major	Minor
Thirds	Sixths	Minor	Major
Fourths	Fifths	Perfect	Perfect
Fifths	Fourths	Diminished	Augmented
Sixths	Thirds	Augmented	Diminished
Sevenths	Seconds		
Octaves	Unisons		
Unisons	Octaves		

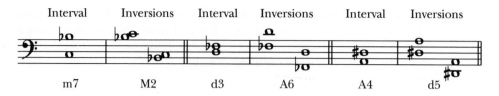

Interval	Inversions	Interval	Inversions	Interval	Inversions
m7	M2	d3	A6	A4	d5

---

exercise 8–10   *Fundamental Skills*
Interval Inversion

A. Invert the given intervals. First, write the upper pitch of the original interval an octave lower; then, reverse the process and move the lower pitch of the original interval an octave higher. Identify both the original interval and the inversions.

1.

_____   _____   _____   _____   _____   _____
      Inversions   Inversions   Inversions

2.

_____   _____   _____   _____   _____   _____
      Inversions   Inversions   Inversions

3.

_____   _____   _____   _____   _____   _____
      Inversions   Inversions   Inversions

4.

_____   _____   _____   _____   _____   _____
      Inversions   Inversions   Inversions

Writing Intervals below a Given Pitch

The type and quality of an interval are always identified by calculating upward from the lower pitch. At times, however, it may be necessary to write an interval below a given pitch. Asked to write a major sixth below F, one could always count down nine half steps, or write the interval type (F to A-flat), identify it in the customary way, and then adjust the lower pitch as necessary.

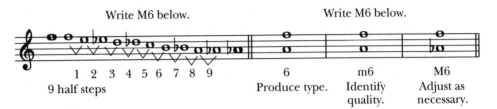

Although these methods may be satisfactory, they offer the potential for errors, since there are several steps. The theory of interval inversion provides a simple, two-step method of writing intervals below a given pitch; moreover, this method is based on Major-Scale Comparison. Since intervals invert in a predictable way, an interval below a given pitch can be produced by first writing the inversion above (in the usual way) and then lowering this pitch an octave. If a major seventh below D were desired, for example, we would calculate a minor second (the inversion of a major seventh) *above* the given pitch and then write this pitch an octave lower.

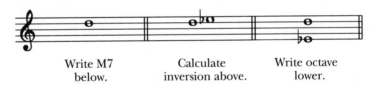

As long as the inversion is determined correctly, and assuming there are no errors in notation, interval inversion combined with octave transposition will always produce the correct pitch below a given note. For instance, the fastest and simplest way to determine a diminished sixth below the pitch G would be to figure the inversion (an augmented third) above G, then write the result below it.

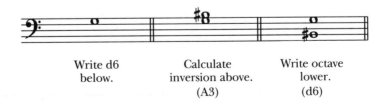

exercise 8–11 Fundamental Skills
Intervals below a Given Pitch

Using either interval inversion or counting half steps, construct intervals below the given pitch as directed. Use the alternative method of constructing intervals (inversion or half steps) to check your answer.

1.   P5   m3   M6   m2   P4   M7   m6   P5

2.   m3   A4   P8   m7   d5   M6   m2   A6

3.   M3   d5   P4   M7   m6   P5   A4   m3

SELF-TEST

1. Write the number of half steps associated with each interval quality given below.

Perfect Intervals		*Major Intervals*	
P4	_____	M7	_____
P1	_____	M2	_____
P5	_____	M6	_____
P8	_____	M3	_____

2. Complete the table.

	Increased One Half Step Becomes	Increased Two Half Steps Becomes	Decreased One Half Step Becomes	Decreased Two Half Steps Becomes
PERFECT	_____	_____	_____	_____
MAJOR	_____	_____	_____	_____
MINOR	_____	_____	_____	_____

3. Identify the following intervals by quality and type.

____   ____   ____   ____   ____   ____   ____   ____

4. Identify the interval in the first measure. Next, duplicate the lower pitch in the second measure, and then write an enharmonic equivalent for the upper pitch. Identify this interval as well.

_____   _____   _____

_____   _____   _____

5. Construct the intervals indicated above the given pitch.

M3   d7   P5   A6   m2   P4   M7   m3

6. Circle pitches that *are not* diatonic in the keys indicated.

         D: Ab: F:

         E: G: Bb:

7. Construct the intervals indicated above the given pitch. In the blank beside the interval, construct its inversion and identify that as well.

    M3_____   m6_____   d7_____   A4_____

8. Write the designated interval below the given pitch.

       m3   M7   A6   P5

9. Identify the following terms:

    a. Melodic interval

    b. Diatonic pitch

    c. Interval inversion

    d. Perfect interval

    e. Interval type

SUPPLEMENTARY EXERCISES

1. Three brief duets follow for analysis. As directed, examine the melodic and harmonic interval content. You might make a list of the intervals most and least frequently encountered in each composition. Consider also whether meter appears to affect interval selection. Do certain harmonic interval types, for example, occur typically on strong or weak beats? Examine the melodic line of each voice. Is melodic motion mostly by step? By leap? Speculate on whether a work was written for voice or for an instrument. Once you have analyzed each composition, compare and contrast the three works in terms of interval content and other areas as directed.

a.

Sweelinck

"In Dorian Mode" from Mikrokosmos *by Béla Bartók. © Copyright 1940 by Hawkes & Son (London) Ltd.;
Copyright Renewed. Reprinted by permission of Boosey & Hawkes, Inc.*

2. Compose an alto voice between the given soprano and bass of the following composition. Use a separate sheet of paper with systems of three staves each. Copy the original two voices on the top and bottom staves, respectively. Use the middle staff for your alto voice. Employ rhythms for the alto that complement the existing voices. Keep the new voice *between* the soprano and the bass if possible (rather than crossing above the soprano or below the bass). Choose pitches for the alto voice based on the intervals you want to create with the soprano and the bass. If you choose predominantly dissonant intervals (seconds, sevenths, and tritones), your finished composition will have a dissonant effect. Using pitches that create thirds, fifths, and sixths with the existing voices, on the other hand, will result in a more consonant sound.

Remember that the purpose of this exercise is to study intervals and their characteristic sounds. You are not expected to compose a trio that maintains the harmony of the duet. If possible, perform the original composition followed by a performance of your trio.

3. On a separate sheet, compose a short duet for piano or wind instruments (as directed) in which certain harmonic interval types predominate. You might write a composition, for example, that uses primarily thirds and sixths. Or for a different effect, you might use mostly fourths and fifths. A dissonant composition will result from seconds and sevenths. You may use a variety of interval types in your duet, but make sure that one type *predominates*.

In addition to the harmonic interval content, you should maintain consistency in the melodic motion of each voice. Use stepwise melodic motion primarily, with occasional leaps for variety. The reverse is also possible: predominant motion by leap with occasional stepwise passages.

You might use one of the rhythmic ensembles in this text as the basis of your composition. Especially recommended are Ensemble 2 on page 101, Ensemble 4 on page 102, and Ensemble 5 on page 135.

Root-Position Triads

The basic unit of traditional harmony is the TRIAD—a collection of three pitches. In the context of Common Practice harmony, the term *triad* is understood to mean *tertian* triad—one built of consecutive thirds. Although other types of triads exist, the tertian triad is the only one employed in traditional music.

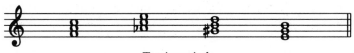

Tertian triads

The tertian triad consists of three elements. The ROOT is the lowest of the three pitches when the triad appears over consecutive lines or spaces. Above the root is the THIRD; the upper pitch of the triad is the FIFTH. The terms *third* and *fifth*, of course, refer to the intervals that these pitches form above the root.

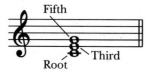

ROOT POSITION

The root is the lowest of the three pitches when the triad occurs over consecutive lines or spaces. When the root of the triad is also the *bass* (the lowest-sounding pitch), the triad is said to be in ROOT POSITION. When a triad is not in root position, it is *inverted*. Inverted triads, in which the root is above the bass, will be discussed in Chapter 10. The following triads are all in root position.

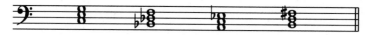

Root - position triads

TRIAD QUALITY

Like intervals, triads occur in a number of qualities—each with a distinct *timbre*. The quality of a triad is determined by the respective qualities of the three component intervals. As shown below, tertian triads consist of two thirds and a fifth.

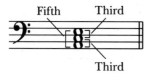

In traditional music, there are four triad qualities: *major, minor, diminished,* and *augmented.*

Major and Minor Triads. A root-position triad is MAJOR if the lower of the two thirds is a major third and if the interval between root and fifth is a perfect fifth. If those two conditions are met, the upper third will always be minor.

Major Triad in Root Position

Triads are identified according to the pitch name of the root and the quality of the triad. The preceding triad is an A-flat major triad. Notice the identification of other root-position major triads shown below.

A major triad   C♯ major triad   F major triad   E♭ major triad

Like the major triad, the root-position MINOR TRIAD has a perfect fifth between root and fifth. The lower third, however, is minor; the upper third, major.

Minor Triad in Root Position

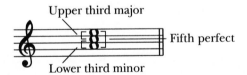

Minor triads are identified by the pitch name of the root and the quality of the triad. Both major and minor triads in root position are heard in Recorded Example 26.

▶ *RECORDED EXAMPLE 26*

Major and Minor Triads

C major triad   C minor triad   E major triad   E minor triad

exercise 9–1 *Fundamental Skills*
Major and Minor Triads

The following triads are either major or minor. Identify the root by writing the correct pitch name in the first blank; identify the quality as "major" (or "M") or "minor" (or "m") in the second blank. Check the lower third of each triad. If the third is major, the triad is major; if minor, the triad is minor.

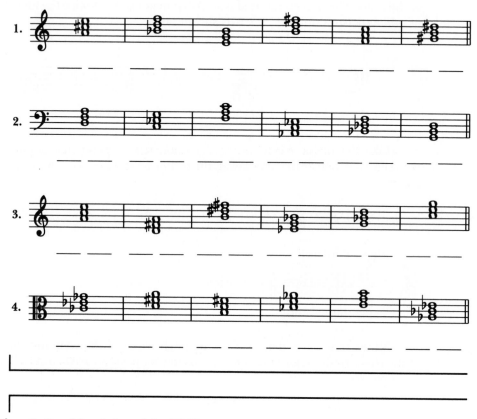

exercise 9–2 *Musicianship Skills*
EAR TRAINING: Major and Minor Triads

Your instructor will play a number of triads. You will hear the pitches first arpeggiated (sounded consecutively), then played simultaneously as a chord. The root-position triads in this exercise are either major or minor. Listen for the lower third and identify the triad as major or minor as appropriate.

1. _____   2. _____

3. _____   4. _____

5. _____   6. _____

7. _____   8. _____

9. _____   10. _____

11. _____   12. _____

13. _____   14. _____

15. _____   16. _____

Diminished and Augmented Triads.   Whereas major and minor triads have in common a perfect fifth between root and fifth, diminished and augmented triads are alike in that their fifths are *not* perfect. The DIMINISHED TRIAD consists of a lower third that is minor and a fifth that is diminished; the upper third is also minor.

Diminished Triad in Root Position

Upper third minor

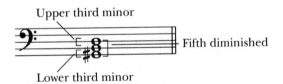

Fifth diminished

Lower third minor

Several diminished triads are identified below.

B diminished triad   F♯ diminished triad   A♭ diminished triad

The AUGMENTED TRIAD consists of a major third and an augmented fifth above the root; the upper third is major.

Augmented Triad in Root Position

Upper third major

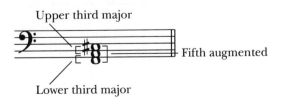

Fifth augmented

Lower third major

Triads of all qualities are heard in Recorded Example 27.

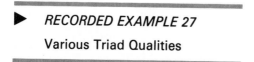

RECORDED EXAMPLE 27

Various Triad Qualities

exercise 9–3 Fundamental Skills
Diminished and Augmented Triads

The following root-position triads are either diminished or augmented. In the first blank, write the pitch name of the root; indicate the quality in the second blank (use "A" for augmented and "d" for diminished, or another system recommended by your instructor). Since this exercise deals only with diminished and augmented triads, if the lower third is major, the quality is augmented; if the lower third is minor, the triad is diminished.

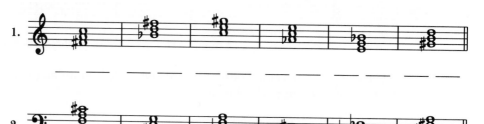

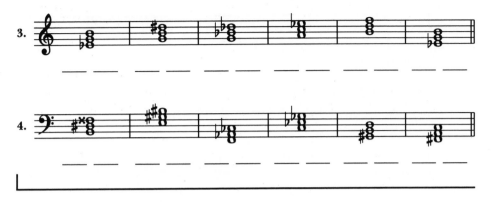

Identification of Triad Quality

Identify triad quality by analyzing the intervals between root and third and between root and fifth. Begin the process with the fifth; if the fifth is perfect, the quality *must* be either major or minor (diminished and augmented triads have fifths of other qualities). If the fifth is *not* perfect, the triad is *neither* major nor minor. An analysis of the lower third (between root and third) differentiates between the two remaining possibilities. If the fifth is perfect and the lower third is major, the triad is major.[1] If the fifth is not perfect and the lower third is major, the triad is augmented. The following chart, which assumes that only the four traditional triad qualities will be encountered, illustrates the identification process.

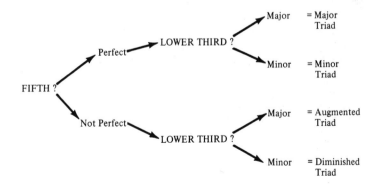

[1] This statement assumes that only the four traditional qualities—major, minor, diminished, and augmented—will be encountered. In music before 1600 and after about 1875, triads of other qualities exist.

exercise 9–4 Fundamental Skills
Triad Quality

All four qualities of root-position triads are included in these exercises. Identify the root name in the first blank and the quality ("M," "m," "d," or "A") in the second blank.

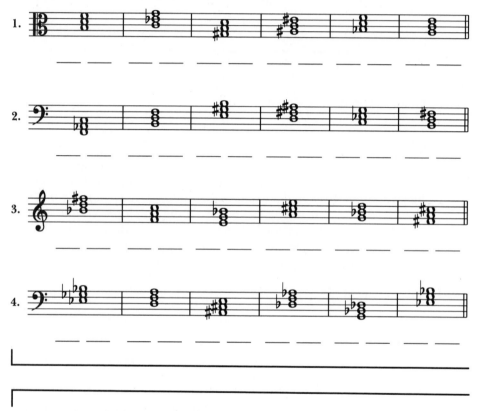

---

exercise 9–5 Musicianship Skills
KEYBOARD: Root-position Triads

Return to the four lines of Skill Exercise 9-4 and play each triad at the keyboard. Use the thumb and the third and fifth fingers for the root, third, and fifth, respectively. Play the triad first melodically (arpeggiated), then harmonically as a chord. Practice hands separately; then, play the triads with left and right hands together. Listen carefully to the characteristic sound of each triad.

▶ *RECORDED EXAMPLE 28*

(See Exercise 9-6.)

---

exercise 9–6 Musicianship Skills

EAR TRAINING: Recognizing Triad Quality

You will hear root-position triads of all four qualities in this exercise. Listen first for the fifth: If it is perfect, the triad is major or minor; if it is not perfect, the triad is diminished or augmented. Listen next for the lower third to separate major from minor or diminished from augmented. Use the standard abbreviations: "M," "m," "d," and "A." Six different triads will be heard in each line.

1. ____   ____   ____   ____   ____   ____

2. ____   ____   ____   ____   ____   ____

3. ____   ____   ____   ____   ____   ____

4. ____   ____   ____   ____   ____   ____

5. ____   ____   ____   ____   ____   ____

CONSTRUCTION OF TRIADS

Triads are constructed by duplicating the appropriate interval pattern for the quality desired. To construct a major triad in root position, begin by writing the basic pitches above the desired root; make sure that all pitches fall over lines *or* spaces. When you have written the basic pitches, adjust the third of the triad if necessary so that it forms a major third above the root. Next, adjust the fifth if necessary so that it is a perfect fifth above the root.

| Construct major triad. | Write basic pitches. | Adjust third if not major. | Adjust fifth if not perfect. | Complete triad. |

| Construct major triad. | Write basic pitches. | Adjust third if not major. | Adjust fifth if not perfect. | Complete triad. |

Triads of other qualities are constructed in a similar manner.

Minor

| Construct minor triad. | Write basic pitches. | Adjust third if not minor. | Adjust fifth if not perfect. | Complete triad. |

Diminished

| Construct diminished triad. | Write basic pitches. | Adjust third if not minor. | Adjust fifth if not diminished. | Complete triad. |

Augmented

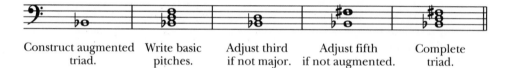

| Construct augmented triad. | Write basic pitches. | Adjust third if not major. | Adjust fifth if not augmented. | Complete triad. |

exercise 9–7 *Fundamental Skills*
Constructing Triads

A. Construct root-position triads of the designated qualities on the given roots. First, write basic pitches above the root; then, adjust the third or the fifth, or both, as necessary.

1.
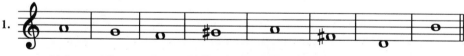

Major   Minor   Major   Diminished Augmented Minor   Diminished Major

2.
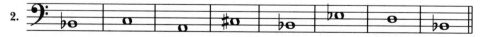

Minor   Major   Diminished Major Augmented Major Augmented Major

3. Major Diminished Augmented Minor Minor Major Diminished Major

4. Augmented Major Minor Dimished Major Major Augmented Minor

B. Begin by writing the designated pitch in the clef indicated. Next, write a triad of the specified quality using the pitch you just supplied as the root. Use the octave designated, and employ the octave sign as necessary to avoid ledger lines.

1. Major on B (bass)
2. Diminished on f (treble)
3. Minor on f♯¹ (bass)
4. Augmented on BB♭ (bass)
5. Diminished on e (bass)
6. Major on d (treble)
7. Minor on A♭ (bass)
8. Augmented on C♯ (bass)
9. Major on g² (treble)
10. Minor on D♭ (bass)
11. Major on a (treble)
12. Diminished on g♯¹
13. Minor on b (bass)
14. Augmented on c¹ (bass)
15. Diminished on g³ (treble)
16. Minor on d♯ (bass)

1.	2.	3.	4.	5.	6.	7.	8.

9.	10.	11.	12.	13.	14.	15.	16.

exercise 9–8 Musicianship Skills
SIGHT SINGING: Triad Outlines

A. Using the syllable system recommended by your instructor, sing the following triad outlines both ascending and descending. You might also use pitch names or the numbers "1," "3," and "5" to designate root, third, and fifth. Play the triad root on the piano; then, sing the triad ascending and descending. Arpeggiate the triad at the keyboard as you did in Skill Exercise 9-4 to check your pitch. In addition to the triads shown, practice others throughout your natural range.

Triad Qualities

1.

Major   Minor   Diminished   Minor

Major   Augmented   Major

2.

Major   Minor   Diminished   Minor

Major   Augmented   Major

B. Sing the following triad outlines. Play the root of the first triad on the piano, arpeggiate the triad vocally, then check your pitch against the piano.

Major Triads

Minor Triads

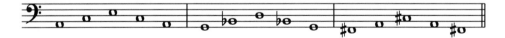

Diminished Triads

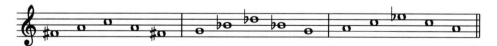

Augmented Triads

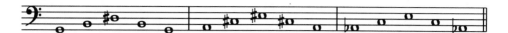

Triads in All Qualities

Triads with Third or Fifth Given

Sometimes you will need to construct a triad not from a given root but from a given third or fifth. If the pitch G is given as the root, for example, a root-position major triad will involve the pitches G, B, and D. When the given pitch G is the *third*, however, the root-position triad is spelled E-flat, G, and B-flat. Given the third of a major triad, you must descend a major third to find the root.

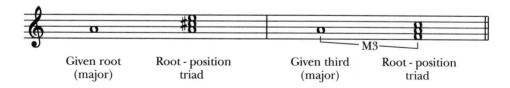

| Given root | Root - position | Given third | Root - position |
| (major) | triad | (major) | triad |

When the fifth is the given pitch of a major triad, descend a perfect fifth to find the root, then fill in the basic pitches and add any necessary accidentals.

Fifth given   Find root.   Complete triad.

Construct minor, diminished, or augmented triads with given third or fifth in the same manner.

Minor Triad

With given third:

• Descend a minor third to find the root.
• Add the root and a perfect fifth above the root to complete the triad.

With given fifth:

• Descend a perfect fifth to locate the root.
• Add the root and a minor third above the root to complete the triad.

| Given third | Root - position | Given fifth | Root - position |
| (minor) | triad | (minor) | triad |

Diminished Triad

With given third:

• Descend a minor third to find the root.
• Add the root and a diminished fifth above the root to complete the triad.

With given fifth:

• Descend a diminished fifth to locate the root.
• Add the root and a minor third above the root to complete the triad.

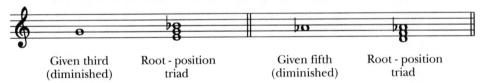

| Given third | Root - position | Given fifth | Root - position |
| (diminished) | triad | (diminished) | triad |

Augmented Triad

With given third:

• Descend a major third to find the root.
• Add the root and an augmented fifth above the root to complete the triad.

With given fifth:

• Descend an augmented fifth to locate the root.
• Add the root and a major third above the root to complete the triad.

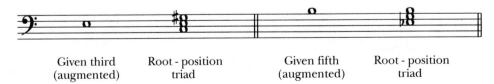

| Given third | Root - position | Given fifth | Root - position |
| (augmented) | triad | (augmented) | triad |

exercise 9–9 *Fundamental Skills*
Triads with Given Third or Fifth

A. Construct root-position triads of the quality indicated from the given third. Be sure to add any necessary accidentals to the root or the fifth or both.

Given Third

1.

Major Minor Major Diminished Major Minor Augmented

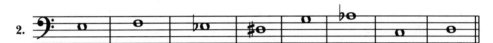

2.

Minor Diminished Augmented Major Minor Major Augmented Minor

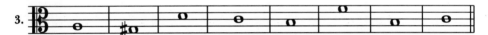

3.

Diminished Minor Major Augmented Minor Major Diminished Major

B. Construct root-position triads of the quality indicated from the given fifth. Be sure to add any necessary accidentals to the root or the third or both.

Given Fifth

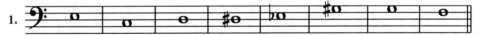

1.

Major Minor Diminished Major Minor Augmented Minor Diminished

2.

Minor Diminished Augmented Minor Major Diminished Augmented Major

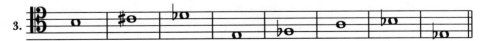

3.

Augmented Minor Major Diminished Major Minor Diminished Major

C. Using pitch names, construct the triads indicated from the given root, third, or fifth. The first pitch name or blank is for the root, the second is for the third of the triad, and the third is for the fifth.

Given Root

	Major	Minor	Diminished	Augmented
1.	F ___ ___	Bb ___ ___	G ___ ___	C ___ ___
2.	Ab ___ ___	B ___ ___	D ___ ___	F ___ ___
3.	C♯ ___ ___	Eb ___ ___	F♯ ___ ___	B ___ ___
4.	Db ___ ___	A ___ ___	C♯ ___ ___	Eb ___ ___

Given Third

	Major	Minor	Diminished	Augmented
5.	___ C ___	___ Eb ___	___ D ___	___ B ___
6.	___ F♯ ___	___ E ___	___ G ___	___ F♯ ___
7.	___ Ab ___	___ B ___	___ C ___	___ Eb ___
8.	___ D ___	___ F♯ ___	___ Bb ___	___ G ___

Given Fifth

	Major	Minor	Diminished	Augmented
9.	___ ___ Eb	___ ___ D	___ ___ C	___ ___ F♯
10.	___ ___ G	___ ___ Ab	___ ___ B	___ ___ E
11.	___ ___ Db	___ ___ E	___ ___ F♯	___ ___ G♯
12.	___ ___ C♯	___ ___ F	___ ___ B	___ ___ D

TRIAD CONSTRUCTION AND IDENTIFICATION THROUGH KEY SIGNATURE

Although triads can be constructed and identified by producing or analyzing the appropriate intervals, that method is time-consuming and may prove unreliable. If the triad is compared with the major key signature represented by its root, however, quality may be apparent immediately. The third and the fifth of a major triad conform to the key signature represented by the root. To write a major triad above a given root, first write basic pitches; next, apply the key signature of the root; and finally, add accidentals to the third and the fifth as necessary. In writing an A-flat major triad, for example, if you know the key signature, you can write the pitch E as E-flat almost without thinking, because E is always flat in A-flat major. With a single accidental, the A-flat major triad is complete without any other computations.

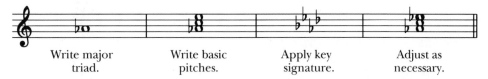

| Write major triad. | Write basic pitches. | Apply key signature. | Adjust as necessary. |

If the A-flat major triad above were written by duplicating intervals, first a major third, then a perfect fifth would be constructed over A-flat; with each step, the possibility for error exists. Using key signatures, the process is more simple.

If the triad is not major, the key-signature approach is still valid. Minor, diminished, and augmented triads differ from major triads in fixed ways:

- A major triad is made *minor* by lowering the third a half step:

| Major | Minor | Major | Minor |

- A major triad is made *diminished* by lowering the third and the fifth a half step:

| Major | Diminished | Major | Diminished |

- A major triad is made *augmented* by raising the fifth a half step:

| Major | Augmented | Major | Augmented |

To write a triad of *any* quality through key signature, begin with the pitches diatonic in the major key represented by the root.[2] If the desired quality is minor, diminished, or augmented, make the necessary half-step alteration(s).

- Major Triads: No changes.
- Minor Triads: Lower the third.
- Diminished Triads: Lower the third *and* the fifth.
- Augmented Triads: Raise the fifth.

exercise 9–10   Fundamental Skills
Triad Construction
through Key Signature

Use the key-signature method to construct triads on the given roots. First, write basic pitches; next, add the key signature of the root. Finally, add accidentals to the third or the fifth, or both, if necessary to make the triad major in quality.

Major Triads

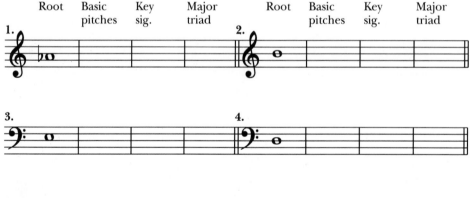

Write minor triads using the process practiced above, but after applying the major key signature to the basic pitches, lower the third.

---

[2] In rare instances where the root of the triad does not correspond to a major key (B♭♭, for example, or G♯), lower or raise the root a half step (B♭♭ = B♭; G♯ = G), construct a triad of the appropriate quality on this root, then lower or raise *each* pitch of the triad accordingly (B♭–D–F = B♭♭–D♭–F♭; G–B–D = G♯–B♯–D♯).

Minor Triads

	Root	Basic pitches	Key signature	Lower third	Minor triad

1.
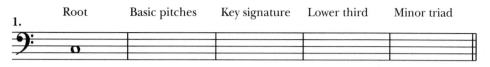

2.

3.

4.
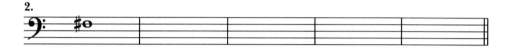

5.

6.

Augmented Triads

	Root	Basic pitches	Key signature	Raise fifth	Augmented triad

1.
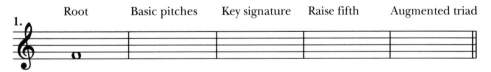

2.

	Root	Basic pitches	Key signature	Raise fifth	Augmented triad

3.

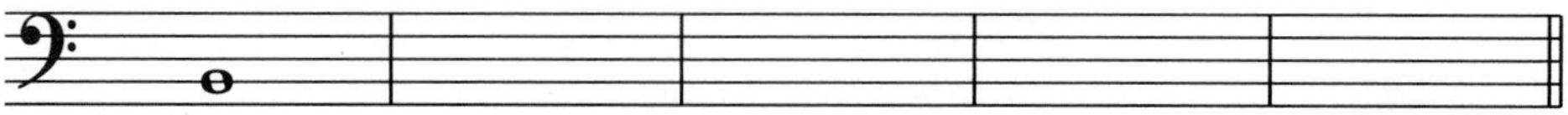

4.

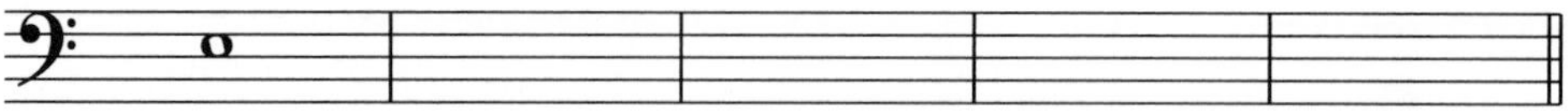

5.

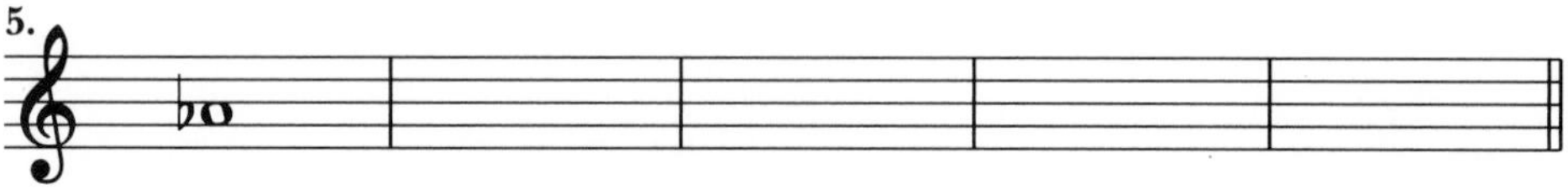

6.

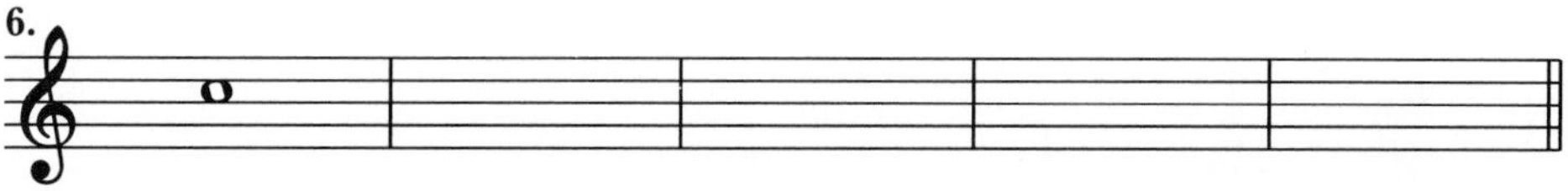

Diminished Triads

	Root	Basic pitches	Key signature	Lower third & fifth	Diminished triad

1.

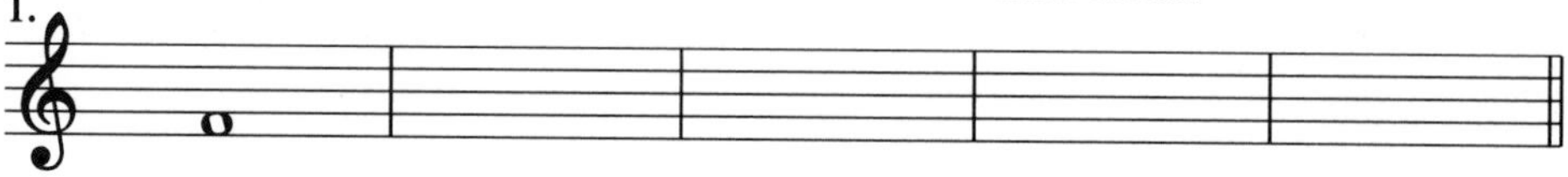

2.

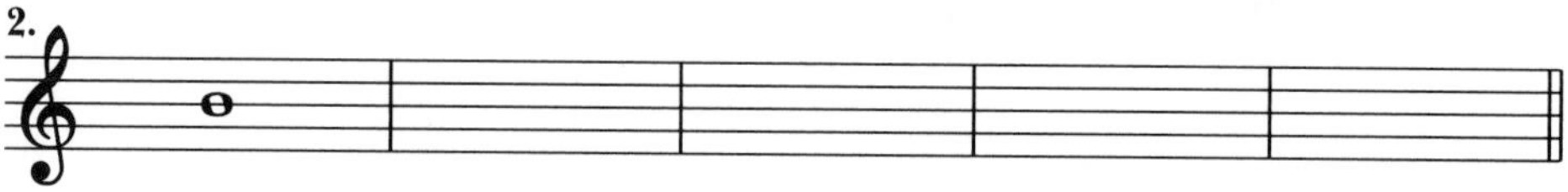

3.

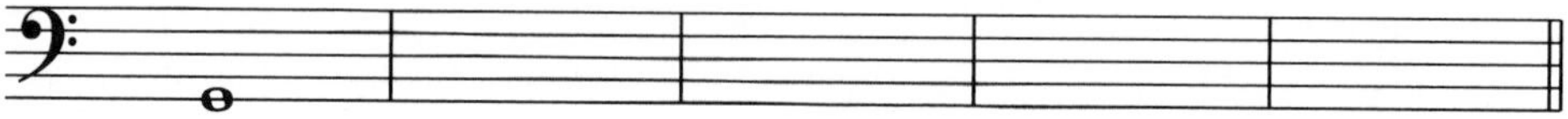

4.

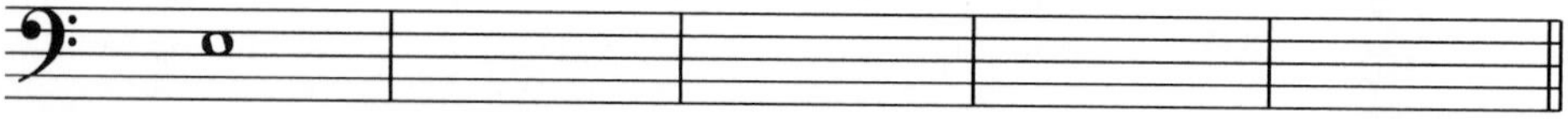

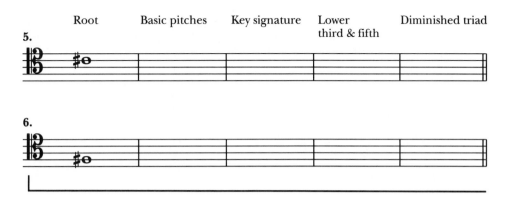

	Root	Basic pitches	Key signature	Lower third & fifth	Diminished triad

5.

6.

Minor Key Signatures

The pitches of a minor triad always conform to the *minor* key signature represented by the root. If minor as well as major key signatures are learned, triad construction and identification are even faster. To construct a minor triad, write basic pitches above the root and apply the appropriate *minor* key signature; no other steps are necessary.

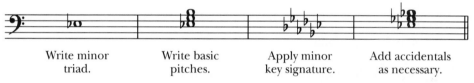

Write minor triad.   Write basic pitches.   Apply minor key signature.   Add accidentals as necessary.

A minor triad is made diminished by lowering the fifth a half step. Through the use of a minor key signature, diminished triads can be written with only one alteration.

Minor   Diminished   Minor   Diminished

Identification of Triads through Key Signature

Triads can be identified through key signature just as easily as they are constructed. Given a triad and the task of determining its quality, ask the question "Is it major?" Apply the major key signature of the root to the third and the fifth of the triad; if both third and fifth are diatonic, the triad is major.

Quality?   Apply key signature.   =   Major triad

If the triad is not major (that is, if the third or the fifth, or both, is not diatonic in the major key represented by the root), determine how these pitches differ from the diatonic pitches. In traditional music, there are but three possibilities:

1. Lowered third (minor)
2. Lowered fifth and lowered third (diminished)
3. Raised fifth (augmented)

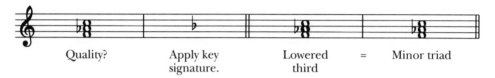

| Quality? | Apply key signature. | Lowered third | = | Minor triad |

If a triad is not major, and if minor key signatures are learned thoroughly, the second question can be "Is the quality minor?" Comparing the pitches of the triad with those of the given minor key represented by the root will reveal the answer immediately.

exercise 9–11 *Fundamental Skills*
Identifying Triads

A. Use the key-signature method to identify the qualities of the following root-position triads.

1.

2.
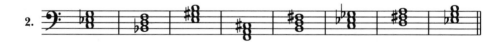

3.

4.

B. Identify the quality of the following root-position triads by letter name.

1. D F A   B♭ D F   G B D♯   A C E   F A C♯   E G B♭

2. C E G♯   A C♯ E   E G B   F A♭ C   B D F   A C E♭

3. C♯ E G   E♭ G B♭   D F♯ A♯   D♯ F♯ A♯   G B♭ D♭   F♯ A C♯

4. C E♭ G   B D♯ F✕   D♭ F A♭   G♯ B D   A♭ C E♭   E G♯ B

SELF-TEST

1. Write the intervals (major third, minor third, and so on) that make up each of the traditional tertian triads.

Triad	Lower Third	Upper Third	Fifth
Major			
Minor			
Diminished			
Augmented			

2. Complete the following statements by indicating how a major triad is altered to produce triads of other qualities.

A major triad becomes minor when _____.

A major triad becomes diminished when _____.

A major triad becomes augmented when _____.

3. All the following triads are major. Without changing the root, rewrite the triad in the second measure using accidentals (including the natural sign if necessary) to make the triad conform to the quality indicated.

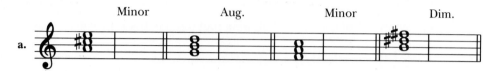

4. Write triads of each of the four qualities on the given roots.

Root Given

5. Write triads of each of the four qualities from the given third.

Third Given

6. Write triads of each of the four qualities on the given fifth.

Fifth Given

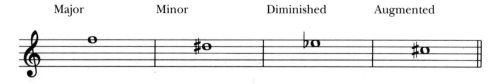

7. Identify the root and quality of the triads.

a.

____   ____   ____   ____   ____   ____   ____   ____

b.

____   ____   ____   ____   ____   ____   ____   ____

8. Identify the following terms:

    a. Tertian triad

    b. Root position

    c. Bass

    d. Fifth

1. Analyze the following triads; then, compare your analysis with the given quality. If necessary, add an accidental to the third or the fifth, or both, to make the quality conform to that specified.

a.

Minor   Major   Dimished Augmented   Minor   Major   Minor Diminished

b.

Diminished   Major   Augmented   Minor   Major Augmented Diminished Major

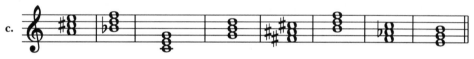

c.

Major   Minor   Diminished Augmented   Major   Minor   Minor Diminished

d.

Augmented Diminished Major Augmented   Major   Minor   Minor   Major

2. The following compositions have been reduced to their basic tertian structures: triads in root position. Identify the root and the quality of each triad, using the blanks provided. That done, analyze the harmony of each composition by counting the total number of triads and the number of times each different diatonic triad occurs (tonic, supertonic, mediant, and so on). How many different triad qualities do you find? How frequent are augmented and diminished triads? Try to draw conclusions regarding which triad or triads are most and least important. Are there some diatonic triads that do not occur at all in one or more of the compositions?

    You will notice that some pitches are not included in the harmonic reduction. These are called *nonharmonic tones*—dissonant pitches that fall into various categories and constitute an important element of a music theory course. Finally, pitches that constitute the seventh of a *seventh chord* have also been omitted from the reduction. Dominant seventh chords will be discussed in a later chapter.

a.

Weber

C major ___ ___ ___ ___ ___

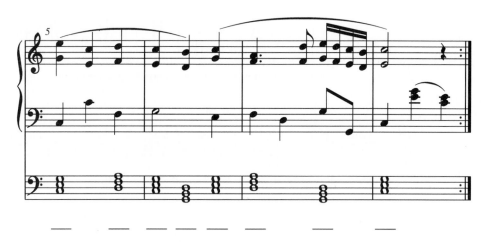

b.

J. S. Bach

D major ___ ___ ___ ___ ___ ___

J. S. Bach

c.

C minor

Schumann

d.

G major

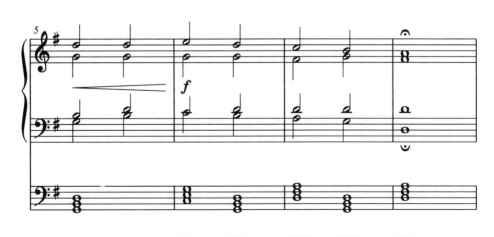

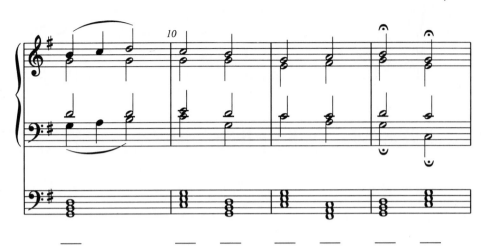

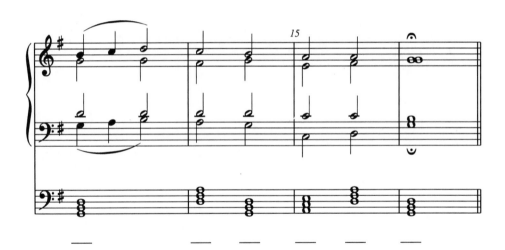

ADDITIONAL TRIAD DRILLS

3. Write root-position major triads on the given pitches. Construct the triads by writing the appropriate intervals above the root for the quality desired.

Major

Minor

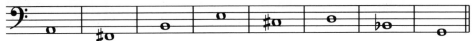

Diminished

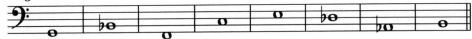

Augmented

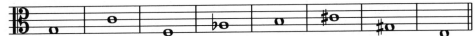

4. Use the given pitch as the *third* and construct root-position triads of the quality indicated.

Minor   Major   Augmented   Minor   Diminished   Major   Minor   Augmented

5. Use the given pitch as the *fifth* and construct root-position triads of the quality indicated.

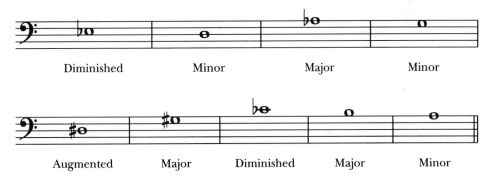

Diminished   Minor   Major   Minor

Augmented   Major   Diminished   Major   Minor

6. Identify the triads by quality and pitch name.

a.

___   ___   ___   ___   ___   ___

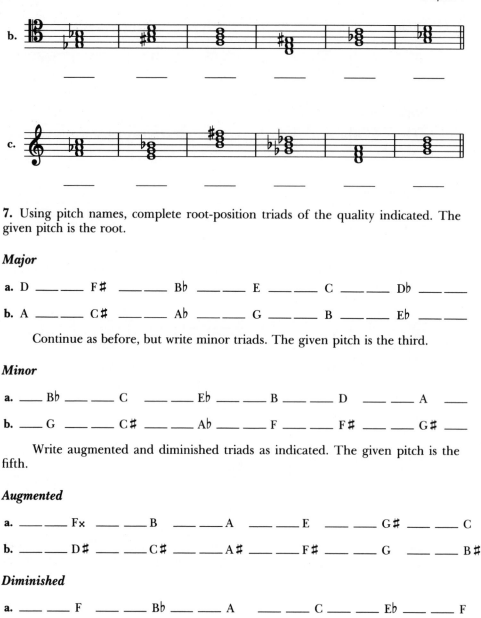

7. Using pitch names, complete root-position triads of the quality indicated. The given pitch is the root.

Major

a. D _____ _____ F♯ _____ _____ B♭ _____ _____ E _____ _____ C _____ _____ D♭ _____ _____

b. A _____ _____ C♯ _____ _____ A♭ _____ _____ G _____ _____ B _____ _____ E♭ _____ _____

Continue as before, but write minor triads. The given pitch is the third.

Minor

a. _____ B♭ _____ _____ C _____ _____ E♭ _____ _____ B _____ _____ D _____ _____ A _____

b. _____ G _____ _____ C♯ _____ _____ A♭ _____ _____ F _____ _____ F♯ _____ _____ G♯ _____

Write augmented and diminished triads as indicated. The given pitch is the fifth.

Augmented

a. _____ _____ F𝄪 _____ _____ B _____ _____ A _____ _____ E _____ _____ G♯ _____ _____ C

b. _____ _____ D♯ _____ _____ C♯ _____ _____ A♯ _____ _____ F♯ _____ _____ G _____ _____ B♯

Diminished

a. _____ _____ F _____ _____ B♭ _____ _____ A _____ _____ C _____ _____ E♭ _____ _____ F

b. _____ _____ D♭ _____ _____ G _____ _____ B♭♭ _____ _____ E _____ _____ D _____ _____ G♭

Inverted Triads

INVERSION

Just as an interval is sometimes inverted, the relationship between the root and the bass of a triad is flexible. As we discussed in the last chapter, a triad is in root position when the root is the lowest-sounding pitch. If the root appears *above* the bass, however, two new versions of the same triad are possible. These new versions—one with the third in the bass, the other with the fifth in the bass—are termed *first* and *second inversions*, respectively.

First Inversion

When the third of a triad is the lowest-sounding pitch, that triad is said to be in FIRST INVERSION. In inverted triads, the root is always above the bass, but whether it is the highest or the middle pitch is not a factor in determining inversion. The basic first-inversion triad contains intervals different from those of the triad in root position. Instead of a third and a fifth above the bass (root), the first-inversion triad has a third and a *sixth* above the bass (which is *not* the root).

| Root position | First inversion | Root position | First inversion |

Second Inversion

If the fifth of a triad appears in the bass, the triad is in SECOND INVERSION. Second-inversion triads contain intervals that differ from those in both root position and first inversion: a fourth and a sixth above the bass. Compare the root-position and inverted triads shown below.

| Root position | First inversion | Second inversion |

Quality. The inversion of a triad changes neither the pitch name nor the quality of that triad. The triads above, for example, all have A-flat as the root; in addition, the quality is major in each case. Because the bass is so important in traditional music, however, the relationship between root and bass (whether these are the same or different) is often designated along with root name and quality.

Root-position and inverted major and minor triads are heard in Recorded Example 29.

▶ *RECORDED EXAMPLE 29*

**Root-position
and Inverted Triads**

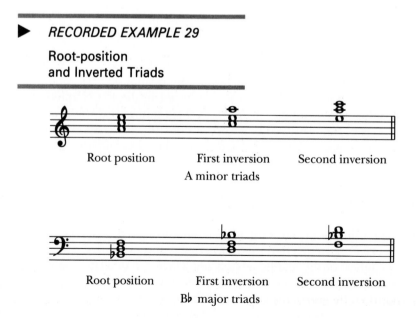

| Root position | First inversion | Second inversion |
| | A minor triads | |

| Root position | First inversion | Second inversion |
| | B♭ major triads | |

Open and Close Position

When the root, third, and fifth of a triad are as close together as possible, the spatial position is termed CLOSE. If the spatial position is not close, it is said to be OPEN. A root-position triad in open position will have more than an octave between the bass (lowest pitch) and the soprano (highest pitch).

C Major Triad in Root Position

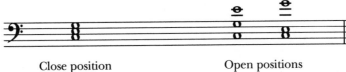

Close position   Open positions

If a triad is in open position, you must rearrange the pitches to be in close position before determining the quality. Although you may need to actually rewrite the triad in close position at first, the eventual goal is to do this step mentally.

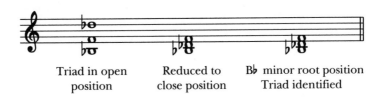

Triad in open   Reduced to   B♭ minor root position
position   close position   Triad identified

CONSTRUCTION OF INVERTED TRIADS

The construction of inverted triads is not a new process but, rather, a further step added to a familiar one. A first-inversion triad is constructed by writing (or visualizing) a root-position triad on the root and of the quality desired, and then rearranging the pitches so that the *third* is in the bass. Inverted triads occur in both open and close positions.

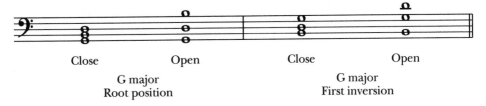

Close   Open   Close   Open

G major   G major
Root position   First inversion

If a second-inversion triad is desired, commence with an appropriate triad in root position; then, rearrange the pitches so that the *fifth* is in the bass. Writing the root directly above the bass and making the third the highest pitch is the closest arrangement, but many other possibilities exist.

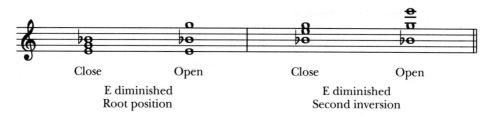

Close   Open   Close   Open

E diminished   E diminished
Root position   Second inversion

exercise 10–1 *Fundamental Skills*
Constructing Inverted Triads

A. Root-position triads of various qualities are given. Beneath the given triad, identify its root and quality. In the first measure, write the triad in first inversion. Use the second measure for second inversion. Employ close position throughout.

1.
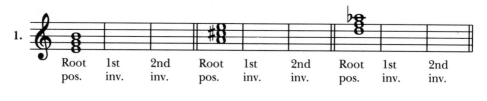

Root   1st   2nd   Root   1st   2nd   Root   1st   2nd
pos.   inv.   inv.   pos.   inv.   inv.   pos.   inv.   inv.

_____   _____   _____

2.
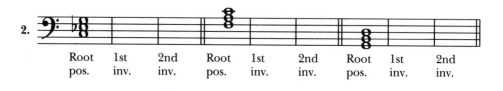

Root   1st   2nd   Root   1st   2nd   Root   1st   2nd
pos.   inv.   inv.   pos.   inv.   inv.   pos.   inv.   inv.

_____   _____   _____

3.
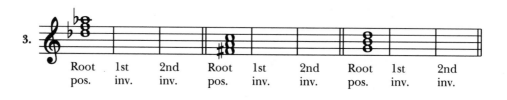

Root   1st   2nd   Root   1st   2nd   Root   1st   2nd
pos.   inv.   inv.   pos.   inv.   inv.   pos.   inv.   inv.

_____   _____   _____

4.
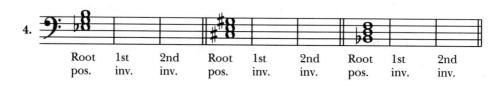

Root   1st   2nd   Root   1st   2nd   Root   1st   2nd
pos.   inv.   inv.   pos.   inv.   inv.   pos.   inv.   inv.

_____   _____   _____

B. Construct root-position or inverted triads as directed. Use close position.

1.

D major	B♭ minor	A dim.	G major	F aug.	A♭ major	D minor	F♯ dim.
Rt. pos.	1st inv.	2nd inv.	Rt. pos.	1st inv.	1st inv.	2nd inv.	Rt. pos.

2.

C♯ major	E minor	G♯ dim.	B major	D minor	E♭ major	D aug.	B dim.
1st inv.	2nd inv.	2nd inv.	1st inv.	Rt. pos.	1st inv.	2nd inv.	Rt. pos.

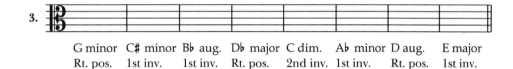

3.

G minor	C♯ minor	B♭ aug.	D♭ major	C dim.	A♭ minor	D aug.	E major
Rt. pos.	1st inv.	1st inv.	Rt. pos.	2nd inv.	1st inv.	Rt. pos.	1st inv.

4.

B♭ major	D♯ minor	F dim.	G aug.	G♯ minor	C♭ major	C minor	A major
1st inv.	Rt. pos.	2nd inv.	1st inv.	2nd inv.	1st inv.	2nd inv.	Rt. pos.

C. For these exercises, first write the specified pitch in the given clef. If necessary, employ the octave sign to avoid ledger lines. Next, use the pitch you wrote as the *root* of a root-position, first-inversion, or second-inversion triad of the quality indicated.

Root Position, Root Given

b^2	CC	E	f	d^1	e	d♯^{1}	a^2
Major	Dim.	Minor	Aug.	Minor	Major	Minor dim.	Aug.

1.

Continue as before, but use the designated pitch as the *third* of a *first-inversion* triad.

First Inversion, Third Given

Use the specified pitch as the *fifth* of a *second-inversion* triad of the quality specified.

Second Inversion, Fifth Given

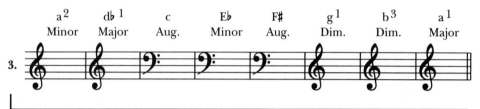

▶ *RECORDED EXAMPLE 30*

(See Exercise 10-2.)

---

exercise 10–2   *Musicianship Skills*
EAR TRAINING: Triad Quality
and Inversion

A. (Recorded) The major and minor triads in this recorded example occur in various inversions. The first four triads are heard first arpeggiated, then as chords. Triads 5–8 are heard chordally. Determine the quality of the triad and write "M" or "m" in the first blank. In the second blank, write "R" if the triad is in root position or "I" if the triad is inverted. In this exercise, it is not necessary to distinguish between first and second inversions. Four different triads will be heard in each line.

Arpeggiated Triads

1. ___ ___   ___ ___   ___ ___   ___ ___

2. ___ ___   ___ ___   ___ ___   ___ ___

3. ___ ___   ___ ___   ___ ___   ___ ___

4. ___ ___   ___ ___   ___ ___   ___ ___

Harmonic Triads

5. ____ ____   ____ ____   ____ ____   ____ ____

6. ____ ____   ____ ____   ____ ____   ____ ____

7. ____ ____   ____ ____   ____ ____   ____ ____

8. ____ ____   ____ ____   ____ ____   ____ ____

B. (Not Recorded) This exercise duplicates the previous one but is not recorded. Your instructor will play the triads on the piano or another instrument. Identify the quality in the first blank, the root–bass relationship in the second ("R" or "I").

Arpeggiated Triads

1. ____ ____   ____ ____   ____ ____   ____ ____

2. ____ ____   ____ ____   ____ ____   ____ ____

3. ____ ____   ____ ____   ____ ____   ____ ____

4. ____ ____   ____ ____   ____ ____   ____ ____

Harmonic Triads

5. ____ ____   ____ ____   ____ ____   ____ ____

6. ____ ____   ____ ____   ____ ____   ____ ____

7. ____ ____   ____ ____   ____ ____   ____ ____

8. ____ ____   ____ ____   ____ ____   ____ ____

TRIAD IDENTIFICATION

When a triad appears in root position and in a close spatial arrangement, the three pitches fall over consecutive lines or spaces. Inverted triads in close position *do not* have such an obvious visual arrangement and are therefore easily distinguished from triads in root position. The pitches of inverted triads in close position always involve lines *and* spaces.

Root position   Inverted

Inverted triads must be restructured to be in root position and close spatial arrangement before the quality and root name can be identified. Because the pitches occur over consecutive spaces within an octave, the first triad below is obviously in root position; the root is A and the quality is major. The second triad, however, is clearly *not* in root position because the pitches, which are in close position, involve lines *and* spaces. The triad is inverted, meaning that the lowest pitch, E-flat, is *not* the root.

A major triad   Root ? Quality ?

To find the root of an inverted triad, first arrange the pitches in close position so that they fall over consecutive lines or spaces. Considering the un-identified triad above, the pitch E-flat is clearly not the root. If the pitch G were the root, the complete triad would be G, B, and D. The triad in question, however, has neither B nor D. The pitches E-flat and G have now been eliminated as possible roots; the only remaining possibility is C.

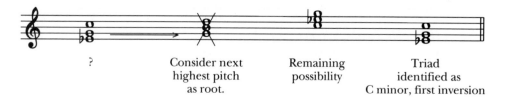

?   Consider next   Remaining   Triad
            highest pitch   possibility   identified as
             as root.   C minor, first inversion

Doubling and Spacing

When triads appear as simple structures, identification is not especially difficult. In the creative process, however, root-position and inverted triads are used in a variety of forms that make the identification of the basic material more complex.

Doubling.   Sometimes composers duplicate, or DOUBLE, one or more pitches of a triad to form a larger structure known as a CHORD.[1] Naturally, any doubling changes the sound of the triad, but the identification of the basic "raw material" is unaffected as long as all three pitches are present at least once. Notice that all three chords below are identified as diminished with A as the root.

A diminished triad   A diminished chords

[1] The simple triad can also be referred to as a chord.

Spacing. In addition to doubling, composers often use alternative *spacings* to affect the timbre of a simple triad. Spacing refers to the choice of octave for the pitches of a triad or chord. Each of the following triads has a different sound, but each is identified as B-flat augmented in root position.

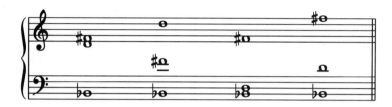

B♭ augmented triads

Triads with a variety of doublings and spacings are heard in Recorded Example 31.

▶ *RECORDED EXAMPLE 31*

**Spacing and Doubling
in Root-position Triads**

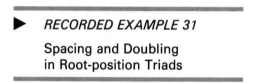

Close position   Open positions

A major triads

When alternative doublings and spacings are combined, the task of triad identification is more complicated but follows the same process. Regardless of the complexity of the chord, the bass is always the lowest-sounding pitch. In identifying triad quality, begin with the bass and move upward to the next different pitch name. Discount any octave duplication of the bass. Mentally (or on paper at first if necessary), write this new pitch immediately above the bass. Continue moving upward through the chord (again, discounting octave duplications) until you encounter a new pitch name. Follow the same process and write this pitch immediately above the bass as well.

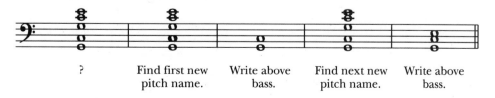

| ? | Find first new pitch name. | Write above bass. | Find next new pitch name. | Write above bass. |

Assuming that no chord has more than three different pitch names, this procedure results in a triad in its closest spatial position.[2] The root and quality of the triad can then be determined in the manner discussed earlier.

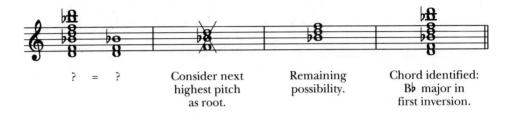

?   =   ?   Consider next   Remaining   Chord identified:
                     highest pitch   possibility.   Bb major in
                     as root.   first inversion.

exercise 10–3 *Fundamental Skills*
Identifying Triads

A. The following triads appear in close position. In the upper blank, identify the root (pitch name) and quality ("M," "m," "d," or "A"). Use the lower blank for a word representing the root–bass relationship (root position, first inversion, or second inversion).

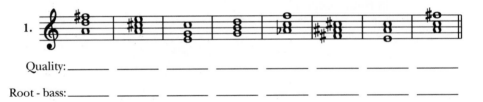

Quality: _____   _____   _____   _____   _____   _____   _____   _____

Root - bass: _____   _____   _____   _____   _____   _____   _____   _____

Quality: _____   _____   _____   _____   _____   _____   _____   _____

Root - bass: _____   _____   _____   _____   _____   _____   _____   _____

Quality: _____   _____   _____   _____   _____   _____   _____   _____

Root - bass: _____   _____   _____   _____   _____   _____   _____   _____

[2] Seventh chords, with four different pitches, will be discussed in Chapter 12.

B. Use the lower staff to reduce the chords to a basic triad in close position; then, identify quality and root–bass relationship as before.

Quality: _____ _____ _____ _____ _____ _____ _____ _____

Root - bass: _____ _____ _____ _____ _____ _____ _____ _____

Quality: _____ _____ _____ _____ _____ _____ _____ _____

Root - bass: _____ _____ _____ _____ _____ _____ _____ _____

Figured Bass

When triads are employed in traditional harmony, the bass line plays a major role in the establishment of a feeling for key. In the early seventeenth century, in fact, composers did not write out chords in full, but merely notated the bass of each chord and added numerals (figures) and other symbols below the bass to indicate how other pitches should be added. This system of shorthand notation is called FIGURED BASS, and although the practice was abandoned by about 1750, some of the figures and other symbols have survived in contemporary musical analysis.

Arabic-Numeral Designations.   In analysis, chords are first reduced to their simplest structure; thus, numeral designations, based on intervals sounding above the bass, always refer to a triad in close spatial position. In root position, a third and a fifth of various qualities appear above the bass (which is also the root). The figures $\frac{5}{3}$, therefore, indicate a triad in root position.

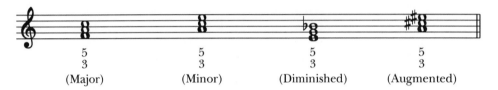

5	5	5	5
3	3	3	3
(Major)	(Minor)	(Diminished)	(Augmented)

Notice in the preceding example that the arabic numerals are the same regardless of the *quality* of the interval. The numeral 5, for example, is used for perfect, diminished, and augmented fifths alike.

If the triad is in first inversion, the root is above the bass. Intervals sounding above the bass in close position will be a third and a sixth. The full designation for a first-inversion triad, therefore, is $\frac{6}{3}$.

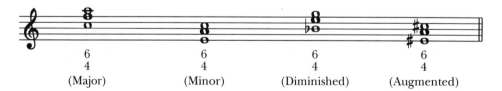

6	6	6	6
3	3	3	3
(Major)	(Minor)	(Diminished)	(Augmented)

In second inversion, the root is again above the bass and the intervals present are a sixth and a fourth. We designate a second-inversion triad with the numerals $\frac{6}{4}$.

6	6	6	6
4	4	4	4
(Major)	(Minor)	(Diminished)	(Augmented)

Various triads in close spatial position are shown below, with their arabic numerals representing intervals sounding above the bass. The analytical symbols identify "raw" harmonic material regardless of how that basic material is varied through doubling or spacing.

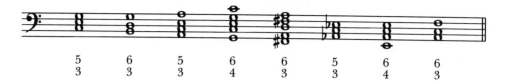

$$\begin{array}{cccccccc}5 & 6 & 5 & 6 & 6 & 5 & 6 & 6 \\ 3 & 3 & 3 & 4 & 3 & 3 & 4 & 3\end{array}$$

exercise 10–4 *Fundamental Skills*
Figured Bass

For each of the triads shown, write the pitch name of the root in the first blank, the quality of the triad in the second blank, and numerals in the third blank to indicate the intervals sounding above the bass ($\frac{5}{3}$, $\frac{6}{3}$, or $\frac{6}{4}$).

Root: ___ ___ ___ ___ ___ ___ ___ ___

Quality: ___ ___ ___ ___ ___ ___ ___ ___

Fig. bass: ___ ___ ___ ___ ___ ___ ___ ___

Root: ___ ___ ___ ___ ___ ___ ___ ___

Quality: ___ ___ ___ ___ ___ ___ ___ ___

Fig. bass: ___ ___ ___ ___ ___ ___ ___ ___

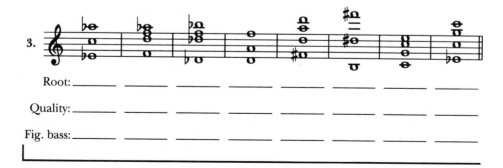

Root: ___ ___ ___ ___ ___ ___ ___ ___

Quality: ___ ___ ___ ___ ___ ___ ___ ___

Fig. bass: ___ ___ ___ ___ ___ ___ ___ ___

exercise 10–5 Musicianship Skills
EAR TRAINING: Root-position
and Inverted Major and Minor Triads

A. Your instructor will play several arpeggiated triads in close position. Identify the quality (major or minor) in the first blank. In the second blank, write $\frac{5}{3}$ if the triad is in root position, $\frac{6}{3}$ if the triad is in first inversion, and $\frac{6}{4}$ in the case of second inversion. Sing the triad to yourself in root position; then, find the bass of the chord played and identify that pitch as root, third, or fifth.

Arpeggiated Triads

1. _____	____	2. _____	____
3. _____	____	4. _____	____
5. _____	____	6. _____	____
7. _____	____	8. _____	____
9. _____	____	10. _____	____
11. _____	____	12. _____	____
13. _____	____	14. _____	____
15. _____	____	16. _____	____
17. _____	____	18. _____	____
19. _____	____	20. _____	____

B. This exercise duplicates the previous one, but you will hear the triad sounded as a chord rather than arpeggiated.

Harmonic Triads

1. _____	____	2. _____	____
3. _____	____	4. _____	____
5. _____	____	6. _____	____
7. _____	____	8. _____	____
9. _____	____	10. _____	____
11. _____	____	12. _____	____
13. _____	____	14. _____	____
15. _____	____	16. _____	____

17. _____   _____   18. _____   _____

19. _____   _____   20. _____   _____

exercise 10–6   *Musicianship Skills*
KEYBOARD: Root-position
and Inverted Triads

Return to the first three lines of Skill Exercise 10-4. Play each of the triads on the piano. Use the left hand for triads written in the bass clef and the right hand for triads notated in the treble clef. First, arpeggiate the triad ascending and descending, using a comfortable fingering pattern. Next, play the three pitches of the triad as a chord. When you can play the triads hands separately, add the right or the left hand in another octave and play hands together.

exercise 10–7   *Musicianship Skills*
SIGHT SINGING: Root-position
and Inverted Major and Minor Triads

Begin by playing the first pitch of each series on the piano. Next, using the syllable or number system recommended by your instructor, sing the root-position, first-inversion, and second-inversion triad outlines in turn. In addition to the triads given, practice other triads within your voice range.

Major

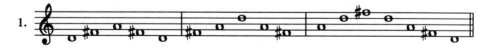

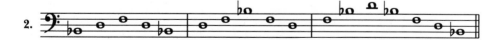

Minor

1.

2.

3.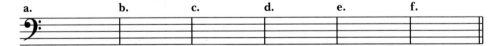

SELF-TEST

1. Write triads on the designated root and of the quality and root–bass relationship suggested.

> **a.** B major, root position
> **b.** D minor, first inversion
> **c.** E-flat augmented, second inversion
> **d.** F minor, second inversion
> **e.** C-sharp diminished, root position
> **f.** A-flat major, first inversion

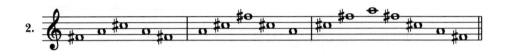

2. Identify the root name, quality, and root–bass relationship of the following triads and chords. Write the pitch name of the root in the first blank, use "M," "m," "d," or "A" to identify the quality in the second blank, and write $\frac{5}{3}$, $\frac{6}{3}$, or $\frac{6}{4}$ in the third blank.

Root:_____ _____ _____ _____ _____ _____

Quality:_____ _____ _____ _____ _____ _____

Root - bass:_____ _____ _____ _____ _____ _____

3. Use the standard figured bass numerals to identify the root–bass relationship of the following chords. First, reduce the chord to its simplest position. Next, identify the root and write that pitch name in the first blank. Identify the quality in the second blank, and use the third blank for the figured bass numerals.

Root:_____   _____   _____   _____   _____   _____

Quality:_____   _____   _____   _____   _____   _____

Root - bass:_____   _____   _____   _____   _____   _____

4. Identify the following terms:

    a. Figured bass

    b. Second inversion

    c. $\frac{5}{3}$

    d. Doubling

    e. Close position

SUPPLEMENTARY EXERCISES

1. Use the specified pitch as the root of a root-position triad of the quality indicated. Use the octave sign as needed.

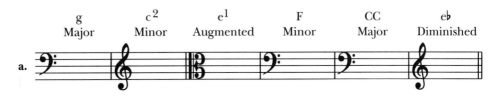

g	c^2	e^1	F	CC	e♭
Major	Minor	Augmented	Minor	Major	Diminished

a.

b	f^2	A	d^1	D	g♭^{1}
Minor	Major	Augmented	Major	Minor	Diminished

b.

2. Use the specified pitch as the third of a first-inversion triad of the quality indicated. Use the octave sign as needed.

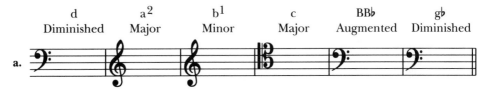

d	a^2	b^1	c	BB♭	g♭
Diminished	Major	Minor	Major	Augmented	Diminished

a.

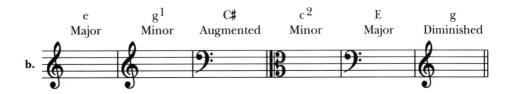

e	g^1	C♯	c^2	E	g
Major	Minor	Augmented	Minor	Major	Diminished

b.

3. Use the specified pitch as the fifth of a second-inversion triad of the quality indicated. Use the octave sign as needed.

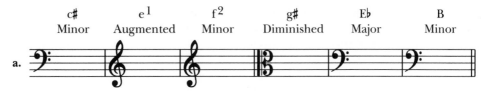

c♯	e^1	f^2	g♯	E♭	B
Minor	Augmented	Minor	Diminished	Major	Minor

a.

a	d^2	F♯	f^2	E	g♭^{1}
Major	Minor	Diminished	Minor	Diminished	Major

4. Identify the pitch name of the root, the quality, and, using figured bass numerals, the root–bass relationship of the following triads and chords.

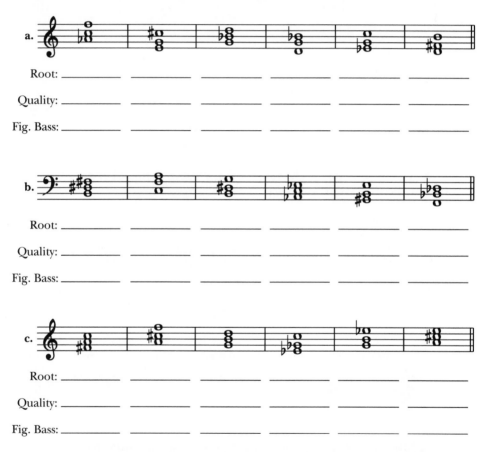

Root: _____ _____ _____ _____ _____ _____

Quality: _____ _____ _____ _____ _____ _____

Fig. Bass: _____ _____ _____ _____ _____ _____

Root: _____ _____ _____ _____ _____ _____

Quality: _____ _____ _____ _____ _____ _____

Fig. Bass: _____ _____ _____ _____ _____ _____

Root: _____ _____ _____ _____ _____ _____

Quality: _____ _____ _____ _____ _____ _____

Fig. Bass: _____ _____ _____ _____ _____ _____

5. Reduce the chords in the following compositions to simple, root-position, or inverted triads. Identify the basic tertian material of each chord with pitch name, quality, and figured bass symbol. Nonharmonic tones and pitches that form the seventh of a seventh chord have been omitted. Stems mark the positions of these omitted pitches in the original compositions.

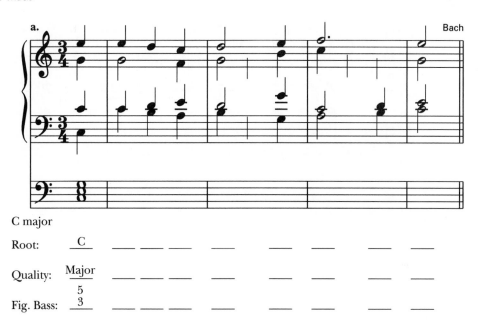

a.   Bach

C major

Root: C   __ __ __ __   __ __   __ __

Quality: Major __ __ __ __   __ __   __ __

Fig. Bass: 5
             3   __ __ __ __   __ __   __ __

b.   Schumann

G major

Root: __ __   __ __   __ __   __ __

Quality: __ __   __ __   __ __   __ __

Fig. Bass: __ __   __ __   __ __   __ __

c.

Kuhlau

B♭ major

Root: ⎯⎯   ⎯⎯   ⎯⎯   ⎯⎯

Quality: ⎯⎯   ⎯⎯   ⎯⎯   ⎯⎯

Fig. Bass: ⎯⎯   ⎯⎯   ⎯⎯   ⎯⎯

Root: ⎯⎯   ⎯⎯   ⎯⎯ ⎯⎯ ⎯⎯

Quality: ⎯⎯   ⎯⎯   ⎯⎯   ⎯⎯

Fig. Bass: ⎯⎯   ⎯⎯   ⎯⎯ ⎯⎯ ⎯⎯

A major

Root: — — — — — — — — — — — — —

Quality: — — — — — — — — — — — — —

Fig. Bass: — — — — — — — — — — — — —

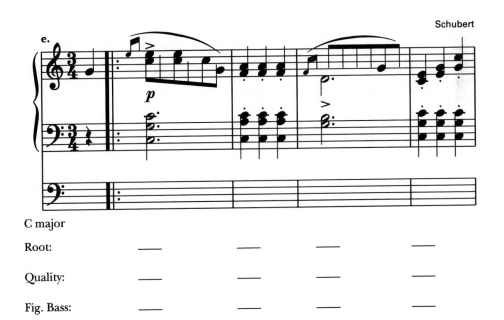

C major

Root: —   —   —   —

Quality: —   —   —   —

Fig. Bass: —   —   —   —

Root: ___   ___   ___   ___

Quality: ___   ___   ___   ___

Fig. Bass: ___   ___   ___   ___

Root: ___   ___   ___   ___

Quality: ___   ___   ___   ___

Fig. Bass: ___   ___   ___   ___

Root: ____   ____   ____   ____   ____

Quality: ____   ____   ____   ____   ____

Fig. Bass: ____   ____   ____   ____   ____

Diatonic Relationships

In several previous chapters, we have discussed intervals and triads as abstract entities. In traditional music, however, these materials are never viewed singly, but as part of a series, or PROGRESSION, of chords. As we will discuss further in Chapter 12, triads have diatonic roles that revolve around the establishment of the tonic pitch and the tonic triad as the most important. The triad built on the first scale degree, of course, is known as the tonic; the names for other diatonic triads reflect their relationship to the tonic.

Tonic Supertonic Mediant Subdominant Dominant Submediant Leading Tone

B♭ Major

Mediant and Dominant. The designation SUPERTONIC TRIAD relates to the tonic; the root of the supertonic triad is one step above the tonic. The designation MEDIANT refers to the third. The root of the mediant triad is a (diatonic) third above the tonic.

B♭ major: Tonic   Supertonic   Tonic   Mediant

The SUBMEDIANT triad is not "below the mediant" but, rather, the *lower* mediant. In B-flat major, the triad a third above the tonic (the mediant) is D minor, but the G minor triad is a third below the tonic (the submediant).

B♭ major: Submediant   Tonic   Mediant   Tonic

The dominant–tonic relationship is one of the most powerful in establishing a feeling for key. The DOMINANT is the triad built on the fifth scale degree—a perfect fifth above the tonic. The subdominant refers to the triad with the same perfect fifth root relationship, but one *below* the tonic; the SUBDOMINANT is the triad built on the fourth scale degree.

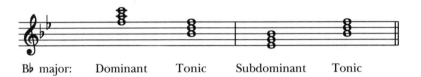

B♭ major: Dominant   Tonic   Subdominant   Tonic

The Leading Tone Triad. By definition, the LEADING TONE is a pitch a half step below the tonic; the diatonic triad built on this pitch is always diminished in quality and is termed the leading tone triad.

B♭ major: Leading tone   Tonic

Quality in Diatonic Triads

The qualities of triads in major keys are inflexible. The tonic, subdominant, and dominant triads are major in quality; the supertonic, mediant, and submediant triads are minor; and the leading tone triad is diminished. Diatonic triads in major are heard in Recorded Example 32.

▶ *RECORDED EXAMPLE 32*

Diatonic Triads in Major

Tonic Supertonic Mediant Subdominant Dominant Submediant Leading tone
MAJOR   MINOR   MINOR   MAJOR   MAJOR   MINOR   DIMINISHED

B♭ Major

The designations for triads within a given key reflect the relationship between the tonic pitch and the root of the triad concerned. Any triad in any key can be identified or constructed through diatonic triad designations. If you are asked to write the supertonic triad in G major, for example, begin with the pitch A (the supertonic pitch in G major); write a triad of basic pitches above it; then, check the key signature of G major to determine whether any of those pitches must be altered.

| Write | Triad root | Basic pitches | Key signature | Add accidentals if necessary. |

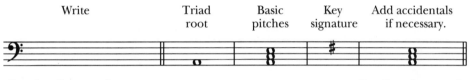

G major: Supertonic   G major: Supertonic

Although the triad above requires no alterations to the basic pitches, accidentals to reflect the key signature would have to be added, for example, to a subdominant triad in A-flat major.

| Write | Triad root | Basic pitches | Key signature | Add accidentals if necessary. |

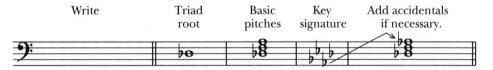

A♭ major: Subdominant   A♭ major: Subdominant

Key Identification in Analysis.   Major keys are identified in analysis by an uppercase letter (and an accidental if necessary) followed by a colon. Use a lowercase letter for minor keys. The keys of C major and E-flat minor, for example, are identified by *C*: and *eb*:, respectively. Once the key is indicated, triads are understood to adhere to this key signature. In E major, the designation *E*: *Submediant* connotes this triad:

E: Submediant

Likewise, the reference *f: Submediant* refers to a triad built on the sixth degree of the F minor scale:

f: Submediant

exercise 11–1 *Fundamental Skills*
Constructing Diatonic Triads

A. Following the procedure described earlier, construct diatonic triads in the keys suggested.

	Triad root	Basic pitches	Key signature	Add accidentals if necessary.

1.

D: Mediant

2.

E♭ : Subdominant

3.

F: Leading tone

4.

A: Submediant

5.

D♭: Dominant

Triad root   Basic pitches   Key signature   Add accidentals
                                                 if necessary.

6.

B: Leading tone

7.

D: Mediant

8.

E♭: Subdominant

9.

F: Leading tone

10.

A: Submediant

11.

D♭: Dominant

12.

B: Leading tone

13.

A♭: Supertonic

14.

C♯: Tonic

B. Continue as before, but perform the steps mentally. Be sure to add any necessary accidentals.

1. Bb: Supertonic   E: Dominant   Eb: Dominant   C: Mediant   A: Leading tone

2. D: Subdominant   Db: Tonic   G: Leading tone   F#: Submediant   Cb: Dominant

3. Gb: Supertonic   A: Tonic   E: Subdominant   Db: Mediant   B: Dominant

4. F: Submediant   C: Subdominant   Bb: Subdominant A: Dominant   Cb: Leading tone

5. B: Supertonic   Db: Mediant   F: Submediant   Bb: Mediant   A: Subdominant

6. F#: Subdominant Cb: Dominant   Ab: Subdominant E: Leading tone   Eb: Mediant

C. Construct triads using pitch names rather than staff notation. The first blank is for the root, the second for the third, and so on. As always, remember to add accidentals if necessary. Check your work by determining the quality of the triad you have written. A dominant triad, for example, must be major; the mediant is always minor.

1. D: Mediant   ___ ___ ___   2. Ab: Supertonic   ___ ___ ___

3. G: Submediant   ___ ___ ___   4. B: Subdominant   ___ ___ ___

5. C: Supertonic   ___ ___ ___   6. E: Tonic   ___ ___ ___

7. G♭: Mediant   _____ _____ _____   8. F: Submediant   _____ _____ _____

9. A: Leading tone   _____ _____ _____   10. E♭: Subdominant   _____ _____ _____

11. F♯: Supertonic   _____ _____ _____   12. C♯: Submediant   _____ _____ _____

exercise 11–2   *Fundamental Skills*
Identifying Diatonic Triads

In the key designated, identify the triads shown with their diatonic names (tonic, supertonic, and so on).

1.   B♭: _____   D: _____   E: _____   F: _____   F♯: _____

2.   G: _____   C: _____   A♭: _____   C♯: _____   D♭: _____

3.   B: _____   A: _____   E♭: _____   C: _____   G♭: _____

4.   G: _____   F♯: _____   B♭: _____   C♭: _____   B: _____

5.   A♭: _____   D♭: _____   E: _____   C♯: _____   B♭: _____

6.   A: _____   F♯: _____   G♭: _____   E♭: _____   D: _____

Roman-Numeral Designations

As a shortcut to writing out the triad names (like supertonic, subdominant, or leading tone), roman numerals can be used to represent diatonic triads. The roman numerals I through VII are ascribed to the triads built on the first through the seventh scale degrees. In addition to identifying the root (V = dominant, IV = subdominant, and so on), the roman numerals are typically adjusted to show the *quality* of the triad as well. Uppercase (capital) roman numerals represent major triads; minor triads are shown by lowercase numerals. A raised circle symbol (°) is added to a lowercase roman numeral to indicate a diminished triad.

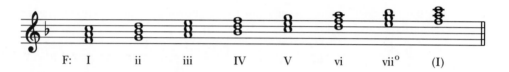

With both a key designation and a roman-numeral reference, a complete triad can be represented through one symbol. View, for example, the triads represented by the symbols shown below. The letter followed by a colon, of course, identifies the key.

Triad Quality in Minor Keys

In major keys, triads appear in three qualities: major (I, IV, and V), minor (ii, iii, and vi), and diminished (vii°). In minor keys, some triads have varying qualities, depending on the form of minor employed. In C minor, for example, the qualities shown below result from building diatonic triads on each degree of a natural minor scale. The designation for a minor key is a *lowercase* letter followed by a colon.

Without raised sixth or seventh, all diatonic triads in minor keys are minor or major in quality. If the raised seventh is applied (which changes B-flat to B-natural, in this case), three triads are affected. The mediant is now augmented, the dominant is major, and the leading tone triad is diminished.[1] If a triad is augmented, a plus sign (+) is added to the uppercase roman numeral.

c: i   ii°   III+   iv   V   VI   vii°   i

If the raised sixth *and* the raised seventh are used (A-natural and B-natural), diatonic triad qualities are again changed.

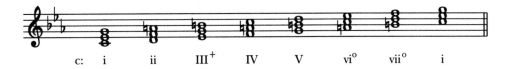

c: i   ii   III+   IV   V   vi°   vii°   i

Although any of the chords shown in the three previous examples is *possible*, the most common choices made by traditional composers are shown below and can be heard in Recorded Example 33.

▶ *RECORDED EXAMPLE 33*

Triad Qualities in Minor

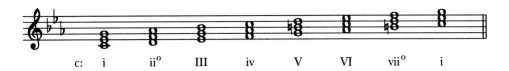

c: i   ii°   III   iv   V   VI   vii°   i

Observe that the raised sixth and seventh, as always, are accidentals. If a major triad on the dominant is specified, the seventh degree (which is the third of the dominant triad) must be raised. Otherwise, the triad is minor—not major.

d: v   V   f♯: v   V   c: v   V

---

[1] Without the raised seventh, of course, there can be no "leading tone" triad. The triad built on the seventh degree of a natural minor scale is known as a SUBTONIC TRIAD.

exercise 11–3 *Fundamental Skills*
Roman-Numeral Analysis: Major Keys

A. In the given key, write roman numerals to designate the chords. Remember to use uppercase numerals for major triads and lowercase for minor. In addition, the circle (°) must be added to the leading tone triad.

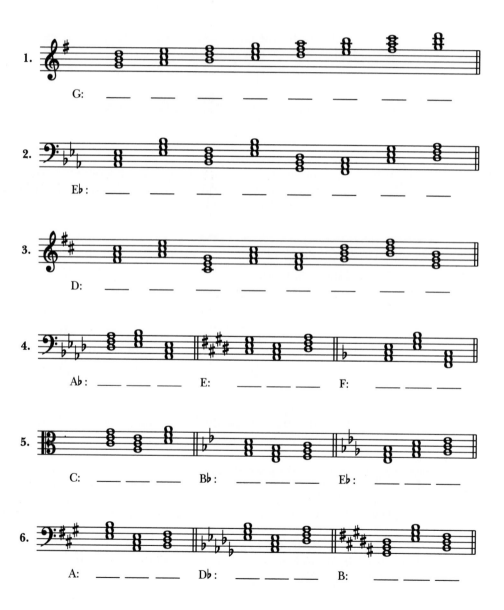

B. Write root-position triads as indicated by the roman numerals. Supply the key signature of the designated major key.

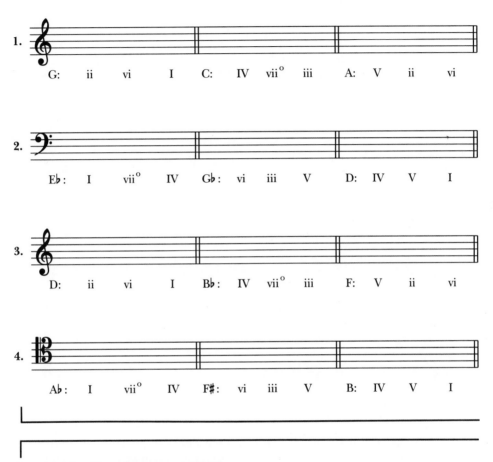

1. G: ii   vi   I   C: IV   vii°   iii   A: V   ii   vi

2. E♭:   I   vii°   IV   G♭:   vi   iii   V   D: IV   V   I

3. D: ii   vi   I   B♭:   IV   vii°   iii   F: V   ii   vi

4. A♭:   I   vii°   IV   F♯:   vi   iii   V   B: IV   V   I

exercise 11–4 *Fundamental Skills*
Roman-Numeral Analysis: Minor Keys

A. At first, it is not easy to remember to add accidentals in a minor key (to reflect a major dominant triad, for example, or the diminished leading tone triad). Considering all three forms of minor, there are many possibilities for various diatonic triads. The subdominant occurs as both a major and a minor triad; the supertonic can be either minor or diminished; and so on.

    Some of the following triads do not correspond to the given analytical symbol. The symbol may indicate a major triad, for example, and an accidental may be necessary to create that quality. If necessary, add an accidental so that the triad corresponds to the quality indicated by the roman numeral and any other symbol. If the triad already corresponds to the analytical symbol, no alterations are necessary.

1. c: v V   e: V iv   f#: ii° iv V   g: V vii° iv

2. d: ii V IV   c#: vii° V   f: vii° ii V   a: V ii IV

3. g#: V vii° iv   eb: V vii° ii   b: ii° IV V   d#: iv V ii

4. f: ii° V IV   bb: vii° V   f#: vii° iv V   e: V VI iv

5. d#: V vii° i   b: V vii° iv   a: ii° IV V   c#: iv V ii

B. Supply roman numerals to designate the given chords. Remember to use uppercase numerals for major triads and lowercase for minor. In addition, the circle (°) may be necessary with the leading tone triad and supertonic triad. An augmented triad, like the mediant, is accompanied by the plus sign.

1. e: ___ ___ ___ ___ ___ ___ ___

2. c: ___ ___ ___ ___ ___ ___ ___ ___

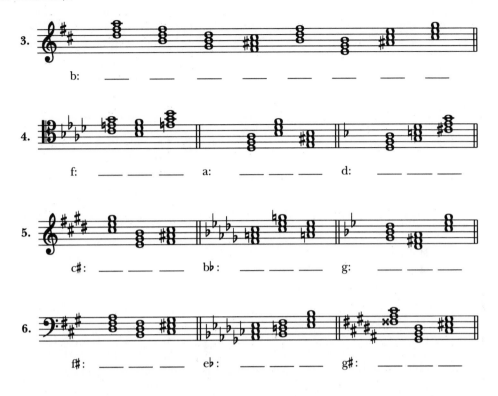

3.

b: ___ ___ ___ ___ ___ ___ ___

4.

f: ___ ___ ___   a: ___ ___ ___   d: ___ ___ ___

5.

c#: ___ ___ ___   bb: ___ ___ ___   g: ___ ___ ___

6.

f#: ___ ___ ___   eb: ___ ___ ___   g#: ___ ___ ___

C. Write root-position triads as indicated by the roman numeral and other symbols. Use a key signature and add any necessary accidentals. Remember that the roman numeral and other symbols dictate the quality of the triad. If the roman numeral is uppercase, the triad must be major; if lowercase, the triad must be minor. The symbol ° indicates a diminished triad.

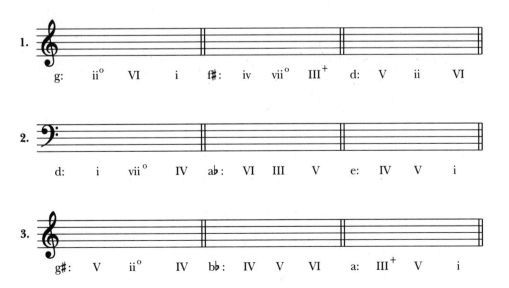

1.

g:　ii°　VI　i　f#:　iv　vii°　III⁺　d:　V　ii　VI

2.

d:　i　vii°　IV　ab:　VI　III　V　e:　IV　V　i

3.

g#:　V　ii°　IV　bb:　IV　V　VI　a:　III⁺　V　i

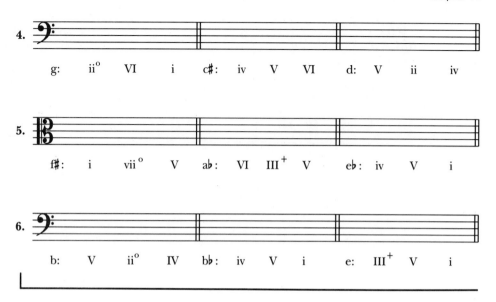

Identification of Inversions

Although roman numerals indicate the quality of the triad and define its relationship with the tonic, they do not reflect the important relationship between root and bass. Arabic numerals, discussed in the last chapter, are used along with a roman numeral to show whether a triad is in root position or inverted. Remember that the arabic numerals always refer to *diatonic* intervals sounding above the bass (not necessarily the root).

Abbreviated Arabic-Numeral Designations. As we discussed in Chapter 10, the arabic numerals $\frac{5}{3}$, $\frac{6}{3}$, and $\frac{6}{4}$ identify triads in root position, first inversion, and second inversion, respectively. Used with roman numerals in analysis, however, some arabic identifications are omitted or simplified. If a triad is in root position, the roman numeral alone designates this root–bass relationship. A roman numeral without an arabic numeral, therefore, is understood to stand for a root-position triad.

In first inversion, the numeral 3 is omitted from the full designation $\frac{6}{3}$; the numeral 6 alone indicates first inversion. Finally, the full identification $\frac{6}{4}$ is used to stand for a second-inversion triad in analysis.

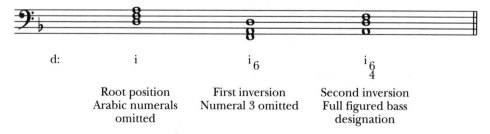

You will recall that other symbols are used in analysis as well. If a triad is diminished, for example, the small superscript circle is added to the arabic and roman numerals. When a triad is augmented, the plus sign accompanies the other analytical symbols. Symbols such as the circle and the plus sign identify triads that are less stable than simple major and minor triads.

Review the use of roman and arabic numerals as shown below.

Roman Numerals

I	i	vii°	III$^+$
major	minor	diminished	augmented

Arabic Numerals

(no numeral)	6	$^6_4$
root position	first inversion	second inversion

exercise 11–5 *Fundamental Skills*
Roman-Numeral Analysis

A. Use roman and arabic numerals along with other symbols to identify the triads in the keys indicated. Begin by supplying the key signature.

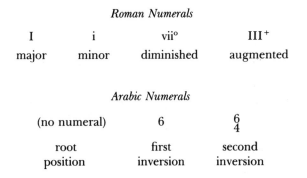

1. a: ___ ___ ___   G: ___ ___ ___   f#: ___ ___ ___

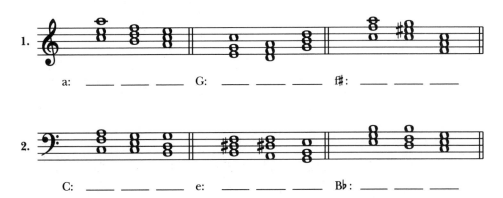

2. C: ___ ___ ___   e: ___ ___ ___   Bb: ___ ___ ___

3.

bb : ____ ____ ____   E: ____ ____ ____   Db : ____ ____ ____

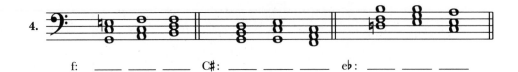

4.

f: ____ ____ ____   C# : ____ ____ ____   eb : ____ ____ ____

5.

b: ____ ____ ____   A: ____ ____ ____   Ab : ____ ____ ____

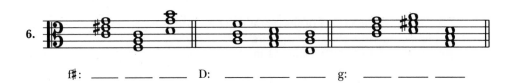

6.

f# : ____ ____ ____   D: ____ ____ ____   g: ____ ____ ____

B. Reverse the process of exercise A and construct triads that correspond to the given analytical symbols. Begin with the key signature, but remember that in some cases, accidentals must be added (to the dominant and leading tone triads in minor, for example).

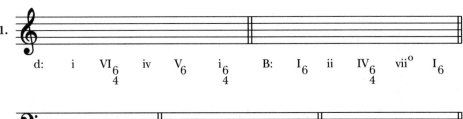

1.

d: i   VI₆₄   iv   V₆   i₆₄   B: I₆   ii   IV₆₄   vii°   I₆

2.

c# : IV₆   V   i₆   b: i   ii°   V₆₄   i₆₄   E: IV   V₆   I

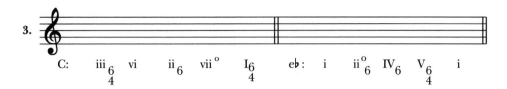

3.

C: iii$_6^4$ vi   ii$_6$ vii$^{\circ}$ I$_6^4$ e♭:   i   ii$^{\circ}_6$ IV$_6$ V$_6^4$ i

4.

D♭:   vi$_6$ I   vii$^{\circ}_6$ I   f: i$_6^4$ VI$_6$ iv   V$_6^4$ a: III$^+$ V$_6$ i

exercise 11–6   Musicianship Skills
EAR TRAINING: Root-position and Inverted Triads

A. Your instructor will play several arpeggiated triads in close position. Identify the quality (major or minor) in the first blank. In the second blank, write $\frac{5}{3}$ if the triad is in root position, $\frac{6}{3}$ if the triad is in first inversion, and $\frac{6}{4}$ if the triad is in second inversion.

Arpeggiated Triads

1. _____   _____   2. _____   _____

3. _____   _____   4. _____   _____

5. _____   _____   6. _____   _____

7. _____   _____   8. _____   _____

9. _____   _____   10. _____   _____

11. _____   _____   12. _____   _____

13. _____   _____   14. _____   _____

15. _____   _____   16. _____   _____

17. _____   _____   18. _____   _____

19. _____   _____   20. _____   _____

B. This exercise duplicates the previous one, but you will hear the triad sounded as a chord rather than arpeggiated.

Harmonic Triads

1. _____   ____   2. _____   ____

3. _____   ____   4. _____   ____

5. _____   ____   6. _____   ____

7. _____   ____   8. _____   ____

9. _____   ____   10. _____   ____

11. _____   ____   12. _____   ____

13. _____   ____   14. _____   ____

15. _____   ____   16. _____   ____

17. _____   ____   18. _____   ____

19. _____   ____   20. _____   ____

SELF-TEST

1. Write the names (tonic, supertonic, and so on) and qualities of the triads on each of the scale degrees listed. On the staff, write a root-position triad on the appropriate scale degree of the given key.

Scale Degree	Triad Name	Quality	Example
2	_____	_____	D major:
7	_____	_____	G major:
5	_____	_____	F major:

Scale Degree	Triad Name	Quality	Example
3	_____	_____	Eb major:
4	_____	_____	B major:

2. Identify the triads with roman and arabic numerals as well as any other necessary symbol.

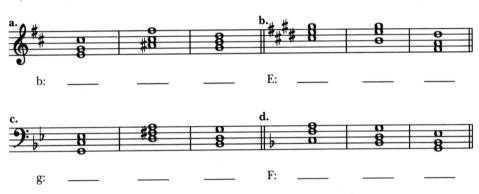

b: ____   ____   ____   E: ____   ____   ____

c.   d.

g: ____   ____   ____   F: ____   ____   ____

3. Write triads as indicated. Use a key signature and add any necessary accidentals.

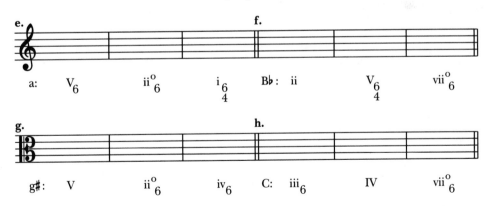

a: V₆   ii°₆   i₆₄   Bb: ii   V₆₄   vii°₆

g#:   V   ii°₆   iv₆   C: iii₆   IV   vii°₆

4. Identify the following terms and symbols:

    a. Progression

    b. Subtonic

    c. Submediant

    d. vii°_{6}

    e. $+$

SUPPLEMENTARY EXERCISES

1. Write diatonic triad names for the chords given. Some of the chords are inverted.

a.

B: _____   g: _____   d: _____   C: _____

b.

D: _____   b: _____   A: _____   f: _____

c.

E♭: _____   B♭: _____   e: _____   C♯: _____

d.

A♭: _____   g♯: _____   F: _____   F♯: _____

2. In the keys given, write the triads indicated. First, write the key signature; then, write basic pitches. Include any necessary accidentals.

    a. F major: Supertonic
    b. D-flat major: Dominant
    c. E minor: Tonic
    d. G major: Submediant
    e. C minor: Subdominant
    f. A-flat major: Leading tone
    g. B major: Mediant
    h. C minor: Tonic

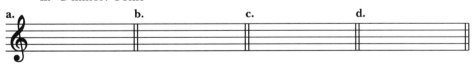

339

3. Write the root-position triads indicated by the key and roman numeral. Begin by supplying the appropriate key signature. Remember that in minor, it may be necessary to add an accidental to achieve the specified quality.

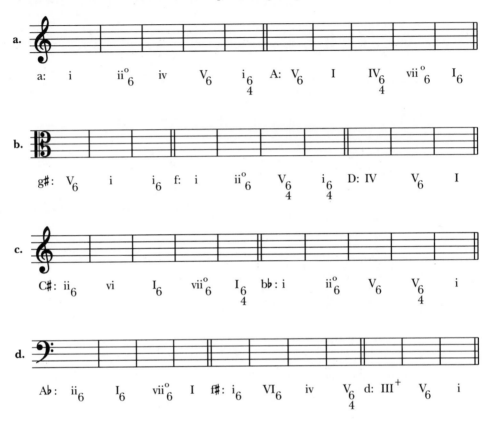

4. With roman and arabic numerals (as well as any other necessary symbols), identify the given chord in the key indicated.

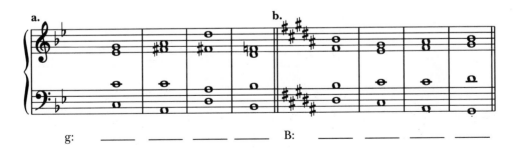

c.   **d.**

d: _____ _____ _____ _____   C: _____ _____ _____ _____

e.   **f.**

e♭: _____ _____ _____ _____   D: _____ _____ _____ _____

Basic Concepts of Tonal Harmony

The terms TONALITY and KEY are synonymous; they refer to the establishment of a pitch reference (the tonic) and the choice between either the major or the minor *mode*. The tonality or key of D major, for example, refers to the establishment of the pitch D as a tonal reference point and indicates that the mode is major. Likewise, the key of G minor signifies that the most important pitch is G and that the mode is minor. Many of the means by which tonality is created lie outside the scope of a music fundamentals text; in a harmonic sense, however, the relationships among the diatonic triads are central to the process of creating a feeling for key.

Consonance and Dissonance

The concepts of consonance and dissonance are relative, but in general, they refer to sounds that are stable (consonance) and to those that are less stable (dissonance). Although in contemporary music the term *dissonance* has varied meanings, a DISSONANCE in traditional tonal music is defined as a pitch, an interval, a triad, or a chord that has a strong tendency to *resolve*—that is, to move or progress toward a more stable sonority.

Medieval theorists grouped intervals into three categories, based on mathematical ratios between the two pitches involved: *perfect consonances*, *imperfect consonances*, and *dissonances*. Although the concepts of consonance are different today, we continue to use the original designations. Notice that seconds and sevenths are classified as dissonances.

Perfect Consonance	Imperfect Consonance	Dissonance
Perfect octave	Major third	Major second
Perfect unison	Minor third	Minor second
Perfect fifth	Major sixth	Major seventh
Perfect fourth	Minor sixth	Minor seventh

The "Devil in Music."   One interval, the augmented fourth, was considered so dissonant by early composers that they referred to it in their writing as "the Devil in Music." Also known as a TRITONE, the augmented fourth (and its inversion, the diminished fifth) was carefully resolved by even Common Practice composers. Typical resolutions of both the augmented fourth and the diminished fifth are shown below. In modern terminology, each interval is known as a "tritone."

augmented fourth   resolution   diminished fifth   resolution

Since dissonances such as the tritone are unstable and have tendencies to resolve, traditional composers used them to create a stronger feeling for key than could be accomplished with consonances alone. The dissonance creates tension; the tension is relaxed as resolution to a consonance occurs. The greater the dissonance, the greater the tension (and, therefore, the stronger the feeling for key when the dissonance is resolved).

THE DOMINANT SEVENTH CHORD

Although major, minor, and diminished triads form the core of traditional harmony, composers use several other chords both for color and as a means of clarifying the tonality. SEVENTH CHORDS, for example, contain not only a third and a fifth above the root but the interval of a seventh as well. The seventh chord that appears above the dominant pitch is the most common in traditional music. The dominant seventh chord is also known as a "major-minor" seventh chord because it is built of a major triad with a superimposed minor seventh.

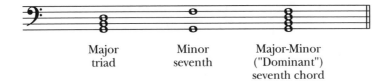

Major triad	Minor seventh	Major-Minor ("Dominant") seventh chord

Roman-Numeral Designations. In analysis, root-position seventh chords are identified as usual with the appropriate roman numeral plus the arabic numeral 7 to designate the dissonant seventh.[1]

Because the dominant seventh chord is a relatively unstable sonority, the chord is classified as a HARMONIC DISSONANCE. In traditional music, the dominant seventh usually moves or *resolves* to the tonic. The seventh itself typically descends by step to the third of the tonic triad. The following progressions are heard in Recorded Example 34. Notice that the dominant seventh in major and parallel minor keys is identical.

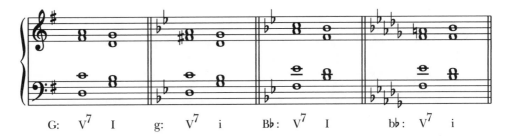

▶ *RECORDED EXAMPLE 34*

Dominant Seventh Chords

---

[1] Although seventh chords can also be inverted, the present discussion will include only those in root position.

Dominant seventh chords must be constructed of a major triad with a minor seventh; if the triad is not major, the chord cannot be a dominant seventh. In minor keys, therefore, you must remember to raise the third of the dominant triad to make the triad major. This altered pitch is the leading tone of the key.

exercise 12–1 *Fundamental Skills*
Constructing Dominant Seventh Chords

Construct root-position dominant seventh chords in the major and minor keys indicated. First, write the appropriate key signature. Next, construct the dominant triad and add a diatonic seventh above the root. In minor, a third step is always necessary: *Raise the third of the triad.*

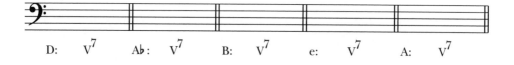

exercise 12–2 *Musicianship Skills*
SIGHT SINGING: Seventh Chords

On the keyboard, play the first pitch of each of the following dominant seventh chords; then, sing the chord melodically both ascending and descending. Check your final pitch against the same pitch on the keyboard. If you find this exercise difficult, play the entire chord on the keyboard before singing the outline. In addition to the chords shown, practice singing dominant seventh chords on other roots.

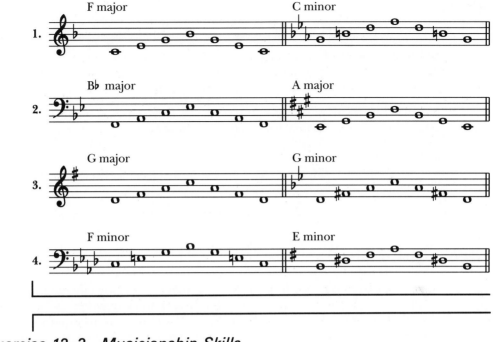

exercise 12–3 Musicianship Skills
EAR TRAINING: Recognizing
Seventh Chords

This exercise centers on differentiating between dominant seventh chords and simple triads. Your instructor will play several series of chords; the number of blanks corresponds to the number of chords in each line. If you hear a dominant seventh chord, write "7" in the blank; otherwise, write "T" to designate a root-position triad *or an inverted* triad without a seventh. All seventh chords are in root position, but some of the triads are inverted.

1. ____ ____ ____ ____

2. ____ ____ ____ ____

3. ____ ____ ____ ____

4. ____ ____ ____ ____

5. ____ ____ ____ ____

6. ____ ____ ____ ____

7. ____ ____ ____ ____

8. ____ ____ ____ ____

exercise 12–4 Musicianship Skills
KEYBOARD: Seventh Chords

Return to Skill Exercise 12-2 and perform the seventh chords at the keyboard. Hands separately, first play the pitches melodically ascending and descending, using any convenient fingering (begin with your thumb in the right hand and little finger in the left). After playing the outlines, sound all four pitches of the chord together. When you have mastered the outlines with right and left hands separately, play hands together.

PRIMARY TRIADS

Composers establish a feeling for key through various melodic and harmonic means; often, harmonic and melodic tendencies work together and cannot be separated clearly. That three of the diatonic triads have an especially strong tendency to establish a key, however, is important in analysis and tonal composition. The tonic, the subdominant, and the dominant are known as the PRIMARY TRIADS; the other diatonic triads are termed SECONDARY.

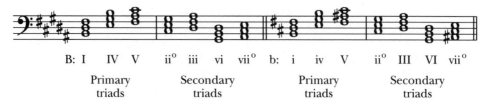

| B: I | IV | V | ii° | iii | vi | vii° | b: i | iv | V | ii° | III | VI | vii° |

Primary triads   Secondary triads   Primary triads   Secondary triads

Harmonic Function.   The root of the tonic triad is the first scale degree; the third of this triad establishes the mode (major or minor). For these and other reasons, the tonic triad is a position of stability in a composition. It is often the first chord and almost invariably the final chord in a tonal work. The tonic chord is a *goal* to which a series of chords moves.

The subdominant triad is often a midpoint or a "digression" in tonal harmony, typically appearing between tonic and dominant. The dominant triad, which contains the leading tone, represents *momentum* in the movement toward tonic. The momentum is relaxed as dominant moves to tonic—the goal of the progression.[2] A basic tonal progression is heard in Recorded Example 35.

---

[2] The concepts of stability, digression, and momentum are from Leonard Ratner's text *Harmony: Structure and Style* (New York: McGraw-Hill, 1961).

► *RECORDED EXAMPLE 35*

**Progression
of Primary Chords**

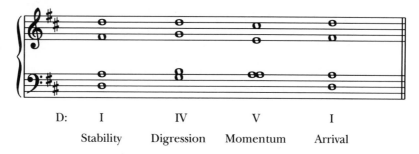

D: I   IV   V   I

      Stability   Digression   Momentum   Arrival

Each of the primary triads has its typical role or function in a series of chords. The tonic represents stability; the subdominant, digression; the dominant, momentum. The term HARMONIC FUNCTION describes the clearly defined roles of chords and how a feeling for key is established through orderly chord progressions. Although many other factors affect harmonic function, the importance of the primary triads is significant.

exercise 12–5 Fundamental Skills
Primary Triads

In the keys specified, write root-position tonic, subdominant, and dominant triads as indicated by the roman numerals. Begin by supplying the key signature. Remember that in minor, you may need to add an accidental.

1.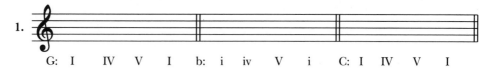

    G: I   IV   V   I   b: i   iv   V   i   C: I   IV   V   I

2.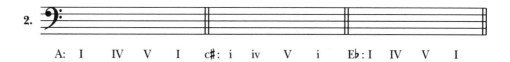

    A: I   IV   V   I   c♯: i   iv   V   i   E♭: I   IV   V   I

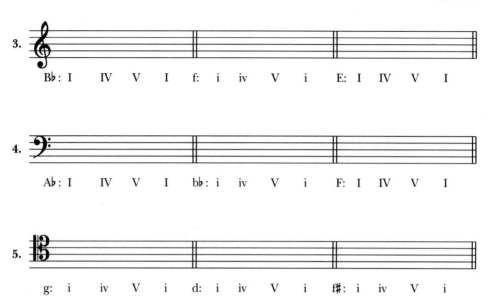

3. Bb: I IV V I   f: i iv V i   E: I IV V I

4. Ab: I IV V I   bb: i iv V i   F: I IV V I

5. g: i iv V i   d: i iv V i   f#: i iv V i

Substitute Triads

In addition to the primary triads, which establish the three basic harmonic functions, other triads serve as substitutes to provide variety. The function of the supertonic triad, for example, is nearly identical to that of the subdominant. The leading tone triad has much the same role as the dominant (momentum), and the submediant triad is sometimes used as a substitute for the tonic.

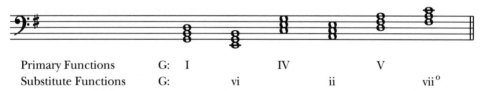

Primary Functions	G:	I		IV		V	
Substitute Functions	G:		vi		ii		vii$^\circ$

Traditional composers use the substitute chords for variety, among other reasons. Where the progression I IV V I is effective in defining a feeling for key, the chords I ii$_6$ vii$_6^\circ$ I have a similar effect. Listen to the three progressions in Recorded Example 36. The first progression, in both major and minor, features the primary triads in a functional harmonic progression. The second progression includes substitute triads in the primary roles. In the third passage, no sense of key is created by the randomly ordered chords.

▶ *RECORDED EXAMPLE 36*

Chord Progressions

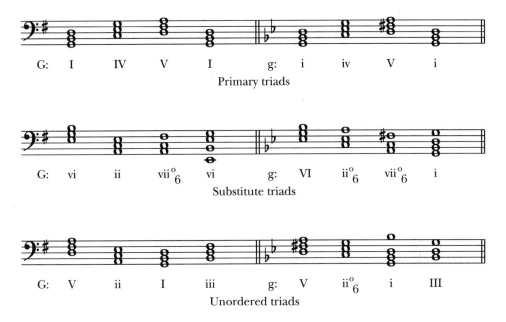

G: I   IV   V   I   g: i   iv   V   i

Primary triads

G: vi   ii   vii°₆   vi   g: VI   ii°₆   vii°₆   i

Substitute triads

G: V   ii   I   iii   g: V   ii°₆   i   III

Unordered triads

CADENCES

One of the reasons that the primary and substitute chord progressions in Recorded Example 36 establish a feeling for key is that they end with a definitive *cadence*. A CADENCE is a musical point of conclusion that can be classified either as *terminal* or as *progressive*. Cadences always involve two different chords: subdominant and dominant, for example, or dominant and tonic. Like punctuation in sentence construction, some cadences create a pause (as a comma does), whereas other cadences are more final (similar to the role of a period).

The Authentic Cadence. A progression of the dominant triad to the tonic creates a strong feeling for key. When these two chords (V–I) *end* a musical phrase, the cadence is termed AUTHENTIC.

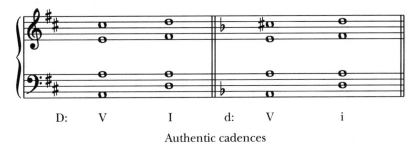

D: V   I   d: V   i

Authentic cadences

The effect of the authentic cadence can be compared to that of a period in sentence construction.

When a seventh is added to the dominant triad in an authentic cadence, the resolution to tonic and the tonal effect are enhanced. In traditional four-part writing, the seventh of a seventh chord almost invariably moves down *by step* to the third of the tonic triad. The dissonant seventh creates tension; the expected resolution clarifies the key.

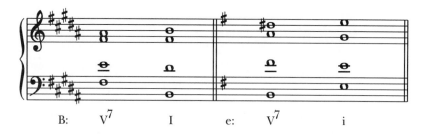

$$\text{B:} \quad V^7 \qquad I \qquad\qquad \text{e:} \quad V^7 \qquad i$$

The Half Cadence.   The HALF CADENCE is a musical comma—a temporary pause. Half cadences conclude with the dominant chord; the dominant is preceded most often by tonic, subdominant, or supertonic.

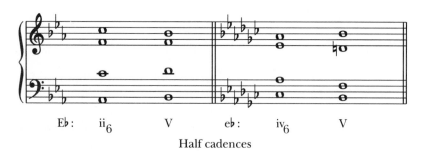

$$\text{E}\flat: \quad ii_6 \qquad V \qquad\qquad \text{e}\flat: \quad iv_6 \qquad V$$

Half cadences

The Plagal Cadence.   A third type of traditional cadence, known as PLAGAL, involves the progression subdominant to tonic (IV–I).

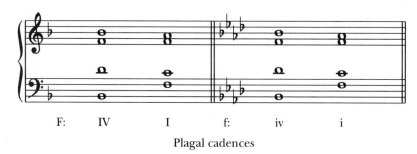

$$\text{F:} \quad IV \qquad I \qquad\qquad \text{f:} \quad iv \qquad i$$

Plagal cadences

Although plagal cadences are less effective in establishing a feeling for key than authentic cadences, they are often used as the final progression in a composition.

The Deceptive Cadence.   Composers sometimes delay arrival at the tonic by using a substitute—usually the submediant—for the tonic. When it occurs at the end of a phrase, the progression V–vi is known as a DECEPTIVE CADENCE.

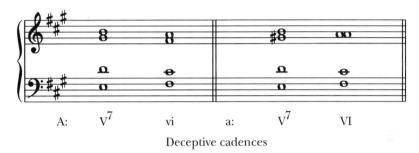

Deceptive cadences

The first phrase below ends with a deceptive cadence. The second phrase ends with an authentic cadence.

---

exercise 12–6 *Fundamental Skills*
Identifying Cadences

Each of the following phrases concludes with one of the cadence types we have just discussed. Analyze the final two chords in each phrase. Write the appropriate roman numerals in the upper blanks, and identify the cadence in the lower blank.

1. Tchaikovsky

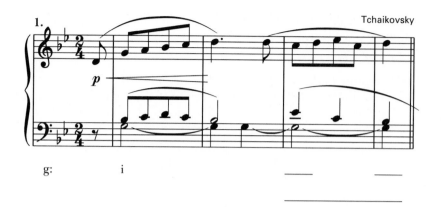

g: i

2. Schumann

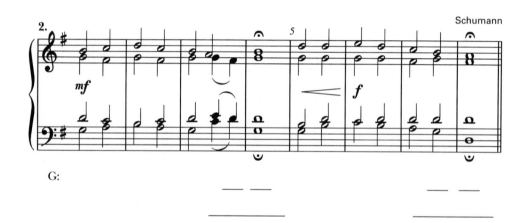

G:

3. Bach

g:

exercise 12–7   Musicianship Skills
EAR TRAINING: Recognizing Cadences

Your instructor will play several phrases, each ending with an authentic, a plagal, a half, or a deceptive cadence. In the first set of exercises, choose between the two possibilities given by circling the cadence played.

1. authentic	plagal		2. authentic	half
3. plagal	half		4. authentic	deceptive
5. plagal	half		6. half	deceptive
7. plagal	authentic		8. deceptive	plagal
9. half	authentic		10. half	plagal

In this group of exercises, use the blank to identify the cadence type heard (authentic, half, plagal, or deceptive).

1. _____   2. _____

3. _____   4. _____

5. _____   6. _____

7. _____   8. _____

9. _____   10. _____

11. _____   12. _____

exercise 12–8   Musicianship Skills
KEYBOARD: Cadences

The following cadences are written in traditional four-part style. Play the bass note with the left hand and the upper three voices with the right. Notice that the motion of the upper voices is generally opposite to that of the bass. The cadences are given first in C major and C minor, then transposed to D major and D minor in the second line. Use the other staffs and additional paper to transpose the cadences to other keys as directed by your instructor. If necessary, practice the right and left hands separately before playing the cadence hands together. The half cadence given is IV–V (iv–V in minor). Remember that a variety of chords can approach the dominant in a half cadence.

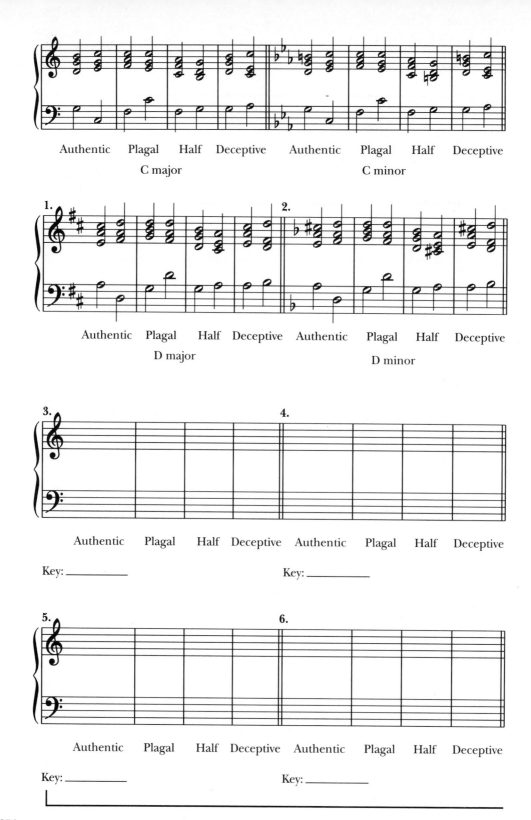

Authentic   Plagal   Half   Deceptive   Authentic   Plagal   Half   Deceptive

C major   C minor

1.   **2.**

Authentic   Plagal   Half   Deceptive   Authentic   Plagal   Half   Deceptive

D major   D minor

3.   **4.**

Authentic   Plagal   Half   Deceptive   Authentic   Plagal   Half   Deceptive

Key: _____   Key: _____

5.   **6.**

Authentic   Plagal   Half   Deceptive   Authentic   Plagal   Half   Deceptive

Key: _____   Key: _____

FOUR-PART HARMONY

Harmony is traditionally studied through the composition and analysis of four-part vocal music written in a simple, chordal style. Although the four voices theoretically should be independent melodies, their vertical arrangement also forms clear harmonies of triads and seventh chords. For the most part, the soprano, alto, tenor, and bass voices should conform to the ranges shown below.

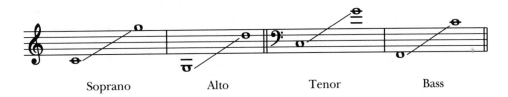

Soprano   Alto   Tenor   Bass

Doubling. When a triad is arranged for four voices, one of the pitches must be doubled. Most often, the root is doubled in major and minor triads. Other conventional procedures apply to inverted triads, however. In first inversion, the soprano is normally doubled (whether this pitch is the root, the third, or the fifth). In second inversion, the fifth of the triad is doubled. *Caution*: Whether root, third, or fifth, the unstable leading tone of a given key must *never* be doubled.

Conventional Doublings in Triads

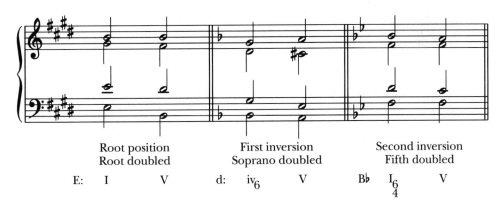

Root position   First inversion   Second inversion
Root doubled   Soprano doubled   Fifth doubled

E: I   V   d: iv$_6$ V   B♭   I$_6^4$ V

All four pitches are normally present in a seventh chord. In some cases, however, composers may omit the fifth and double the root if the chord is in root position. As with triads, the leading tone is never doubled.

Conventional Doublings in Root-position Dominant Seventh Chords

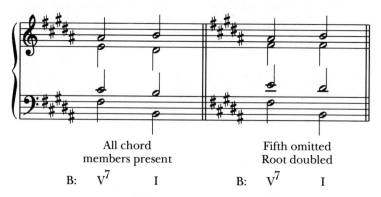

Voicing. Although the four voices should conform to the ranges given earlier, composers typically treat the bass separately from the three upper voices (soprano, alto, and tenor). The bass and tenor voices are often separated by intervals greater than an octave, for example, while adjacent upper voices are rarely more than an octave apart. Notice that the soprano and tenor voices are written with stems up and the alto and bass have stems down.

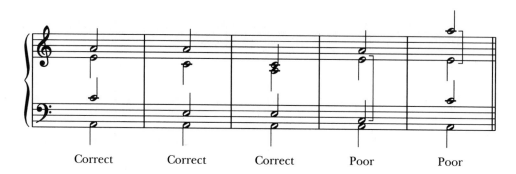

Open and Close Position. CLOSE POSITION in four-part writing indicates that the upper three voices are as close together as possible, with tenor and soprano separated by *less than an octave*. If the distance between tenor and soprano is an octave or more, the four-part arrangement is known as OPEN POSITION. In general, composers retain the same spatial position for several chords rather than alternating frequently between open and close or the reverse. The bass voice is not a factor in differentiating between open and close position.

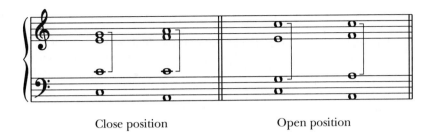

Close position   Open position

Voice Leading

One of the most important aspects of traditional harmony is VOICE LEADING—
the melodic movement of individual voices. Good voice leading means that although the four voices retain their independence, the melodic movement is
smooth and relatively easy to sing. If the voice leading is poor, voice independence
is less effective or the movement of individual lines is awkward and difficult.
Voice leading is a complex topic best reserved for a music theory course, but
three general principles will suffice for writing cadences and short progressions:

1. The upper voices should move to the closest pitch in the next chord—by stepwise
   motion contrary to the bass if possible.

G: I   IV   I   V   I   IV   I   V

Good: Stepwise motion   Poor: Stepwise motion ignored

2. Common tones (the same pitch appearing in two consecutive chords) should be
   retained in the same voice or voices.

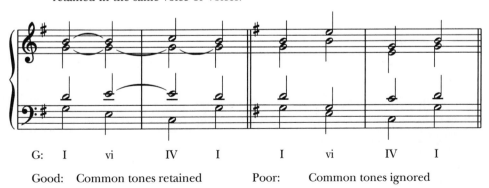

G: I   vi   IV   I   I   vi   IV   I

Good: Common tones retained   Poor: Common tones ignored

3. The three upper voices should move generally in contrary motion (the opposite direction) to the bass. If the bass descends, for example, the three upper voices should ascend. When the bass ascends, move the upper three voices in descending stepwise motion if possible.

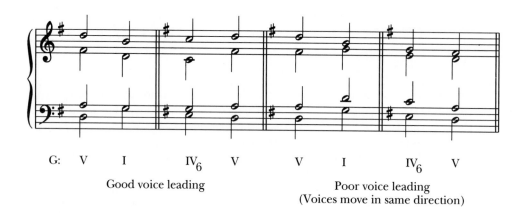

G: V   I   IV₆   V   V   I   IV₆   V

Good voice leading   Poor voice leading
                                                 (Voices move in same direction)

Parallel Perfect Intervals.   Voices that move in the same direction by the same interval are termed PARALLEL. When two voices (whether adjacent or not) move in parallel motion by a simple or compound perfect fifth or perfect octave, voice independence is reduced. Parallel fifths and octaves are considered serious voice-leading errors and should be avoided. Do this by moving the bass and the upper three voices in contrary motion. Note that parallel perfect fourths are acceptable.

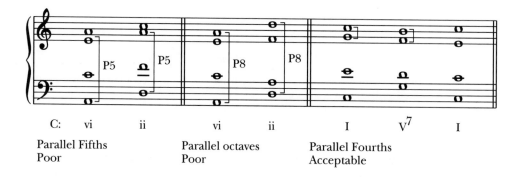

C: vi   ii   vi   ii   I   V⁷   I

Parallel Fifths   Parallel octaves   Parallel Fourths
Poor   Poor   Acceptable

Awkward Melodic Intervals.   Certain melodic intervals, such as the tritone and the augmented second, are difficult to sing and should be avoided in melodic writing.

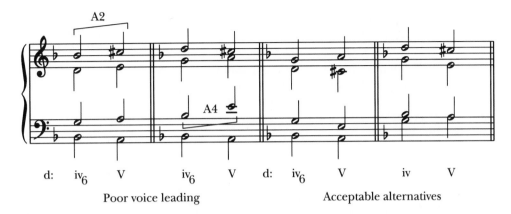

d: iv₆   V   iv₆   V   d: iv₆   V   iv   V

Poor voice leading   Acceptable alternatives

Seventh Chords.   Although any chord may theoretically have a root-position or inverted seventh above its root, only the dominant seventh chord will be discussed in this volume. For present purposes, the seventh of the dominant seventh should resolve down by step to the third of the tonic triad. In a deceptive cadence, the seventh resolves down by step to the fifth of the submediant chord.

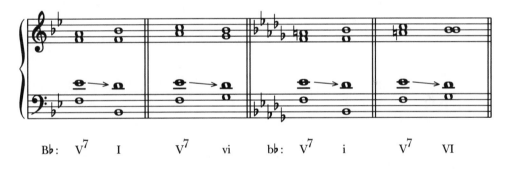

B♭:   V⁷   I   V⁷   vi   b♭:   V⁷   i   V⁷   VI

---

exercise 12–9 *Fundamental Skills*
Errors in Voice Leading

Many of the following cadences contain one or more errors in voice leading. Although the chords are spelled correctly, there may be errors such as parallel fifths or octaves, awkward melodic intervals (a tritone, a seventh, or an augmented second, for example), incorrect doublings or spacings, and the improper resolution of a seventh. Use the list below to identify errors. Circle the incorrect pitch or pitches, then write the letter(s) of the error(s) in the blank. Use another sheet to rewrite the cadences without errors.

A. Parallel octaves
B. Parallel fifths
C. Incorrect resolution of seventh
D. More than octave between adjacent upper voices
E. Incorrect doubling
F. Awkward melodic interval (specify)
G. Doubled leading tone
H. Common tones not retained

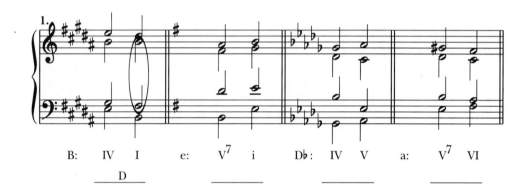

1.

B: IV   I   e: V⁷   i   D♭:   IV   V   a: V⁷   VI
     ___D___   _____   _____   _____

2.

C: V   vi   d: V   i   F♯:   ii   V   c♯:   i   V
     _____   _____   _____   _____

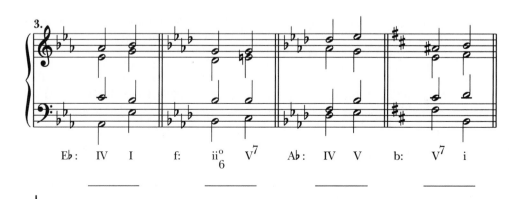

3.

E♭:   IV   I   f: ii°₆   V⁷   A♭:   IV   V   b: V⁷   i
      _____   _____   _____   _____

exercise 12–10 *Fundamental Skills*
Voice Leading in Alto and Tenor

The following cadences have soprano and bass given. Using effective voice leading and conventional doubling, add the alto and tenor voices. Remember that there should be no interval greater than an octave between alto and tenor or between alto and soprano. Write the name of the cadence in the blank.

1.

G:　V　vi　　B♭:　V　I　　f:　iv₆　V　　C:　IV　I

_____　_____　_____　_____

2.

d:　iv　V　　E♭:　V　I　　A:　IV　I　　c♯:　V　i

_____　_____　_____　_____

3.

e♭:　IV　V　　F:　V　vi　　a:　iv　i　　D:　V　I

_____　_____　_____　_____

exercise 12–11 *Fundamental Skills*
Cadences in Four Parts

In the keys indicated, write cadences in four parts with smooth voice leading. Begin
with a key signature. In the blanks, write the type of cadence specified by the given
roman numerals; then, write the necessary bass pitches. Next, choose notes for the
soprano that will create smooth melodic motion in the highest voice as well as contrary
motion between the soprano and the bass if possible. Finally, fill in the alto and tenor
voices in both chords—moving stepwise in contrary motion to the bass if possible.
All the chords should be in root position (meaning that the root must be doubled).
Be careful to avoid parallel fifths and octaves.

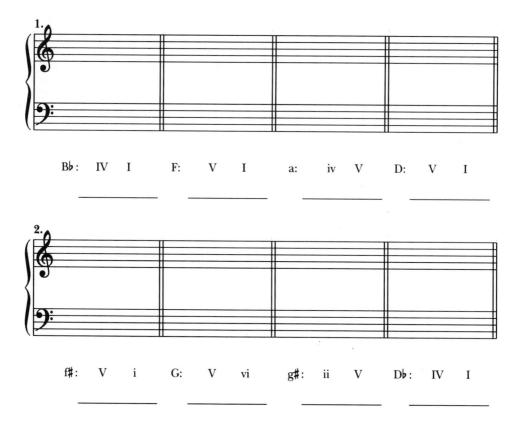

1.

B♭: IV I   F: V I   a: iv V   D: V I

_____   _____   _____   _____

2.

f♯: V i   G: V vi   g♯: ii V   D♭: IV I

_____   _____   _____   _____

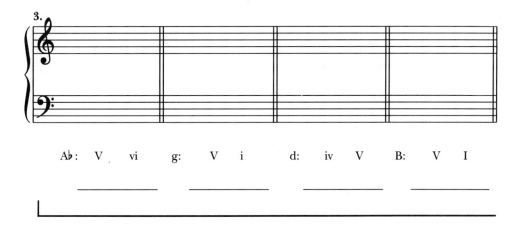

3.

Ab: V   vi   g: V   i   d: iv   V   B: V   I

SELF-TEST

1. Use roman and arabic numerals (as well as additional symbols if necessary) to identify the following chords in the keys indicated.

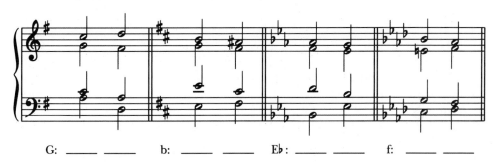

G: ____ ____   b: ____ ____   Eb: ____ ____   f: ____ ____

2. Write the chords indicated by the given analytical symbols. Remember to add accidentals as necessary in minor keys.

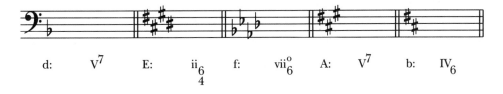

d: V^7 E: ii^6_4 f: vii^o_6 A: V^7 b: IV_6

3. Provide roman numerals and identify the cadences.

A: _____ _____   g: _____ _____   C: _____ _____

_____   _____   _____

4. Using correct four-part procedures, write cadences as indicated. Provide roman numerals and add any necessary accidentals.

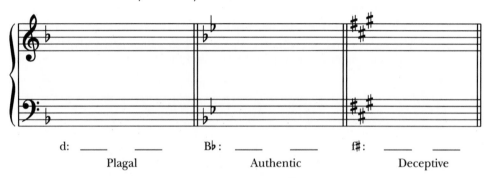

d: _____ _____   B♭: _____ _____   f♯: _____ _____

Plagal   Authentic   Deceptive

5. List the three primary triads in the first column. In the second column, write the secondary triad that serves as a substitute.

Primary Triads   *Secondary Triads*

_____   _____

_____   _____

_____   _____

6. Identify the following terms:

    a. Half cadence

    b. Tonality

    c. Voice leading

    d. Consonance

    e. Imperfect consonance

SUPPLEMENTARY EXERCISES

1. Analyze the cadences that end the following phrases. The points of cadence are indicated with blanks. Write the appropriate roman and arabic numerals and identify the cadence type.

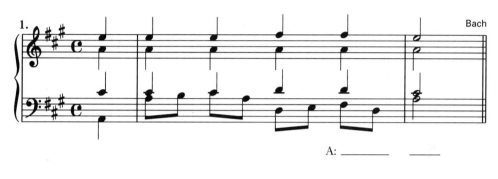

Bach

A: _____ _____
_____

Bach

A: _____ _____
_____

Beethoven

G: _____ _____
_____

Menuetto

Haydn

D: _____ _____

_____

D: _____ _____

_____

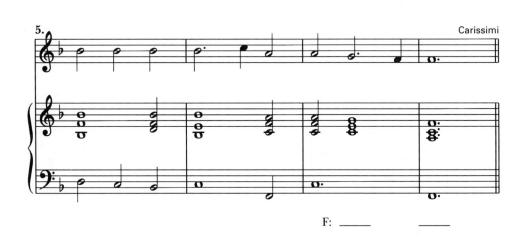

Carissimi

F: _____ _____

_____

6.

Mozart

g: _____ _____

_____

7.

Haydn

A: _____ _____

_____

8.

Bach

D: _____ _____

_____

e: _____   _____

_____

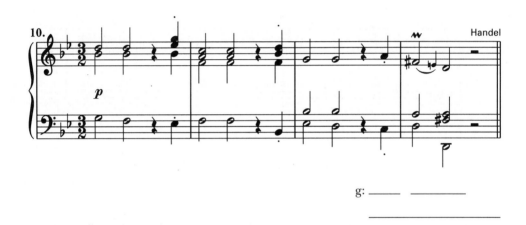

g: _____   _____

_____

2. Write the cadences and progressions indicated. Use correct four-part voice leading, and avoid parallel fifths and octaves, awkward melodic intervals, and incorrectly resolved sevenths. Retain common tones, and move the bass and the upper three voices in contrary motion where possible.

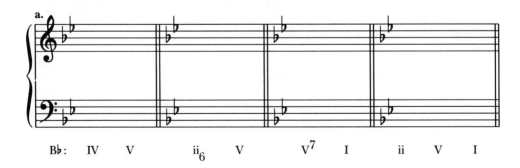

B♭:   IV   V   ii₆   V   V⁷   I   ii   V   I

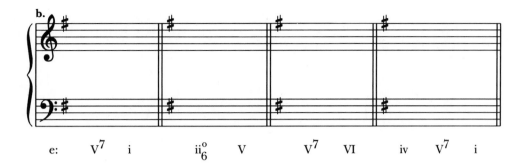

e: V⁷   i   ii°₆   V   V⁷   VI   iv   V⁷   i

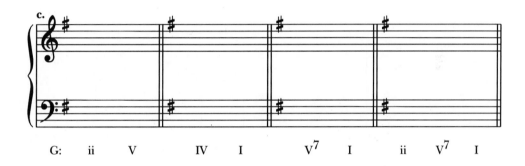

G: ii   V   IV   I   V⁷   I   ii   V⁷   I

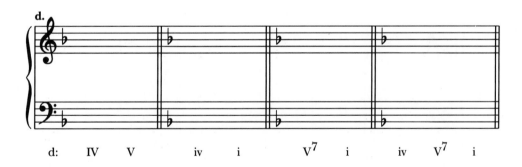

d: IV   V   iv   i   V⁷   i   iv   V⁷   i

3. Locate part-writing errors in the following progressions using the list of errors on page 362. Circle the pitch or pitches concerned and write the appropriate letter(s) in the blank.

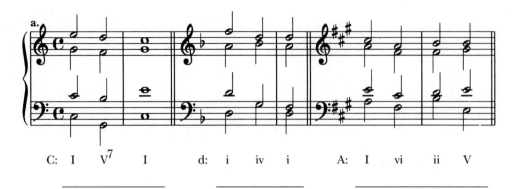

C: I   V⁷   I   d: i   iv   i   A: I   vi   ii   V

_____   _____   _____

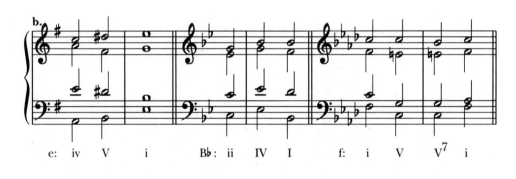

e: iv   V   i   B♭: ii   IV   I   f: i   V   V⁷   i

_____   _____   _____

G: IV   V   I   f♯: i   iv   V   A♭: I   IV   V⁷   I

_____   _____   _____

The Nature of Sound

ACOUSTICS AND PSYCHOACOUSTICS

In addition to possessing measurable *physical* properties, sounds, such as those of a clarinet or an automobile horn, make an impression on us *psychologically*. Since duration can be measured with precision, it is a physical property; the duration of a sound might be exactly seven seconds, for example. Hearing the sound as loud, soft, or somewhere in between, on the other hand, is a relative psychological sensation. Exposed to the same sound, one listener might think it loud; another might consider it relatively soft. ACOUSTICS is the branch of science that deals with the physical properties of sound; PSYCHOACOUSTICS is a relatively new field through which the psychological responses to sound are explored.

Sound Waves

Before sound can be transmitted, the air surrounding the sound source must be set in motion. On the violin, the vibrations of a string disturb the air molecules; in the flute and other wind instruments, the air inside the instrument itself vibrates. The vibrating string or column of air causes the surrounding air particles to be set in motion in regular patterns of vibration. These patterns of molecular motion are known as SOUND WAVES. Like waves in the water, sound waves travel spherically from the source, growing more and more faint until they die out completely. If the sound is a musical tone (as opposed to noise), the patterns or waves are regular and controlled. Counting the number of these vibrations within a given timespan measures the *frequency* of the sound.

Frequency. FREQUENCY is determined by the number of sound waves (patterns of molecular vibration) created by the vibrating string or air column. The frequency of a sound wave is measured in cycles or vibrations per second (c.p.s.). A more modern term for this measurement is *hertz* (Hz). Most musical sounds lie between about 50 Hz and 2000 Hz. A tone in the upper register of a flute, for example, produces about 1600 sound waves per second (1600 Hz). The lowest note on the double bass, on the other hand, produces only about 40 sound waves per second (40 Hz). The limits of human audition fall between approximately 20 Hz and 20,000 Hz.

Pitch. The frequency of a sound produces the psychological response we call PITCH. The greater the frequency of a sound, the higher the pitch; sounds with lesser frequencies produce tones of lower pitch. An electronic instrument known as an oscilloscope is used to measure the frequency of sound waves. The first representation below is of a relatively high pitch as it might appear on an oscilloscope; the second is lower; the third, lower still.

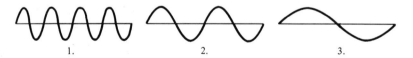

Amplitude and Intensity

Sounds differ not only in pitch but in other respects as well. The acoustical property known as *amplitude*, for example, plays a role in most musical works. AMPLITUDE is the degree of disturbance in air molecules caused by the sound. We translate differences in amplitude into perceptions of a sound's being loud or soft. If a sound has relatively greater amplitude (that is, if it creates a relatively great disturbance of the air particles), we perceive the sound as loud. Lesser amplitude creates the sensation of a softer tone. Notice that the two sounds represented below are of the same frequency; they differ in amplitude. The first would be the louder; the second, the softer.

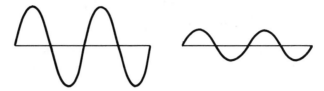

Timbre and Quality

Almost any musical sound is made up of many different frequencies—some relatively strong, others weaker. The various frequencies present in a tone are known as HARMONICS. A flute can be distinguished from a trumpet even if the sounds are of identical frequency and amplitude. This is primarily because the harmonics present in the tone of the trumpet are greater in number and relatively stronger than those of the flute. Differences in harmonics largely determine the acoustical property known as TIMBRE. We perceive differences in timbre as differences in the QUALITY of a tone—the corresponding psychological response. Even if we cannot see the performers, we can identify most orchestral instruments by the qualities of their tones. The same phenomenon allows us to recognize a familiar voice over the telephone.

The Harmonic Series

One of the most important factors affecting tone quality is the natural *harmonic series*. When a tone is sounded on an acoustic musical instrument such as the flute or the trumpet, in addition to the FUNDAMENTAL (the lowest frequency heard), there are other, weaker frequencies that are audible as well. The frequencies sounding above the fundamental are termed PARTIALS; the strength and quantity of these partials determine the quality or timbre of a musical tone. The higher frequencies above a fundamental are called OVERTONES. The fundamental is included in the counting of partials but excluded in the counting of overtones.

The HARMONIC SERIES is a natural phenomenon that occurs when a sound source is set into motion. The relationship of the partials and the overtones to the fundamental is invariable. Each fundamental produces exactly the same range of partials and overtones. The harmonic series for the fundamentals C and A♭ are shown in the next example. Harmonic series for other fundamentals are merely transpositions of these series.

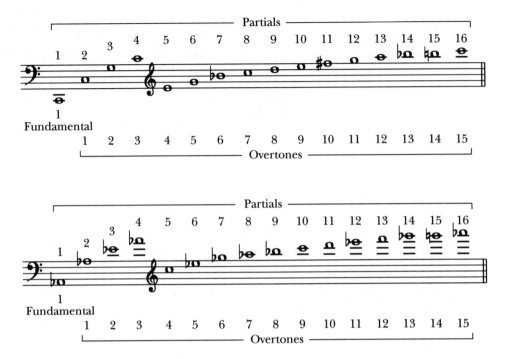

Duration and Length

Whereas the frequency, amplitude, and timbre of a tone cannot be measured without the use of electronic equipment, the fourth acoustical property—DURATION—can be calculated easily in minutes or seconds. The duration of a tone determines its LENGTH.

Other Modes and Scales

In addition to major and minor scales, past and present composers have used other scale series as the basis of a composition. Although composers of the Common Practice Period limited themselves to two modes (major and minor), other melodic series were employed before 1600 and after about 1900.

CHURCH MODES

The earliest patterns used to organize Western music were the CHURCH MODES—series of whole steps and half steps beginning on the basic pitches, C through A (heard in Recorded Example 37). Three of the original modes are classified as minor; three are classified as major. Major modes have two whole steps between the first and third degrees; minor modes have a whole step plus a diatonic half step between those same pitches.

Major Modes.   The basic pitch series beginning on C, F, and G are major modes known as IONIAN, LYDIAN, and MIXOLYDIAN, respectively. Ionian mode is the equivalent of the major scale.

Ionian   Lydian   Mixolydian

Minor Modes.   Minor modes occur on the basic pitch series beginning on D, E, and A. The DORIAN MODE has a tonic on D, the PHRYGIAN MODE begins on E, and the tonic of the AEOLIAN MODE is A. The Aeolian mode corresponds to the natural minor scale.

Dorian   Phrygian   Aeolian

LOCRIAN MODE, found in the basic pitch series B–B, was not employed by early musicians but is a melodic resource in contemporary music. The Locrian is a minor mode.

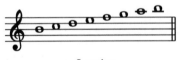

Locrian

▶ *RECORDED EXAMPLE 37*

Modes

Ionian (Major)   Dorian

Phrygian   Lydian

Mixolydian   Aeolian (Minor)

Locrian

Transposition of Modes. Transpose modes by noting the difference between the given mode and a major or natural minor scale. Except for the Locrian, other modes differ by one flat or sharp from the corresponding major or minor key signature.

Major Modes

IONIAN	Major scale
LYDIAN	Major scale with raised fourth degree (with sharp added to key signature)
MIXOLYDIAN	Major scale with lowered seventh degree (with flat added to key signature)

Minor Modes

AEOLIAN	Natural minor scale
DORIAN	Natural minor scale with raised sixth (with sharp added to key signature)
PHRYGIAN	Natural minor scale with lowered second (with flat added to key signature)
LOCRIAN	Natural minor scale with lowered second and lowered fifth (with two flats added to key signature)

OTHER SCALES

The Pentatonic Scale

Whereas major and minor scales as well as the modes have seven different pitches, the PENTATONIC SCALE has only five. The pitches of a pentatonic scale are derived from a series of perfect fifths reduced to a single octave.

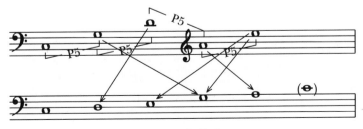

Pentatonic Scale

Various forms of the pentatonic scale are possible, but the most common form can be written as a major scale with fourth and seventh scale degrees omitted.

D Major Scale

D Pentatonic

The pentatonic scale (Recorded Example 38) is ancient; it forms the basis of many folk and popular melodies. Two such melodies are heard in Recorded Example 39.

▶ *RECORDED EXAMPLE 38*

Pentatonic Scale

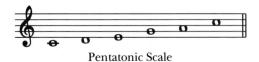

Pentatonic Scale

▶ *RECORDED EXAMPLE 39*

Pentatonic Melodies

Korean Folk Song

American Folk Song

The Whole-tone Scale

In the late nineteenth century, some composers began using a scale with only one type of interval: the whole step. The WHOLE-TONE SCALE consists of six whole steps. The seventh pitch is an enharmonic octave duplication of the first pitch. Double flats and double sharps are not used in constructing whole-tone scales.

Whole - tone Scales

Melodies based on a whole-tone scale have a distinctive sound. Both the whole-tone scale and a whole-tone melody are heard in Recorded Example 40.

▶ *RECORDED EXAMPLE 40*

Whole-tone Scale and Melody

Whole - tone Scale

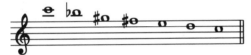

Whole - tone Melody   Debussy

The Chromatic Scale

A scale consisting entirely of half steps is the CHROMATIC SCALE. Tradition dictates that the scale be written with sharps ascending and flats descending.

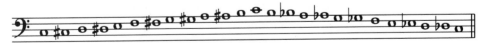

Chromatic Scale on C

Chromatic Scale on E♭

Calligraphy

One of the most important aspects of music fundamentals is the development of an individual approach to notating music—a process known as CALLIGRAPHY. In many instances, student errors on exams and projects are due not so much to a misunderstanding of the theoretical concept as to inaccurate calligraphy. In writing a scale, for example, if the student makes a notehead too large, the note may be misinterpreted and one of the scale degrees may be omitted inadvertently. An accidental on the wrong line or space may likewise cause a later error.

Notes

Noteheads—whether solid or open—should be oval in shape and approximately the width of a space on the staff in thickness. Noteheads vary in size, depending on the type of manuscript paper being used.

Stems

Stems are affixed to either the right or the left side of the notehead and may extend above or below it. A simple rule permits a correct placement of individual stems:

Notes on the third line and above have stems down from the left side. Notes below the third line have stems up from the right side.

When several notes are beamed together, the majority of the notes should have the correct stem direction.

The beams themselves are usually slanted if there is a definite ascending or descending pattern.

Beams should be thicker than stems.

Stems should extend from the notehead about an octave in length.

Flags

Flags are always placed on the right side of the stem (whether the stem is up or down). Notating flags as music engravers do takes some practice, but a simple arc, or even a slanted line, is usually sufficient for legible student manuscript.

Accidentals

Accidentals precede the note they affect and appear close to the notehead on the same line or space. The sharp sign is made with two vertical strokes and two slanted ones of the same length. The flat sign is like the lowercase letter *b* with an oval head. The natural sign is the combination of an uppercase letter *L*, and another upside down.

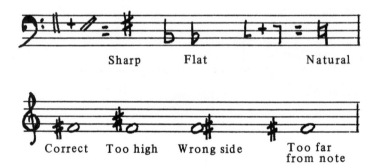

Clefs

The treble clef is made with two strokes; the end of the second stroke should encircle the second line.

The bass clef is even more simple. Make sure that the two dots occur above and below the fourth line.

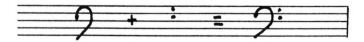

The movable C-clef (discussed in Chapter 2) has several manuscript forms:

Rests

Remember that the whole rest appears below the fourth line; the half rest is notated above the third line.

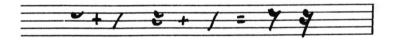

Whole   Half

The quarter rest is made much like an angular numeral *3*.

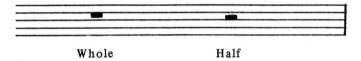

Eighth, sixteenth, and thirty-second rests are made by writing first the "flag" or "flags," then adding a slanted line of proportional length.

Clefs, Barlines, Key and Meter Signatures

The clef is placed at the beginning of each line. The key signature follows the clef at the beginning of *every* line. The meter signature, however, occurs only on the first line of a composition, where it follows the key signature.

Barlines precede each new measure. At the end of sections of a composition, a double bar often appears; at the end of the composition, the double bars are of unequal thickness.

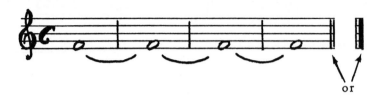

or

Repetition

Several symbols in traditional notation are used to indicate repetition. The REPEAT SIGN :‖: specifies that material between the double bars is to be repeated. When the repeat is to the beginning of the composition or movement, the first set of double bars may be omitted (as seen below). If the repeat is to a point other than the beginning, however, both sets are used (as in the Schubert example).

Written   Played

When only part of the material is repeated, the composer may use FIRST and SECOND ENDINGS. The first ending specifies a repeat to the beginning or to the first set of double bars. On the second playing of the material, however, the performer omits the first ending and goes instead to the second ending.

Schubert

Da Capo. The designation *D.C.* stands for *Da Capo* (Italian, meaning "from the head or top") and instructs the performer to repeat from the beginning of the composition. Often this abbreviation is used with the phrase *al fine* ("to the end"). The notation *D.C. al fine* requests a repeat from the beginning of the composition to the word *fine*.

Dal Segno. The notation *D.S.* stands for *Dal Segno* ("from the sign"). On seeing this designation, the performer returns not to the beginning but to the 𝄋 sign. If the instruction is *D.S. al fine*, the composition ends at the word *fine*.

Terms and Symbols of Tempo and Expression

ESSENTIAL TERMS

- *dynamics*
- *expression*
- *metronome*
- *tempo*

One of the most complex aspects of notating music concerns nuance. Although the composer can designate a certain group of specific pitches and even indicate the precise length of each of those pitches, the performer ultimately decides on certain less exact parameters, such as loudness, articulation (the manner in which the note is begun), and general effect. Over the centuries, composers developed a vocabulary of terms and symbols to aid the performer in understanding how to approach musical nuance. Many of these terms are Italian—reflecting an almost total domination by Italian musicians during the seventeenth and early eighteenth centuries.

Tempo

Although many twentieth-century composers have used their native languages to indicate the tempo—the general *speed* of the beat—Italian terms for this purpose are still predominant. Terms for tempo are relative. The word *Andante* (It.: "going"), for example, is usually interpreted as a "walking speed," giving the performer a good, but general, idea of the composer's intentions. The word *Lento* (It.: "slow") indicates a relatively slow tempo, and *Presto* (It.: "quick") suggests a fast beat.

The Metronome.   In the early part of the nineteenth century, the METRO-NOME was invented—a device that permits the composer to indicate a specific number of beats per minute. Rather than relying on the performer's interpretation of general tempo indications, composers simply write the letters *M.M.* (for Maelzel Metronome) followed by a note and the number of those notes to be played in one minute. Sometimes the letters *M.M.* are omitted.

M.M. ♩ = 132   M.M. ♩ = 72   ♪ = 100   ♩. = 60

Dynamics

Like terms for tempo, indications of dynamic level are relative. In addition to abbreviations of Italian terms, composers employ symbols to indicate a gradual increase or decrease in volume.

pianissimo (*pp*): very soft	*mezzo forte* (*mf*): medium loud
piano (*p*): soft	*forte* (*f*): loud
mezzo piano (*mp*): medium soft	*fortissimo* (*ff*): very loud
Gradually louder	Gradually softer

Expression

Composers often indicate a specific effect they want the performer to achieve, such as "tender" or "detached." Again, such commonly used terms are primarily Italian.

Composers also often add symbols to notes to indicate the manner of performance.

short   long   unbroken   accented   heavy

Solfège

ESSENTIAL TERMS
• fixed do solfège
• movable do solfège

Solfège

Over the ages, musicians have devised various methods for teaching sight singing. One such system is called SOLFÈGE; you may recognize the familiar syllables that are used for a major scale:

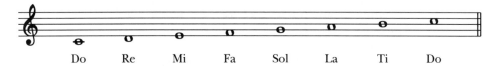

In movable *do* solfège, shown above, the tonic of any scale is named *do*; this system corresponds to scale degree numbers. In fixed *do* solfège (below), the pitch C is always *do* (regardless of where C falls in the scale).

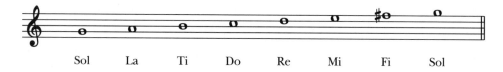

Today, instructors often prefer to have students sing scale degree numbers or pitch names rather than solfège syllables.

Solfège in Minor. Many instructors teach sight singing in minor with the same syllables used for major: *do, re, mi, fa, sol, la, ti, do*. Pitch names and scale degree numbers are also commonly used for sight singing. In true solfège, however, one of two sets of syllables is used. In movable *do* solfège, the tonic is always *do* and syllables are altered if they are raised or lowered. Raised a half step, the syllable *la* becomes *le*. A subtonic pitch is *te* instead of *ti*.

Natural Minor

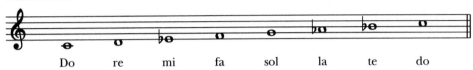

Do   re   mi   fa   sol   la   te   do

Harmonic Minor

Do   re   mi   fa   sol   la   ti   do

Melodic Minor

Do   re   me   fa   sol   la   ti   do   te   le   sol   fa   me   re   do

In movable *do* solfège, the syllables *la, ti, do, re, mi, fa, sol,* and *la* are used for natural minor. If the seventh degree is raised, *sol* becomes *si*; if the sixth is raised, *fa* becomes *fi*.

Natural Minor

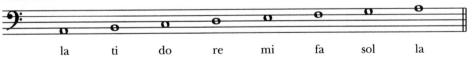

la   ti   do   re   mi   fa   sol   la

Harmonic Minor

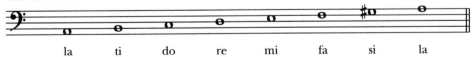

la   ti   do   re   mi   fa   si   la

Melodic Minor

la   ti   do   re   mi   fi   si   la   sol   fa   mi   re   do   ti   la

Glossary

NOTE: Terms in *italics* are defined elsewhere in the glossary.

accent   A stress or emphasis given to a *note*. See also *metric accent*.

accidental   A symbol, such as the *sharp*, the *flat*, or the *natural sign*, that raises or lowers a *basic pitch* one or more *half steps*.

acoustics   A branch of science that deals with the physical properties of sound.

Aeolian mode   The octave series of *half steps* and *whole steps* beginning on A: A B C D E F G and A.

alla breve   An old term for $\frac{2}{2}$ *meter*, still used today and indicated by the symbol ¢. Also known as "cut time."

alto   The second highest voice category in traditional four-part writing.

alto clef ( ) A *movable C-clef* that identifies the position of the pitch C on the *staff*.

amplitude   The degree of molecular disturbance caused by a sound source that produces the psychological sensation of loudness.

anacrusis   An incomplete *measure* that begins a composition or section.

analysis   The systematic study of one or more aspects of a musical composition.

arabic-numeral identification   The use of arabic numerals to represent *intervals* sounding above a given *bass* note.

augmented interval   A *major interval* or a *perfect interval* that has been increased in size by one half step.

augmented second   An interval formed by a *whole step* plus a *chromatic half step*.

augmented triad   A type of *triad* that is constructed of a major *third* and an augmented *fifth* above the *root*.

authentic cadence   A concluding harmonic formula consisting of the *dominant* or the *leading tone* to tonic (V–I).

bar   See *measure*.

barline   A vertical line used to separate *measures*.

basic pitch   A pitch without an *accidental*, such as A B C D E F or G.

bass   (1) The lowest-sounding pitch in a *triad* or *chord*. (2) The lowest voice in traditional *four-part harmony*.

bassa   A term often used with the *octave sign* to indicate notes to be performed an *octave* lower than written.

bass clef (𝄢)   A symbol that identifies the fourth line on the *staff* as the position of the pitch F.

beam   A thick horizontal line that connects two or more stemmed notes and indicates lesser rhythmic values. Beams are equivalent to *flags*.

beat   A monotonous pulse that underlies the rhythmic structure of a traditional composition.

beat division   The use of rhythmic values of less than one *beat*. Beat division is either *simple* or *compound*.

beat subdivision   The use of rhythmic values smaller than the *beat division*.

borrowed division   A division of the *beat* into three parts (a *triplet*) in a *simple meter* or into two parts (a *duplet*) in a *compound meter*.

breve (◻)   An older note value, little used in modern music, having twice the value of the *whole note*.

cadence   A musical point of conclusion. See *authentic cadence, half cadence, plagal cadence,* and *deceptive cadence*.

calligraphy   The process of notating music by hand.

chord   A group of three or more pitches. See also *tertian triad* and *seventh chord*.

chromatic   A term usually associated with music in which the *half step* predominates.

chromatic half step   A *half step* formed between pitches with the same letter name (G and G-sharp, for example).

chromatic scale   An *octave* series of half steps written typically with *sharps* ascending and *flats* descending.

church modes   The half-step and whole-step patterns through which early Western music was organized and the predecessors of our modern *major scale* and *minor scale*. See also *Dorian, Phrygian, Lydian,* and *Mixolydian modes*.

circle of fifths   A sequence of major and minor *keys* whose *tonics* lie a *perfect fifth* (seven half steps) from their closest neighbor above and below. Adjacent keys on the circle of fifths have all but one pitch in common.

clef   A symbol that designates the precise position of one note on the *staff*.

close position   The spatial arrangement of a *triad* or *chord* so that the highest and lowest pitches are as close together as possible. See also *open position*.

common time   An alternative term for $\frac{4}{4}$ meter, represented by the symbol C.

common tone   In traditional *four-part harmony*, a pitch heard in two consecutive *chords*.

compound beat division   A division of the *beat* into three smaller parts.

compound interval   An *interval* that is larger than an *octave*.

compound meter   A meter that employs *compound beat division*.

conductor   The leader of a musical *ensemble*.

consonance   A *pitch*, an *interval*, or a *chord* that is relatively stable. See also *perfect consonance* and *imperfect consonance*.

contrary motion   The linear movement of voices in opposite directions.

counting   The mental or audible assignment of rhythms to various *beats, divisions,* or *subdivisions* for accuracy in performance.

deceptive cadence   A harmonic concluding formula consisting of a progression of the *dominant triad* to the *submediant* (V–vi).

diatonic   A *pitch*, an *interval*, or a *triad* that conforms to the notes found in a given *scale*. In C major, for example, the pitches C D E F G A and B are diatonic; all other pitches are *nondiatonic*.

diatonic half step A *half step* formed between two pitches with different letter names (F-sharp and G, for example).

diminished interval A *perfect interval* or a minor interval that has been decreased in size by one half step.

diminished triad A *triad* that is constructed of a minor *third* and a diminished *fifth* above the *root*.

dissonance (1) A *pitch*, an *interval*, or a *chord* that is relatively unstable. (2) A traditional category of interval that includes the *second*, the *seventh*, and the *tritone*.

division See *beat division*.

dominant The fifth scale degree or the *triad* with the fifth *scale degree* as its *root*.

dominant seventh chord A type of *seventh chord*, consisting of a major *triad* with the addition of a minor *seventh* above the *root* of that triad.

Dorian mode The series of basic pitches beginning on D: D E F G A B C and D.

dot (·) A symbol added to a *note* or a *rest* to increase its value by one half.

double barline Two vertical lines that indicate the end of a composition or section.

double flat (♭♭) An *accidental* symbol used to indicate a note one *whole step* lower than the corresponding *basic pitch*.

double sharp (×) An *accidental* symbol used to indicate a note one *whole step* higher than the corresponding *basic pitch*.

doubling The octave duplication of one or more pitches in *triads* and *chords*.

duple meter A recurring metric pattern that is strong–weak.

duplet A *borrowed division* in *compound meter* wherein the beat is divided into two equal parts.

duration The length of a sound.

eighth note (♪) A relative rhythmic value that is one-eighth the duration of the *whole note*.

enharmonics Pitches notated differently but having the same *frequency*.

ensemble A composition intended for two or more performers.

fifth (1) A type of *interval* that usually consists of six or seven *half steps*. (2) A *triad* member that lies a *fifth* above the *root*.

figured bass An eighteenth-century system of abbreviated *chord* notation using arabic numerals. Figured bass is employed today in musical *analysis*.

first inversion The arrangement of a *tertian triad* with the *third* in the *bass*.

flag (♩) A curved line added to the *stem* of a *note* to indicate a reduced rhythmic value. Flags are equivalent to *beams*.

flat (♭) An *accidental* symbol that lowers pitch *one half step*.

form The term for the organized growth of musical elements over a given time span.

four-part harmony A traditional style of composition based on four independent voices: *soprano*, *alto*, *tenor*, and *bass*.

fourth A type of *interval* that usually consists of five or six *half steps*.

frequency The number of molecular vibrations per second produced by a sound source to create a musical tone. Greater and lesser frequency produces the psychological sensation of higher and lower *pitch*.

grand staff A combination, usually of one treble and one bass *staff*, used for the notation of piano and other *keyboard* music.

half cadence   A harmonic concluding formula that consists usually of a progression of *supertonic*, *subdominant*, or *tonic* to the *dominant* chord (IV–V or I–V, for example).

half note (♩)   A relative rhythmic value that is one-half the duration of the *whole note*.

half step   The smallest *interval* in Western music. On the *keyboard*, a half step is found between any two adjacent keys. See also *diatonic half step* and *chromatic half step*.

harmonic dissonance   A relatively unstable *chord* containing a dissonant *interval* such as a *seventh*.

harmonic function   The arrangement of *triads* and *chords* into *progressions* that establish a feeling for *key*.

harmonic interval   Two pitches heard simultaneously.

harmonic minor scale   A form of *minor scale* in which the seventh degree has been raised a half step to provide a *leading tone*.

harmony   The vertical arrangement of pitches into *intervals*, *triads*, and *chords*.

hertz   A measurement of *frequency* (abbreviated Hz) equivalent to the number of molecular vibrations per second.

imperfect consonance   A category of *interval* comprising the major and minor *third* and the major and minor *sixth*.

interval   The distance between two pitches.

interval inversion   An alternative version of an original *interval* in which the relative positions of the two notes are reversed (the higher pitch is now the lower, for example).

interval quality   A precise measurement of interval size dependent on the number of *half steps* between pitches.

interval type   A general measurement of interval size dependent on the number of lines and spaces between pitches.

Ionian mode   The octave series of *half steps* and *whole steps* beginning on C: C D E F G A and B.

key   An effect produced when the *tonic* of a *scale* is heard as the most important pitch.

keyboard   The black- and white-key manual arrangement found on the piano, the organ, and other instruments.

key signature   A listing of the *accidentals* necessary to produce the effect of a given *key*.

leading tone   The pitch or the *triad* built on the seventh *scale degree* that lies a *half step* below the *tonic*.

ledger line   A temporary extension of the *staff* beyond the customary five lines and four spaces.

loco   A term that indicates a return to standard notation after an *ottava* passage.

Locrian mode   The octave series of *half steps* and *whole steps* beginning on B: B C D E F G A and B.

Lydian mode   The octave series of half steps and whole steps beginning on F: F G A B C D E and F.

major interval   A category of *interval* consisting of *seconds*, *thirds*, *sixths*, and *sevenths*.

major scale   An organized series of pitches in which the arrangement of *whole steps* and *half steps* is Whole, Whole, Half, Whole, Whole, Whole, Half.

major triad   A type of *triad* consisting of a major *third* and a perfect *fifth* above the *root*.

measure   One complete metric pattern (also called a "bar"). In traditional music, measures are delineated by *barlines*.

mediant   The third *scale degree* or the *triad* with the third scale degree as its *root*.

melodic interval   Two pitches heard consecutively.

melodic minor scale   A *minor scale* in which both the sixth and the seventh degrees have been raised a *half step* in the ascending form. Descending melodic minor is identical to descending *natural minor*.

melody   An organized series of pitches in a single voice.

meter   A recurring pattern of strong and weak beats. See also *duple meter* and *triple meter*.

meter signature   Two numbers placed at the beginning of a composition to indicate the note receiving one *beat*, the manner of *beat division*, and the number of beats in a *measure*. Also called a "time signature."

metric accent   The regular strong and weak patterns of beats that create *meter*.

metronome   A device for producing a steady pulse at a given *tempo*.

minor scale   An organized series of pitches in which the *whole-step* and *half-step* pattern is Whole, Half, Whole, Whole, Half, Whole, Whole. See also *harmonic minor scale*, *natural minor scale*, and *melodic minor scale*.

minor triad   A type of *triad* consisting of a minor *third* and a perfect *fifth* above the *root*.

Mixolydian mode   The octave series of half steps and whole steps beginning on G: G A B C D E F and G.

mode   (1) The establishment of either the major or the minor effect within a given *key*. (2) One of eight specific arrangements of the seven basic pitches. See also *church modes*.

movable C-clef   A symbol that identifies the pitch C on the *staff*. See also *alto clef* and *tenor clef*.

music   Organized sound in time.

natural division   A division of the *beat* according to the metric plan: a two-part division in a *simple meter* and a three-part division in *compound meters*.

natural minor scale   A minor scale that conforms to the *interval* pattern Whole, Half, Whole, Whole, Half, Whole, Whole. See also *harmonic minor scale* and *melodic minor scale*.

natural sign (♮)   An *accidental* symbol that cancels the effect of a *sharp* or a *flat*.

noise   Uncontrolled sound produced by irregular *sound waves*.

nondiatonic   Pitches that lie outside a given *scale*. In C major, for example, all pitches except C D E F G A and B are nondiatonic.

notation   A system through which sounds are represented by symbols.

note   The symbol for sound. Notes vary in appearance according to their rhythmic value.

notehead   The oval portion of a *note*.

octave   The purest and most stable *interval*, which forms the basis of practically all musical systems. Pitches that appear in different places on the *staff* but have exactly the same letter names (F–F or E♭–E♭, for example) are one or more octaves apart.

octave designation   A system of identifying *pitches* within a specific *octave* range.

octave sign (8va)   A symbol that indicates that a note or notes are to be played an *octave* higher or lower than written.

open position   The spatial arrangement of a *triad* or *chord* so that the highest and lowest pitches lie an *octave* or more apart. See also *close position*.

ottava   An indication that notation is to be performed an *octave* higher or lower than written. See also *octave sign*.

parallel fifths   In *four-part harmony*, the movement from one chord of any two voices forming a *perfect fifth* to a perfect fifth in the same voices in the next chord.

parallel octaves In *four-part harmony*, the movement of any two voices forming a perfect *octave* in one chord and moving to a perfect octave in the same voices in the next chord.

parallel relationship Major and minor *keys* having the same *tonic* (G major and G minor, for example).

pentatonic scale An ancient scale form that includes no half steps and that can be played over five consecutive black keys on the piano.

perfect consonance A category of *interval* comprising the perfect octave, perfect fifth, perfect fourth, and perfect unison. See also *imperfect consonance*.

perfect fifth An *interval* that is a fifth in type and comprising seven *half steps* between pitches.

perfect interval An *interval* category consisting of *octaves, unisons, fourths,* and *fifths.*

Phrygian mode The octave series of half steps and whole steps beginning on E: E F G A B C D and E.

pitch The psychological sensation of perceiving a note as relatively higher or lower as determined by the *frequency*.

plagal cadence A concluding harmonic formula consisting of a progression of the *subdominant triad* to the *tonic* (IV–I).

primary triad In traditional *harmony*, the three most important *triads* in establishing a *key*: the *tonic*, the *subdominant*, and the *dominant*. See also *secondary triad*.

progression A series of *chords* that establishes a feeling for key.

pure minor See *natural minor scale*.

psychoacoustics A study of the psychological properties of sound.

quadruple meter A metric pattern that is a strong–weak–semistrong–weak accent scheme.

quarter note (♩) A relative rhythmic value that is one-quarter the duration of the *whole note*.

relative relationship Major and minor *keys* having the same *key signature* but different *tonics* (C major and A minor, for example). See also *parallel relationship*.

rests The symbols employed to notate periods of silence. Like notes, rest symbols vary according to the length of silence they represent.

rhythm The element of time in music.

roman-numeral identification A system of musical *analysis* in which roman numerals and other symbols stand for various *diatonic triads* and *chords*.

root The lowest member of a *triad* when the three pitches are arranged over consecutive lines or spaces. See also *root position*.

root position The arrangement of a *tertian triad* with the *root* as the *bass*.

scale A series of pitches arranged in a fixed order. See also *major scale* and *minor scale*.

scale degree A number assigned to each pitch in a *scale* to define its relationship to the *tonic* pitch.

second A type of *interval* usually comprising one or two *half steps*.

secondary triad In traditional *harmony*, any *triad* other than those considered *primary*. The *supertonic, mediant, submediant,* and *leading tone* are secondary triads. See also *primary triads*.

second inversion The arrangement of a *tertian triad* so that the *fifth* is in the *bass*.

seventh A type of *interval* that usually consists of ten or eleven *half steps*.

seventh chord A *chord* that is constructed of four different pitches: a *root*, a *third* and a *fifth* above the root, and also a *seventh* above the root. See also *dominant seventh chord*.

sharp (♯)   An *accidental* symbol that raises pitch one *half step*.

simple beat division   A division of the *beat* into two smaller parts.

simple meter   A meter with a *duple*, or strong–weak, accent pattern.

sixteenth note (♪)   A relative rhythmic symbol that is one-sixteenth the duration of the *whole note*.

sixth   A type of *interval* that usually consists of eight or nine *half steps*.

solfège   A system of teaching sight singing through syllables.

soprano   The highest of the four traditional voice categories. See also *alto*, *tenor*, and *bass*.

sound waves   Regular patterns of molecular motion created by a sound source.

spacing   In *triad* and *chord* construction, the arrangement of the pitches over one or several octaves. See also *open position* and *close position*.

staff   A grid of five lines and four spaces used for the precise *notation* of music. The plural of staff is "staves."

stem   A vertical line added to a *note* to indicate a decrease in rhythmic value.

subdivision   See *beat subdivision*.

subdominant   The fourth *scale degree* or the *triad* with the fourth scale degree as its *root*.

submediant   The sixth *scale degree* or the *triad* with the sixth scale degree as its *root*.

subtonic   The seventh *scale degree* that lies a *whole step* below the *tonic* or the *triad* with this pitch as its *root*.

supertonic   The second *scale degree* or the *triad* with the second scale degree as its *root*.

syncopation   The intentional misplacement of natural metric *accents*.

system   A set of two or more staves. See also *grand staff*.

tempo   The speed of the *beat*.

tenor   The next to lowest voice in traditional *four-part harmony*.

tenor clef (𝄡)   A *movable C-clef* that identifies the position of the pitch C on the *staff*.

tertian triad   A group of three pitches that can be arranged to fall over consecutive lines or consecutive spaces.

third   (1) A type of *interval* usually consisting of three or four *half steps*. (2) A *triad* member that lies a third above the *root*.

tie (⌒)   A symbol that combines the rhythmic values of two or more notes of the same pitch.

timbre   The term used to describe the quality of a musical tone.

time signature   See *meter signature*.

tonality   The establishment of *key* and *mode* (the key of E-flat major, for example).

tonic   The first pitch of a *scale* or the *triad* built on the first *scale degree*.

transcription   The process of revising the notation of music so that although the sound is the same, the visual appearance is different. The term "transcription" is also applied to music written for one medium that has been rewritten to be performed in a different medium (an orchestral work transcribed for piano, for example).

transposition   The process of moving a series of pitches to a different *tonic* (and therefore a different *key*) without changing the original pattern of *intervals*.

treble clef (𝄞)   The symbol that identifies the second line on the *staff* as the position of the pitch G.

triad   A group of three pitches. See also *tertian triad*.

triad inversion   A *tertian triad* arranged so that the *root* is above the *bass*. See also *first inversion* and *second inversion*.

triple meter   A recurring metric pattern that is strong–weak–weak.

triplet   A *borrowed division* in a *simple meter* wherein the beat is divided into three equal parts.

tritone   An augmented fourth or a diminished fifth consisting of six *half steps*.

unison   The *interval* between two or more pitches of the same *frequency*.

upper voices   The *soprano, alto,* and *tenor* voices in traditional *four-part harmony*.

voice leading   The horizontal movement of individual voices in traditional *four-part harmony*.

whole note (o)   The greatest rhythmic value commonly used in traditional music.

whole step   An *interval* consisting of two *half steps*.

whole-tone scale   A series of six consecutive whole steps and ending with an octave duplication of the first pitch.

Index

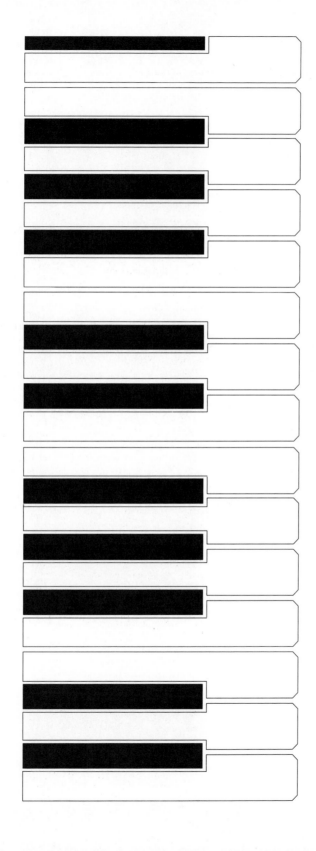